The Rise and Fall of Britain's North American Empire

Gerald Pollio

The Rise and Fall of Britain's North American Empire

The Political Economy of Colonial America

palgrave
macmillan

Gerald Pollio
London, UK

ISBN 978-3-031-07483-7 ISBN 978-3-031-07484-4 (eBook)
https://doi.org/10.1007/978-3-031-07484-4

This Palgrave Macmillan imprint is published by the registered company Springer Nature Switzerland AG.
The registered company address is: Gewerbestrasse 11, 6330 Cham, Switzerland

The Wildest chimera that ever disturbed a Madman's Brain has not less Foundation in this opinion (because) there are not five Men of Sense in America who wou'd accept of Independence if it was offered (George Mason, 1770).[1]

If we search the whole history of human events, we shall not meet with an example of such a sudden change, from the most perfect loyalty to universal disaffection. On the contrary, in every instance where natural attachment has been generally effaced, it has been effected by slow degrees, and a long continuance of oppression, not in prospect, but in actual existence.[2]

The sense of historical destiny that surrounds the Revolution challenges our capacity to think our way back into the contingencies of the past and to appreciate how improbable an event it was. Part of that improbability lies in the record of misguided decisions that led the British government to fulfil its worst fears by driving the colonists down the road to independence. It took a peculiarly flawed process of framing bad policies and reacting to the

[1] Cover image, 'Arrival in Jamestown, 1607,' D. Scott, *A School History of the United States* (New York, NY: Harper & Brothers, 1883).

R. Rutland (Ed), *The Papers of George Mason, 1725-1792.* Vol. 1 (Chapel Hill, NC: University of North Carolina Press, 1970), p. 129.

[2] Joseph Galloway, *Letters to a Nobleman on the Conduct of the War in the Middle Colonies.* Second Edition. (London: J. Wilkie, 1779), p. 10.

resulting failures to convince the government of George III and Lord North that the best way to maintain the loyalty of the North American subjects to make war on them.[3]

The long story of the bickerings of British politicians both in and out of office might be told for still another decade, until the colonies were lost, not wholly for lack of men of understanding to govern them more wisely, but because, being divided on other questions, they were seldom able to unite to do what they knew ought to be done for the salvation of the empire.[4]

[3] J. Rakove, *Revolutionaries: Inventing and American Nation* (London: William Heineman, 2010), p. 17.

[4] W. Laprade, "The Stamp Act in British Politics," *American Historical Review*, **35** (1930), 735-757, p. 757.

Acknowledgements

The author and publishers would like to thank the following for allowing the use of copyright material.

Bank of England for Charts 3 and 4 from *A Millennium of Macroeconomic Data*, V3.1, 2 March 2017.

Econ Journal Watch for Chart 6 from F. Grubb, "Theory, Evidence, and Belief—The Colonial Money Puzzle Revisited: Reply to Michener and Wright," *Econ Journal Watch*, **3** (2006).

Elsevier Science for:

Table 6 from Peter. M. Garber, "Alexander Hamilton's Market-based Debt Reduction Plan," *Carnegie-Rochester Conference Series on Public Policy* **35** (1991).

Chart 10 from G. Hall and T. Sargent, "Fiscal Discrimination in Three Wars," *Journal of Monetary Economics*, **61** (January 2014).

Tables 2 and 4 from J. Shepherd and G. Walton, "Economic Change after the American Revolution: Pre- and Post-War Comparisons of Maritime Shipping and Trade, *Explorations in Economic History*, **13** (1976).

Table 5 from Ohio State University Press from E. Perkins, *American Public Finance and Financial Services, 1700–1815* (1994).

Table 7 from Duke University Press "State Issues of Paper Money During the Revolutionary War" from in B. Ratchford, *American State Debts* (1941).

Contents

Part I Introduction 1

1 Historical and Political Background 3

Part II The Economy of Colonial America 13

2 Labour 15

2.1 Slave Labour 21

3 The Slave Trade and Britain's Industrial Revolution 47

4 Economic Impact of Slavery 53

5 Industry 75

6 Land Values, Tenancy, and Private Ownership 91

Part III The Politics and Economics of British Trade and Revenue Policies 97

7 The End of Salutary Neglect 99

8 Trade and Navigation Acts 113

9 The Stamp Act 127

10 The Townshend Duties 149

11 Nonimportation 157

Part IV Rebellion: Revolution and Its Aftermath 169

12 Confiscation 177

13 Repudiation 195

14 Foreign Loans 203

15 Fiat Money? 213

16 Trade and Trade Policy 225

Conclusion 235

Index 237

List of Charts

Chart 2.1	British American and West African Slave Prices, 1638/1642–1773/1775 (pounds sterling). (Note: Quadrennial averages. Blue line: West African Prices; Red Line: British American (landed) Prices. Source: *Historical Statistics of the United States*, Series Z165–168, p. 1174)	23
Chart 4.1	British cotton imports, total and from the United States, 1860–1867 (1000 pounds) (Notes: Blue bars: Total British cotton imports; Brown line: Imports from the United States. Source: John Pender and Co., *Statistics of Trade of the UK with Foreign Countries from 1840* (London: Simkin Marshall, 1869), *Historical Statistics of the United States (HSUS)*)	58
Chart 4.2	US Middling Uplands cotton prices, Liverpool, 1840/1841–1867/1868 (pence per lb). (Source: J. Watkins, *King Cotton: A Historical and Statistical Review, 1790 to 1908* (New York: J. L. Watkins and Sons, 1908), p. 30)	59
Chart 7.1	National debt of Great Britain, 1692–1815 (per cent of GDP) (Source: Bank of England, *A Millennium of Macroeconomic Data*, March 2017)	109
Chart 7.2	Public income sources during decades of the 1700 (per cent of total income). (Bank of England, *A Millennium of Macroeconomic Data*, V3.1, 2 March 2017)	111
Chart 8.1	English imports of American Tobacco and Maryland Tobacco prices. Imports: 1697–1776 (thousands of pounds sterling). Maryland Tobacco prices, 1697–1775 (pence sterling/lb.). (Source: *Historical Statistics if the United States*, Chart A: Series Z 471–478; Chart B: Series Z 578–582)	117

Chart 9.1	Colonial currency exchange rates vis-à-vis sterling. (Source: F. Grubb, "Theory, Evidence, and Belief—The Colonial Money Puzzle Revisited: Reply to Michener and Wright," *Econ Journal Watch*, **3** (2006) 45–72, p, 56, Fig. 1)	144
Chart 10.1	Lexical analysis, 1763–1776 ('Taxation,' 'Representation,' 'Tyranny': American English) (**a**) Unadjusted data. (**b**) Smoothed data. (Source: Google Ngram)	152
Chart 11.1	Colonial trade with Great Britain, 1760–1770 (pounds sterling). (Source: *Historical Statistics of the United States*, "Colonial and Pre-Federal Statistics," Series Z 213–226, p. 1176)	161
Chart 15.1	Nominal and Specie Value of Continental Dollars. (Source: G. Hall and T. Sargent, "Fiscal Discriminations in Three Wars," *Journal of Monetary Economics*, **61** (2014) 148–166)	222
Chart 16.1	Federal debt outstanding, 1790–1816 (thousand dollars). (Source: US Treasury Department)	232

List of Tables

Table 2.1	Vessel Tonnage, Outbound Crew, and Number of Slaves Landed, Bristol, 1746–1748 and 1766–1769	37
Table 5.1	Pig iron exports from the American colonies, 1768 and 1772 (hundredweight)	79
Table 5.2	Shibuilding in America's Thirteen Colonies, 1769–1771 (tonnage)	82
Table 14.1	Foreign debt and arrears, 1 January 1790	204
Table 15.1	Annual supply of continental dollars, 1775–1779	219
Table 15.2	Annual state issues of paper money, 1775–1783 (thousands of dollars)	220
Table 16.1	Geographic and commodity distribution of American trade, pre- and post-revolutionary war	227

PART I

Introduction

Britain's North American colonies were initially conceived of as commercial investments, much like Britain's Caribbean possessions, but over time became increasingly populous, self-confident, and prosperous, so much so that by the mid-eighteenth century it encouraged a sense of resentment at the British government's determination to shift the fiscal burden resulting from recent wars with France from English to American taxpayers. Less clear is whether the colonies' opposition to successive tax measures reflected principle or opportunism or some combination of the two. American colonists had long accepted the premise that Parliament could impose taxes on maritime trade but not excises unless approved by those being taxed. In reaction to enactment of the Stamp Act, James Otis of Massachusetts provided in 1765 what is still regarded by many as the main justification for American opposition to the various imposts enacted by Parliament: 'taxation without representation is tyranny.' Seen from the British perspective, it was more likely a matter of 'no representation without taxation.'

American hostility could, of course, just as easily be construed as resentment against repeated parliamentary attempts to inhibit their economic and commercial development. The Trade and Navigation Acts, for example, imposed various restrictions on colonial commerce in keeping with the prevailing mercantilist doctrine that trade was meant primarily to serve the mother country's economic interests. Colonial merchants, for example, were barred from trading directly with non-British regional colonies while all European exports had first to go through Great Britain. True, these restrictions were counterbalanced with concessions that in the aggregate eased significantly the burden the Acts imposed on the colonies, but the more important point is that the distribution of benefits and costs was not symmetrical.

Official restrictions encouraged smuggling, a refusal to remit the revenues imposed in the successive tax measures and, finally, the adoption of nonimportation agreements or boycotts of British goods. The progressive escalation of colonial reactions, culminating in rebellion, underlines the growing economic power of the colonies vis-à-vis Great Britain, and the rising costs to the British economy connected with the pursuit of fiscal policies known to be strongly opposed by Americans. Some contemporaries argued that had the British government acted more forcefully to suppress colonial opposition it would have discouraged local resistance. All that can be known for sure is that when Parliament finally resolved to bring the colonies to heel via the punitive measures adopted in the aftermath of the Boston Tea Party the policy failed miserably and triggered open rebellion.

To be sure, some British statesmen, merchants, and others encouraged the government to consider colonial representation in Parliament. After all, a previous government had conceded the principle in the Acts of Union with Scotland, even to the point of approving substantial and disproportionate political and financial concessions to ensure Scottish endorsement of the proposed Union. By the mid-eighteenth century, the number of white Americans equalled or exceeded the population of Scotland, were almost certainly wealthier, while many of the concessions formalised in the Acts of Union were not dissimilar to what the colonists were demanding.

The truth is support for American representation was not very strong owing in part to the fact the mainland colonies never achieved the same level of parliamentary influence as enjoyed by Britain's West Indian colonies. Of greater importance is that American representation would have encouraged major British cities, such as Birmingham, Liverpool, and Manchester, which likewise lacked formal parliamentary representation, to demand equal treatment, while the combined influence of representatives from the American colonies and major British urban centres would have tilted the legislative agenda in a direction inimical to the interests of the ruling landowning elites. The great irony is that all attempts to get the Americans to assume a greater share of the costs of empire involved Britain in a war with the colonies the costs of which exceeded the revenues foregone by the failure to implement the proposed tax measures.

CHAPTER 1

Historical and Political Background

The development of Britain's American colonies dictated the Empire's pattern of trade, the bulk of which was meant to benefit the metropolitan centre, although it is arguable whether that objective was achieved. Certainly, many individuals became wealthy and politically influential, but whether the British economy benefitted is another matter. Even if colonial agriculture was profitable, as demonstrably was the case, once the costs of protecting the island and mainland colonies and the subsidies paid by consumers in the form of higher tariffs are included in the assessment, the net economic impact was more likely than not negative.

The balance of evidence suggests that the economic impact of the mercantilist policies that governed imperial commercial relationships, while not overly burdensome, do appear to have inhibited colonial economic development. The restrictions imposed on the colonies by the Trade and Navigation Acts were largely or entirely offset by the bounties paid to mainland colonists to produce goods required by the British economy. By contrast, any attempt to develop industries that competed with English manufactures was discouraged by the Board of Trade, whose records up to the Revolution provide an indication of those sectors that in the absence of official obstruction were most likely to have flourished. It is true that throughout most of the seventeenth century the colonial economy was probably too small to support a significant manufacturing base. Even so, the extent to which a local manufacturing industry could have developed appears limited, certainly with respect to those industries that were exposed

G. Pollio, *The Rise and Fall of Britain's North American Empire*,
https://doi.org/10.1007/978-3-031-07484-4_1

to international competition. This, in turn, had significant implications for the development of the new Republic's industrial policies.

More to the point, during the later antebellum era, the development of major manufacturing industries was supported by direct state intervention, including the adoption of trade restraints, the justification for which were contained in Alexander Hamilton's 1791 *Report on the Subject of Manufactures.*[1] Hamilton's proposed tariffs were not especially protectionist, as they were intended to 'encourage' the development of industry, not 'protect' it.[2] His opposition to highly restrictive trade policies was motivated both by principle and expediency, above all, the fact that high tariffs would have discouraged imports, or encouraged smuggling (or both), the critical tax base upon which Hamilton planned to fund the public debt. Still, the principles upon which Hamilton's 'moderate measures' were based were subsequently adopted and expanded by Jeffersonian Republicans, albeit not for the reasons set out in Hamilton's original *Report*,[3] the cumulative impact of which was that by the early 1830s average rates on dutiable imports were the highest in Republic's history, and were reduced only against the backdrop of the Nullification Crisis of 1832–1833, one of the major regional crises leading to the American Civil War.

Later Imperial policies contributed to growing political and commercial tensions between Britain and its American colonies. As the Whig policy of 'salutary neglect' was abandoned following the conclusion of the French and Indian (or Seven Years) War, England's difficulties with the colonies intensified to the point that rebellion, inconceivable up to the 1770s, became a reality. The main source of contention was taxation.

[1] On the background and impact of Hamilton's *Report* see L. Hacker, "The Report on Manufactures," *The Historian*, **19** (1957) 144–167 and D, Ben-Atar, "Alexander Hamilton's Alternative: Technology Piracy and the Report on Manufactures," *William and Mary Quarterly*, **52** (1995) 389–414.

[2] G. Clarfield, "Protecting the Frontiers: Defense Policy and the Tariff Question in the First Washington Administration," *William and Mary Quarterly*, **32** (1975) 443–464, p. 459.

[3] 'Hamilton was not as much of a protectionist as he is sometimes made out to be. Although Hamilton's moderate tariff policies found support among merchants and traders, the backbone of the Federalist party, disappointed domestic manufacturers soon came to embrace the much more draconian trade policies of the Republican party led by Jefferson and Madison,' D. Irwin, "The Aftermath of Hamilton's "Report on Manufactures", *Journal of Economic History*, **64** (2004) 800–821, pp. 820–821. On the differences in Hamiltonian and Jeffersonian economic policies see J. Dorfman, "The Economic Philosophy of Thomas Jefferson," *Political Science Quarterly*, **55** (1940) 98–121.

Notwithstanding that tax rates varied widely across American colonies, the overall tax burden was significantly lower than that in England. The British government maintained that in consequence considerable fiscal capacity existed; moreover, the expenditure it was meant to support was their own defence. Americans resisted all such measures, as they were viewed not only as an attempt to shift the burden of expenditure from the Exchequer to the colonies but, in doing so, affronted their rights as Englishmen. Customs duties, the principal and traditional source of colonial revenues, were acceptable, excises were not, since under English law they required the consent of those being taxed.

Unlike the Scots, Americans were not represented in Parliament. True, neither were the principal English cities, which nevertheless accepted the principle of 'virtual representation,' something the Americans were unwilling to do. Prominent English statesmen and merchants argued in favour of American representation in Parliament, which the government refused to consider. Nor were such arguments predicated on constitutional principles alone. America had become an economic power so that the boycotts and nonimportation agreements adopted in reaction to the policies enacted by Parliament threatened British prosperity, compelling the government to rescind each of the major fiscal measures approved during the 1760s. The possibility for compromise evaporated following the Boston Tea Party to which the British government responded with the passage of the Intolerable (or Coercive) Acts, Parliament's vain attempt to reimpose strict British control over the American colonies; after ten years of vacillation, the decision to be firm with the American colonies was too late. Rather than coercing compliance, the measures became the justification for convening the First Continental Congress later in 1774.

The British treasury anticipated revenue of more than £2 million from the Sugar, Stamp, and Townshend Acts, the actual amount collected totalled £343,000, about a sixth of the hoped-for sum; adding in revenues from the earlier Navigation Acts contributed an additional 7 per cent.[4] Bounties, drawbacks, and export subsidies in the form of cash benefits to colonial planters and consumers of imported goods more than offset the total amount of revenue collected. Even the more nuanced assessments of the impact of the Navigation Acts conclude the losses associated with the

[4] A. Rabushka, *Taxation in Colonial America* (Princeton University Press, 2008), Table 25.4, p. 755.

legislation were modest,[5] but nevertheless antagonised America's social and commercial elites, domestic manufacturers, and urban artisans who, in response, collectively became active supporters of rebellion; almost all of the Founding Fathers, for example, were to varying degrees affected by these measures. Douglas Irwin's recent survey of the era concluded that 'while most colonists accepted Britain's long-standing regulation of America's trade, they resisted British attempts to put more of the financial burden of supporting the colonies onto the colonists themselves. By discounting the benefits of protection within the British Empire, the colonists saw the new taxes and regulations as a threat to their prosperity and future well-being.'

In retrospect, it appears that the British government would have been better advised to have followed Walpole's policy of 'salutary neglect,' and the pro-American policies of Pitt and Newcastle.[6] Many prominent Britons, statesmen and merchants, so advised successive Tory governments but to no avail, suggesting the country's economic interests were subordinate to other, more significant, parliamentary objectives. Among the more pressing were preservation of the interests of the landed gentry who by then made up the government. Major concessions to the Americans, such as permitting their direct representation in Parliament, which would have averted war, albeit at the cost of upsetting the existing political balance as the Americans almost certainly would have aligned themselves with the emerging democratic movement.

Adam Smith for one saw no danger in conceding parliamentary representation to the American colonists. He thought it would pose no risk that would threaten the British constitution; on the contrary, he argued, 'it would be completed by it, and seems to be imperfect without it.' Despite the obvious advantages, Smith doubted, but without providing any formal explanation, that 'this union … could be easily effectuated, or that difficulties and great difficulties might not occur in [its] execution, I do not

[5] Thomas and McCloskey estimate that if Virginia planters could trade freely with other European nations, they would have earned a third more on their tobacco sales. Enumerated commodities accounted for c. one-half of the colonies' commodity exports; commodities were three-quarters of all exports (shipping included), and exports constituted one-seventh of colonial income. Altogether the Trade and navigation Acts raised colonial income by about 1.8 per cent. R. Thomas and D. McCloskey, "Overseas Trade and Empire, 1700–1860," in R. Floud and D. McCloskey (Eds.) *The Economic History of Britain since 1700* (Cambridge, UK and New York: Cambridge University Press, 1981).

[6] Rabushka, *Taxation in Colonial America*, p. 764.

pretend' (*Wealth of Nations* [WN]:IV:7). British merchants, likewise, favoured a peaceful resolution of the conflict because they recognised the colonies wielded considerable economic power, mainly through nonimportation, that once exercised could threaten British prosperity. Unleashed, nonimportation agreements cut deeply into British exports, forcing the government to rescind unpopular policies. Following the repeal of the Stamp and Townshend duties, exports rebounded strongly, indicating the main objective of the colonists was to pressure Parliament into eliminating the offending measures. But the most obvious resolution, Parliamentary representation, was rejected in favour of still more coercive measures that shifted the balance of colonial opposition from considerations of fiscal equity to political independence.

The colonies were in a position of 'economic strength, not weakness, and this gave them the confidence to confront their overseas rulers.'[7] But all such singular explanations miss the point. The ill-conceived Townshend duties further incensed Americans, as they were meant to raise colonial revenues as a means towards both covering the costs of maintaining troops in North America while reducing land taxes in England. Americans were simply unwilling to accept the principle that Parliament had the right to impose taxes without their consent. Parliament's dilemma was succinctly summarised by Edmund Burke: while conceding that Parliament had a constitutional right to tax the colonies, he argued they should refrain from doing so as a means of improving relations with Americans.[8]

The same 'spendthrift humour' that led to the rise of the consumer revolution in seventeenth-century England spread across the Atlantic to Colonial America. As in England (and later Britain) rising prosperity in the

[7] D. Irwin, *Clashing Over Commerce: A History of U.S. Trade Policy* (Chicago: University of Chicago Press, 2017), p. 38. Irwin provides a balanced assessment of the impact of the Navigation Acts in the light of current research. See especially Chapter 1, pp. 35–38.

[8] E. Burke, *Observations on a Late State of the Union* (London: J. Dodsley, 1769). As late as 1775 Burke continued to advocate a conciliatory policy towards the American colonies. His attempts at conciliation were rejected by Parliament. Welbore Ellis speaking for the majority argued that 'the greater disposition Great Britain shewed towards conciliation, the more obstinate, rebellious, and insolent America would become.' Criticism of Burke's proposals outside Parliament was even more scathing. On 22 March 1775, Josiah Tucker observed: 'Why truly, if we will grant the Colonies all that they shall require, and stipulate for nothing in Return; they will be at Peace with us. I believe it; and on these simple Principles of simple Peace-making I will engage to terminate every Difference throughout the World.' Pp. 6–7. Cited in H. Dickinson. "The Failure of Conciliation: Britain and the American Colonies 1763–1783, *Kyoto Economic Review*, 79 (2010) 2–20.

American colonies converted former luxuries into everyday staples, many of which were manufactured in England, thus sustaining the momentum towards industrialisation. Indeed, the impact was much greater than would have been the case had Britain's colonies never existed, principally because average per-capita incomes were higher in the thirteen North American colonies than in Great Britain.[9] This was true of all regions with the exception of New England. Trade growth, significantly, was underwritten by the liberal provision of credit. As major creditors English factors quite obviously had a strong interest in ensuring the stability of commercial relations with the American colonies as a guarantee of eventual repayment.

The larger question is whether these policies, however beneficial they may have been to the mother country, ultimately cost England the loss of its North American empire. For some scholars, British trade and revenue policies had a largely benign impact on the American colonies being measured as a few percentage points at most of the colonies' combined GDP. Moreover, they affected only a small proportion of the colonial population, while in some instances they actually benefitted American consumers and producers, the former via lower prices, and the latter via direct subsidies. Much research has been devoted to quantifying the overall impact of the various measures adopted by Parliament while ignoring the fact the burden would not have fallen uniformly on the population. Merchants and planters would have been the most directly affected, thus uniting important sections of the northern and southern colonies in opposition to British policies. If we assume these two together groups accounted for one-quarter of the total colonial population,[10] an overall economic impact of, say, 1 per cent of GDP translates to a fourfold impact on the most directly affected groups.

Group size and cohesion provide the best assurance of being able to generate collective goods. Small groups are more likely to further their common interest than larger groups because of the attraction to individual members.[11] This perspective is especially applicable to the groups most directly affected by parliamentary legislation, above all, wealthy merchants,

[9] P. Lindert and J. Williamson, *Unequal Gains: American Growth and Inequality since 1700* (Princeton University Press, 2016), Figure 3–3, p. 64.

[10] The estimate is from Reid, "Economic Burden: Spark to the American Revolution?" *Journal of Economic History,* **38** (1978) 81–100, p. 95, fn. 35.

[11] M. Olson, *The Logic of Collective Action* (Cambridge, MA: Harvard University Press, 1965).

to whom were joined, for example, other prominent social elites, newspaper publishers, and clergymen.[12] Richard Brown long ago compiled data on the occupational distribution of those signing the Declaration of Independence (1776) and delegates who attended the Constitutional Convention (1777).[13] With respect to the former, lawyers were the most numerous, being slightly outnumbered by merchants and planters; the three groups together accounted for four-fifths of the total number present. As to the Constitutional Convention, lawyers made up one-half of delegates, while merchants and planters accounted for half that number; even so the three occupations made up three-quarters of Convention participants. Collectively, lawyers and merchants dominated delegates from all three regions: the merchant share was the highest in New England, while lawyers made up more than half the attendees from the Middle Atlantic colonies. As expected, the planter-and-farmer share was the highest among southern delegates.

Even if British commercial policies were benighted, there is no question foreign trade contributed positively to the sustained growth of the Atlantic economy.[14] Trade, Adam Smith argued, addressed two important matters that together establish its benefit to the nation: it provides an outlet for surplus goods for which there is no local demand in exchange for goods for which there is and, by enlarging the market for local production, engenders greater specialisation leading, in turn, to an improvement in productivity.[15] Trade thus contributed to both the growth of Great Britain and its North American colonies, but over time became the main source of friction that led ultimately to the colonies declaring their independence. Economic factors are widely considered as having contributed to growing colonial resistance to Parliamentary rule. Few, however, would accord it primacy, not the least because so much of the debate was concerned with

[12] C. Robbins. "Decision in '76: Reflections on the 56 Signers". *Proceedings of the Massachusetts Historical Society.* Vol. 89 pp. 72–87, p. 86. Key personal and occupational statistics on the signers is given in R. Brown, "The Founding Fathers of 1776 and 1787: A Collective View," *William and Mary Quarterly*, **33** (1976), 465–480.

[13] R. Brown, "The Founding Fathers of 1776 and 1787: A Collective View," *William and Mary Quarterly*, **33** (1976), 465–480, p. 478, Table IV.

[14] See, for example, D. Açemoglu, S. Johnson, and J. Robinson, "The Rise of Europe: Atlantic Trade, Institutional Change, and Economic Growth," *American Economic Review*, **95** (2005): 546–579.

[15] R. Schumacher, "Adam Smith's 'Two Distinct Benefits' from Trade: The Dead-End of 'Vent-for-Surplus' Interpretations," *History of Political Economy*, **47** (2015): 577–603 for a recent survey of Smith's views on the gains from trade.

constitutional issues, which thus must be counted as having contributed, perhaps even more so than economics, to the Revolution. But largely unnoticed is that constitutional rhetoric was always closely entwined with issues of trade and taxes, suggesting that at bottom the Revolution was at least as much a matter of economics as abstract political philosophy.

Within the context of the Atlantic system, the American colonies exported high value to weight primary commodities (principally rice and tobacco) in exchange for goods manufactured in England. Rising prosperity stimulated the demand for consumption goods so much so that by the end of the eighteenth century mercantilist doctrine was discarded in favour of the view that consumption had become 'the sole end and purpose of all production; and the interests of the producer should be attended to, only so far as it may be necessary for promoting that of the consumer (WN:IV:xiii).' To that end, Adam Smith was even willing to countenance American representation in the British Parliament (WN:IVxii), and while there was support among some political elites for such a compromise, Parliament opposed the reform.

The general rise in wealth throughout the Atlantic economy encouraged greater luxury consumption as well as a more accepting attitude towards it, especially as demand for luxuries spread throughout society. 'Luxury extends itself even to the lowest ranks of the people, and that the labouring poor will not now be contented with the same food, clothing and development.' They are now keen on 'satisfying the other wants and fancies' such as '[c]loathing and lodging, household furniture, and what is called Equipage' (WN:I:x11). As to the affluent, 'the rich man consumes no more food than his poor neighbour. In quality it may be very different … but in quantity it is very nearly the same. … The desire of food is limited in every man by the narrow capacity of the human stomach; but the desire of the conveniencies (*sic*) and ornaments of building, dress, equipage, and household furniture, seems to have no limit or certain boundary. … What is over and above satisfying the limited desire is given for the amusement of those desires which cannot be satisfied, but seem to be altogether endless' (WN:I:xi:2). In short, 'in times of wealth and luxury what is rare, with only nearly equal merit, is always preferred to what is common' (WN:I:11).

Beyond that, Smith recognised a second important aspect of extravagant expenditure, namely, that it can be used to signal rising social prominence. According to Smith, there is a natural tendency among people to enhance their social distinction and prestige and thus prefer attractive goods for the sake of conspicuous consumption, which 'naturally increases with the increase of riches' (XI.2). 'The chief enjoyment of riches,' Smith concludes, 'consists in the parade of riches, which in their eyes is never so compleat (*sic*) as when they appear to possess those decisive marks of opulence which nobody can possess but themselves.'

Following the conclusion of the Seven Years War, luxury consumption affected British perceptions that took for granted the vast sums Americans were spending on such goods signified they had the resources and therefore should contribute more to covering the costs of Britain's military presence in the New World. The various revenue acts passed by Parliament post-1763 aroused colonial ire and in due course were all repealed. By any standard, England's trade and revenue measures were an abject failure. 'From the standpoint of securing an American tax, the efforts of Parliament clearly failed, not to mention the loss of sales to British merchants and the Revolution that severed the colonies from the empire. Moreover, bounties, drawbacks, and export subsidies to British merchants more than offset the amount of revenue collected in the American tax in the form of cash benefits to colonial planters and consumers of imported goods.'[16]

But more than that in due course American's 'weaponised' consumption expenditure, responding to each parliamentary provocation by boycotts or nonimportation agreements that were meant to, and did, harm British industry, and thus must be accounted among the principal reasons for their repeal. True, local tensions abated almost immediately after each crisis passed, but the fact is that they became an integral part of the colonial response to any attempt to tax the American colonists. Later on, and under different circumstances, Lord North was prepared to concede what seemed impossible only three years earlier, namely, America's right to self-rule, including parliamentary representation within the British Empire.[17]

Whether the decision to reject Lord North's attempt at conciliation was unanimous or not, the fact is matters had reached the point where anything short of full independence was inconceivable, as adamantly opposed by the British as it was supported by the Americans. All such efforts at reconciliation failed because of this fundamental dichotomy. 'No

[16] Rabushka, *Colonial Taxation*, p. 764.

[17] On the Peace Commission of 1778 see N. Einhorn, "The Reception of the British Peace Offer of 1778." *Pennsylvania History* 16 (1949)191–214, A. Gregory, "'Formed for Empire': The Continental Congress Responds to the Carlisle Peace Commission." *Journal of the Early Republic* **38** (2018): 643–672.

significant group or powerful individual in Britain could devise a means of solving the question to the satisfaction of majority opinion in Britain or the American colonies of which person, legislature or institution could legitimately exercise sovereign authority in the American colonies. The vast majority of politicians and commentators agreed with William Blackstone, the foremost constitutional thinker of the age, that there could be only one absolute, irresistible, and uncontrolled sovereign authority in any orderly state and it was widely agreed that in Britain history had shown that this authority was best located in the combined legislature of the King-in-Parliament.'[18] What was inconceivable to the British was impossible for the Americans.

[18] H. Dickinson, "The Failure of Conciliation: Britain and the American Colonies 1763–1783," *Kyoto Economic Review*, 79 (2010) 2–20, pp. 22–23.

PART II

The Economy of Colonial America

Colonies exist according to mercantilist doctrine to serve the needs of the home country. They were thus expected to provide the metropole with the goods and services it required, typically raw materials, luxury consumables (such as sugar or tobacco), and intermediate goods, in exchange for finished manufactures. Central to the mercantilist doctrine was the conviction that prosperity depended upon a country's stock of bullion, so that the avoidance of commercial deficits or, better still, the generation of surpluses, should be the ultimate objective of national trade policy. Britain's colonial empire in the New World appears to have prospered within this framework, while upholding the bullion constraint. The island colonies of the West Indies produced mainly sugar consumed in Britain or transhipped to continental Europe. The West Indian islands used the proceeds from its sale to import luxury goods from England, and food and raw materials from Britain's North American colonies, while the latter recycled the West Indian revenues via the purchase of manufactures produced in Britain. The triangular trade that developed between Britain and its American colonies is thus seen as having contributed to Britain's Industrial Revolution, although the precise mechanism by which this was achieved is disputed.

For some historians, it was not so much trade that mattered, but rather the system of slave labour used to produce the commodities exported from Britain's American colonies. The strong form version of this hypothesis argues that the profits derived from the use of slaves effectively financed the Industrial Revolution. This hypothesis is now rejected by most historians, albeit without denying the profitability of the sugar island plantations. 'While some curious mechanisms have been proposed to solve this problem such as the Williams' … thesis, which attributed the "original accumulation" to profits generated in the slave trade, the difficulty seems a bit overstated, since in the early stages of the industrial revolution the fixed-cost requirements to set up a minimum-sized firm were modest and could be financed from profits accumulated at the artisan level.'[1] Instead, the vital connection is now viewed as the relationship between slave labour and the cultivation of cotton in the southern regions of North America. Cotton was critical to the rise of the Lancashire textile industry. In the absence of steady increases in production and stable real prices, the English cotton textile industry could never have achieved the scale it attained and, by extension, contributed to the growth and development of the overall British economy in the nineteenth century. More recently, the focus of the debate over slavery has shifted to its contribution to the rise of capitalism, especially in the United States.

The flaw common to all these theories is that reliance on a single causal explanation is unlikely, for several reasons, to explain a phenomenon as complex as the Industrial Revolution. First, the Industrial Revolution spread rapidly to other European countries that did not depend upon either the capital provided by slave production or its principal outputs. Second, it diminishes the importance of invention, the steam engine, or Arkwright's Water Frame or Compton's Mule, for example, the latter two the motive force behind the growth of Britain's cotton textile industry and its diffusion throughout Europe and the American Republic. Third, changing factor price relationships, above all, the cost of capital in relation to wages, encouraged innovation, while the low price of energy, in the form of coal, sustained the transition. And finally, it ignores the technical and organisational developments in the antebellum period that contributed to stable real cotton prices and, notwithstanding the abolition of slave labour, the continued increase in cotton cultivation and exports in the post-Civil War era.

[1] J. Mokyr, "The Industrial Revolution and the New Economic History," in Joel Mokyr (Ed.) *The Economics of the Industrial Revolution* (London: George Allen and Unwin, 1985), p. 35. Thomas was even more forthright, dismissing William's thesis as 'a brilliant jeu d'esprit. After all, the slave trading entrepreneurs of Lisbon and Rio, or Seville and Cadiz, did not finance innovations in manufacture.' H. Thomas, *The Slave Trade: The History of the Atlantic Slave Trade 1440–1870* (London: Picador, Pan Macmillan,1997), p. 795.

CHAPTER 2

Labour

Labour scarcity was the main factor inhibiting colonial development in the Americas, and while Europeans were willing to emigrate to the New World, many were discouraged by the high transportation costs involved in getting there: data compiled by Farley Grubb indicate the fare to America amounted, on average, to half or a full year's earnings for English and German emigrants, respectively.[1] Labour problems surfaced almost immediately after Jamestown, England's first permanent settlement in mainland America, was established where colonists reportedly shirked their responsibilities, even to the point of inviting starvation, cannibalism, and death; historians have described 1609–1610 as the 'Starving Time.'[2] Four principal reasons have been adduced to explain the colony's 'tragicall historie,' lack of leadership,[3] disease,[4] poor work ethic,[5] and communal

[1] F. Grubb, "he Market for Indentured Immigrants: Evidence on the Efficiency of Forward Labour Contracting in Philadelphia, 1745–1773." *Journal of Economic History* **45** (1985) 855–68, p. 859, fn. 12.

[2] E. Morgan, "The Labour Problem at Jamestown, 1607–18," *American Historical Review*, **76** (1971) 595–611, pp. 596–597.

[3] W. Gookin, "The First Leaders at Jamestown," *Virginia Magazine of History and Biography*, **58** (1950) 181–193.

[4] I. Noel Hume, *The Virginia Adventure: Roanoke to Jamestown, An Archaeological and Historical Odyssey* (New York, NY: Alfred A. Knopf, 1984).

[5] Morgan, 'Labour Problem.'

G. Pollio, *The Rise and Fall of Britain's North American Empire*,
https://doi.org/10.1007/978-3-031-07484-4_2

property,[6] all of which have attracted their fair share of scholarly attention. More recently, drought has been added to the list of early Jamestown's travails.[7] One year after the turmoil, the cultivation of tobacco, which ultimately became one of Virginia's principal exports, was introduced. It stretches credulity that following the deaths of four-fifths of the original settlers ostensibly from starvation, the colony prioritised the production of a single cash crop over subsistence agriculture. Either the Virginia Company's investors were extraordinarily venal or the event was grossly exaggerated or non-existent.[8]

In due course, the labour shortages were addressed in four distinct ways. The first involved an individual's decision to migrate to the Americas with all of the costs connected with embarkation covered out of the expatriate's own resources (Free Labour). The second, indentured servitude, which achieved the same result albeit having a third party, typically a British shipper or merchant, to cover the upfront transportation costs via a fixed term, labour contract, negotiated either prior to departure or upon arrival in Britain's mainland or island colonies, where the contract for service was auctioned to the highest local bidder. The price paid ultimately reflected the immigrant's perceived economic value, determined in keeping with various observable personal characteristics, such as age, health, gender, skills, and so forth. Since contract length was variable, it served as the principal valuation metric by which individual characteristics could be arbitraged. The decision to emigrate was the same, regardless of which indenture option was selected, and dictated by economic conditions in England and perceived prospects in the New World.

Four sources contributed to the increase in the population of colonial America. Immigration over the course of the seventeenth century consisted mainly of free and indentured servants, which collectively accounted

[6] R. Ellickson, "Property in Land" *Yale Law Journal*, **102** (1993) 1315–1400, p. 13361338. T. Bethell, *The Noblest Triumph: Property and Prosperity Through the Ages* (London, UK: Palgrave Macmillan, 1999).

[7] D. Blanton, "Drought as a Factor in the Jamestown Colony, 1607–1612," *Historical Archaeology*, **34** (2000), 74–81. J. Sheller, "Rethinking Jamestown," *Smithsonian Magazine* (2005), 1–5.

[8] A recent study has shown that there are clear differences in the various accounts used to build up the traditional picture of these events in early Jamestown, including the details of the possible cannibalism. Her study establishes that, inter alia, reputational and economic interests suggest clear reasons for propagating or denying stories about cannibalism. R. Hermann, "The 'tragicall historie': Cannibalism and Abundance in Colonial Jamestown," *William and Mary Quarterly*, **68** (2011) 47–74.

for four-fifths of the indicated increase, with the latter accounting for *c.* 60 per cent of the total. Slaves represented only one-fifth of colonial American immigrants, while convicts accounted for barely 1 per cent. The pattern changed drastically in the eighteenth century, with the total number of immigrants increasing nearly threefold over the previous century. Slave numbers increased *c.* eightfold and accounted for nearly one-half of the increase.[9] Convict numbers, too, rose sharply from 1 to 10 per cent of the total number of immigrants. The records of London's central jail, the Old Bailey, indicate that included among the 52,000 convicts transported to the New World were 4700 women, most of whom apparently were convicted for having committed what would now be regarded as petty crimes, the bulk of which involved theft of one sort or another.[10]

This pattern appears to have applied equally to all of England's New World colonies in the seventeenth century; the following century, induced mainly by the growing importance of sugar production, the demographic shifts were more pronounced in the island than the mainland colonies. According to estimates compiled by Stanley Engerman, net slave imports in Britain's Caribbean Island settlements increased from 264,000 prior to 1700, more than doubling over the next sixty years, and rising 1.5 times again between 1761 and 1810.[11] These shifts drastically altered the racial composition of Britain's American colonies. On the eve of the American Revolution, the black proportion of the island colonies had already reached its long run average of 90 per cent, compared with the mainland colonies where the proportion, although exhibiting wide variation across individual

[9] A. Fogleman (1998): "From Slaves, Convicts, and Servants to Free Passengers: The Transformation of Immigration in the Era of the American Revolution," *Journal of American History*, **85** (43–76), p. 44, Table 1. These figures exclude Scotland, which was a sovereign polity in the seventeenth century and was not covered by the Transportation Act of 1718. Even so, 'some (Scottish) offenders were specifically ordered "beyond the seas" or to "his Majesty's plantations in America," most were merely banished "furth of the Kingdom," largely because Scotland lacked legal claim to the colonies before its union with England in 1707. Post-1718, only an estimated 700 convicts were transported to the American colonies in the during the period 1718–1775.' A. Ekirch, "The Transportation of Scottish Criminals to America during the Eighteenth Century," *Journal of British Studies*, **24** (1985) 366–374, p. 367.

[10] J. Lodine-Chaffey, *From Newgate to the New World: A Study of London's Transported Female Convicts, 1718–1775* (Master's thesis, University of Montana, 2006), p. 79, Table 1.

[11] S. Engerman, "A Population History of the Caribbean," in M. Haines and R. Steckel (Eds.) *A Population History of North America* (Cambridge University Press, 2000), p. 489, Table 11.1.

regions—from 3.4 per cent in the Northeast to 35.2 per cent in the South in 1790—the national average amounted to *c.* one-fifth of the population.

Declining interest in indentured servitude can be attributed to a combination of developments that collectively reduced the demand for unskilled contract labour, while concurrently increasing the demand for skilled workers. As population growth in England slowed, the parallel rise in industrial demand for labour reversed the declining real wage trend, even among unskilled workers; these shifts, moreover, coincided with falling slave prices as private traders augmented the numbers despatched by the Royal African Company. Prices paid for indentured servants rose by 60 per cent in the 1680s[12] while slave prices declined to less that £15, and in terms of sugar even further in the 1690s.[13] And, finally, there was a change in the ultimate destination of newly arrived immigrants as increasing numbers self-selected Pennsylvania and the Middle Atlantic region over the Chesapeake colonies, contributing to an even greater rise in the price of skilled labour in the southern colonies that encouraged regional planters to train and substitute slaves for contract labour even in skilled occupations.[14]

The transportation alternative, by contrast, depended upon the migrant's financial circumstances. With respect to contract labour, it should be clear the first option was superior to the alternative, affording the migrant the opportunity to reject the terms offered, in contrast to the second where no such flexibility existed. Under either option, transportation charges had to cover the shipper's opportunity cost, in effect, the income foregone by shipping passengers instead of freight, conditional on the amount of unused shipping capacity. The third option consisted of the transportation of convicts, which appeared to serve to two principal objectives, namely, minimising the costs of penal administration and populating territories that had vast economic potential.

[12] D. Galenson, 'Indentured Servitude,' p. 11.

[13] D. Eltis, F. Lewis and D. Richardson, "Slave Prices, the African Slave Trade, and Productivity in the Caribbean, 1674–1807," *Economic History Review*, **58** (2005) 673–700, p. 679, Table 2.

[14] D. Galenson, "White Servitude and the Growth of Black Slavery in Colonial America," *Journal of Economic History*, **41** (1981) 39–47, p. 46. 'The timing of both parts of the process can apparently be explained primarily with reference to the increasing relative costs first of unskilled, and later of skilled, indentured white labour. It might be added that differences in the timing of these changes across colonies can similarly be attributed to regional differences in relative labour costs.'

The final option was to employ slaves. However, the figures mentioned above relate only to those imported from Africa, notwithstanding that in the seventeenth and early eighteenth centuries, Native Americans ('Indians') were widely used as slaves and traded throughout Britain's New World Empire. In fact, the distribution of Indian slaves within England's mainland colonies was more widespread during those years than those that arrived later from Africa. Various estimates of their numbers range from 147,000–340,000 in North America (excluding Mexico)[15] to 2.5–5.5 million enslaved throughout the Americas.[16] These figures cannot in any way be considered definitive. Whatever the truth one conclusion is inescapable: 'There was a domestic traffic in humans that preceded the mass importation of Africans in the later seventeenth and early eighteenth centuries. Even concurrent with that traffic, there was another one, just as tragic, flowing just as insidiously, but often in the opposite direction. Indeed, … as Thomas Jefferson once exclaimed, "An inhuman practice once prevailed in this country of making slaves of the Indians."'[17]

> New England and the southern colonies were the sections that employed Indian slave labour most extensively, the south taking precedence, for climatic conditions there were more favourable, and economic conditions made necessary a larger quantity of servile labour than was required in the north. Yet New England made use of the natives as slaves as long as they lasted, and drew further supplies from Maine, the Carolinas, and other districts. Among the English colonies, the Carolinas stood first in the use of Indians as slaves. Such use began with the founding of the colony. The need for laborers was great; the source of supply was near at hand and the colonists availed themselves of their opportunity.[18]

[15] A. Resendez, *The Other Slavery: The Uncovered Story of Indian Enslavement in America* (Bostin, MA: Houghton, Mifflin Harcourt, 2016), p. 324.

[16] Brown University press release (15 February 2017) re article published by L. Fisher, 'Why shall wee have peace to bee made slaves': Indian Surrenderers during and after King Philip's War," *Ethnohistory,* **64** (2017):91–114.

[17] C. Everett, "'They Shalbe Slaves for their Lives:' Indian Slavery in Colonial Virginia," in A. Gallay, Indian Slavery in Colonial America (Lincoln, NE: University of Nebraska Press, 2009), p. 98.

[18] A. Lauber, *Indian Slavery in Colonial Times within the Present Limits of the United States* (New York, NY: Columbia University, 1913), pp. 105–107. Lauber presents estimates on the comparative valuations of African and Indian slaves derived mainly from probate inventories, the point being to illustrate the former were more highly valued and thus how they came to displace the latter. Probate valuations are of only limited usefulness in assessing rela-

We will probably never know the full extent to which Native Americans were enslaved, although it undoubtedly was much greater than is widely believed. Native Americans, whether in North America or the West Indies, were familiar with slavery, albeit not necessarily on the same terms as among Europeans. Most tribes in both regions held slaves: some were captured members of enemy tribes or punished members of their own tribes. Other than the fact itself, little else is known about the practice of slavery among the Indians prior to their encounter with Europeans. By contrast, recent studies have dismissed the conventional wisdom, partly retailed by Lauber, that Indians made poor slaves because they could easily escape and return to their tribes. Some undoubtedly did, but the reality is that many were often shipped to places far from their original homeland. Nor is there any reason to suppose that escapees would have been accepted by any neighbouring tribes to which they may have fled. Given that slavery existed among Native American tribes, it is more than likely that many among these tribes would have been involved in their original capture and enslavement. In which case, the runaways would most likely have been returned to their masters against some sort of compensation or retained for their own use.

Of far greater importance in terms of their unsuitability as slaves was the fact that they were especially susceptible to diseases contracted from both European colonists and their African slaves, notwithstanding those in the southeast physically interacted with Europeans at least a century before the English arrived. Whole tribes may have been decimated in this way, thus necessitating obtaining replacements from tribes located further away. Given these multiple interchanges, Wright has argued that the culture of the black population of the south-eastern United States should be understood as amalgamating elements of Native American, white, and African culture, concluding that Indian contribution to this amalgam, both cultural and genetic, is far greater than is generally recognised.[19]

tive values since they depend largely upon the skill and experience of the valuer, which can and does vary quite considerably.

[19] J. Wright, *The Only Land They Knew: The Tragic Story of the American Indians in the Old South* (Lincoln, NE: University of Nebraska Press, 1999.

2.1 Slave Labour

The use of slave labour in the Americas has been analysed in detail by a number of scholars; much less, however, is known about the circumstances of their capture, pricing, and trade in West Africa. There are three key aspects of the trade that need to be explained and integrated within a coherent framework: (1) the low prices paid by traders for slaves on the West Coast of Africa; (2) the absence of commodity alternatives to slaves that could have covered the region's trade deficit with Europe; and (3) the employment of slaves more or less exclusively on the plantations of the Caribbean islands and the southern mainland colonies.[20]

The first characteristic has been explained primarily in terms of the low productivity of African labour or, alternatively, the high cost of internal transportation would have significantly increased the cost of moving commodities from the African interior to the coastal regions; in other words, it was cheaper to transport slaves than the commodities they could have produced. The second issue is concerned with the production regime most suitable for the employment of slaves. The principal output produced by slave labour in the New World was cash crops, mainly sugar. One explanation that connects the two phenomena emphasises the fact that most agricultural regimes can be classified either as effort-intensive or care-intensive.[21] The principal difference lies in the nature of inducements required to motivate workers, the former relying mainly on pain-incentives and the latter on ordinary rewards. 'It is thus cheaper to buy effort than to buy care through the slave market, which is why the advantage of slaves

[20] Some scholars favour the view that the Atlantic slave trade differed from slave regimes. Recent research challenges that contention whether in respect of the Middle East or East Asia, regions where slavery existed long before Europeans entered the trade. With respect to the latter, 'the dynamics of the West African and wider Atlantic slave trade are not that different from what we encounter in the Indian Ocean and Indonesian archipelago worlds. Local inequalities (caste, indebtedness, slave lineage) and conflicts (warfare, punishment) were sources for an expanding long-distance slave trade in West Africa, as well as different parts of Southeast Asia, South Asia, and the Western Indian Ocean.' T. Chakraborty and M. van Rossump, "Slave Trade and Slavery in Asia—New Perspectives," *Journal of Social History*, **54** (2020) 1–14, p. 9. On the Middle East see M. Hopper, *Slaves of One Master: Globalization and Slavery in Arabia in the Age of Empire* (New Haven, CT and London: Yale University Press, 2015).

[21] S. Fenoaltea, "Slavery and Supervision in Comparative Perspective: A Model," *Journal of Economic History*, **44** (1984) 635–668.

over free labour would be greatest in highly physical activities.'[22] There is another possibility, namely, the climate was so harsh, and the work so backbreaking, that free or contract labourers were unwilling to emigrate to the West Indies; the same was true of the southern mainland colonies as settlers were likewise put off by the climate. In which case, the type of agricultural regime, although obviously of importance, may have counted for less than the combined impact of the arduous nature of the work and the environment in which it was carried out.[23]

The main feature of pre-colonial Africa that sustained the slave trade was that in contrast to most other global regions, the continent was highly fragmented politically, linguistically, and culturally. In contrast to Eurasia, where cultural areas were large, slaves could only be acquired via extremely costly long distance military operations. Culturally fragmented Africa, by contrast, implied that small-scale operations, involving no more than a few dozen men attacking villages from a nearby region, would be a much cheaper way of obtaining slaves. Thus, the role of Africa in the slave trade derived from several sources: a historical tradition of having commercialised slave raiding, a high degree of cultural fragmentation that kept slave acquisition costs low, and a desire for manufactured goods produced in Europe with little other than slaves to offer in exchange.

The catalyst that involved the Europeans in this trade was, of course, the discovery and development of the territories acquired in the New World. The growth of the transatlantic slave trade in the sixteenth and seventeenth centuries is widely considered to have benefitted Britain in a number of ways. Not only did it generate British manufactured exports to the regions in Africa where slaves were sourced, it also produced income on ancillary services such as shipping and insurance and, as a significant component of the traded goods in Africa consisted of textiles produced in India, gave a fillip to the latter's textile industry. There is some question as to the number of slaves imported into Britain's American colonies. While there are numerous estimates as to the scale of the trade, the earliest of these suggested the cumulative total amounted to 15–20 million up to the beginning of the American War for Independence; later research lowered

[22] L. Angeles, "On the Causes of the African Slave Trade," Adam Smith School of Business, University of Glasgow Working Paper (2012), p. 10.

[23] On the impact of climate on emigrant destination choices see K. Kupperman, "Fear of Hot Climates in the Anglo-American Colonial Experience," *William and Mary Quarterly*, **41** (1984) 213–240.

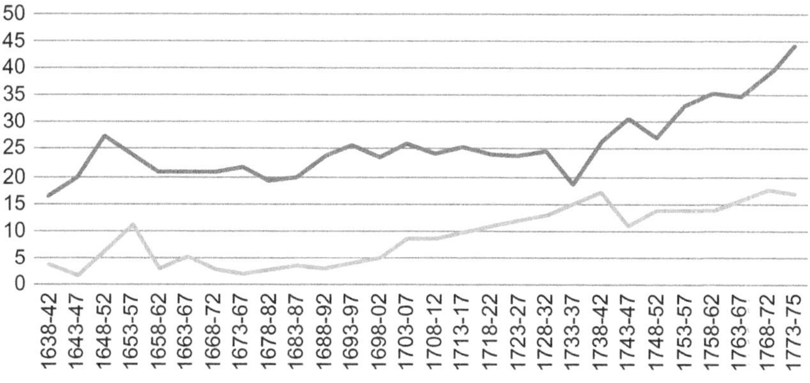

Chart 2.1 British American and West African Slave Prices, 1638/1642–1773/1775 (pounds sterling). (Note: Quadrennial averages. Blue line: West African Prices; Red Line: British American (landed) Prices. Source: *Historical Statistics of the United States*, Series Z165–168, p. 1174)

the figure to a maximum of 10 million.[24] Kenneth Stetson maintains the importation of slaves to the British colonies, both in the Caribbean and on the mainland, amounted to less than 1.5 million between 1700 and 1773,[25] while more recent estimates based upon Emory University's *Slave Voyages* database increase the figure slightly by 200,000. On one matter there is broad agreement among historians, namely, that the mainland's share amounted to less than one-fifth of the British total, and that post-independence there is no evidence of an increase in the North American share (Chart 2.1).[26]

Quantitative analysis of the use of slave labour in Britain's sugar islands, which attracted the largest share of the trade, indicates the economic impact while positive was modest. Eltis and Engerman, for example, estimate the value added in West Indian sugar production in 1805 to be

[24] P. Curtin, "Epidemiology and the Slave Trade," *Political Science Quarterly*, **83** (1968) 190–216, p. 191.

[25] Cited in M. Rothstein, "The Cotton Frontier of the Antebellum United States: A Methodological Battleground," *Agricultural History*, **44** (1970), 149–165 p. 155.

[26] According to the *Slave Voyages* data base, 273,419 slaves disembarked in North America between 1651 and 1775, and accounted for c. 6 per cent of the total New World slave trade. Charleston, NC was the principal port of disembarkation, although slaves were also landed in several northern ports, including Newport, RI and Boston, MA.

around £5.4 million, equivalent to *c.* 2 per cent of Britain's GDP,[27] subsequently increased to 4 per cent in a later study employing the same methodology.[28] Even so, the upgrade does little to alter Eltis and Engerman's overall conclusion that notwithstanding its regional importance 'the value added by the Caribbean sugar sector was less than 2.5 percent of British national income, meaning that more than 97.5 percent of income was generated by domestic and other foreign markets. As a share of the U.K. labour force Caribbean sugar comes out slightly higher, at 3.7 percent. Even if we include British refining enterprises in the calculations, sugar production was no more important than were several other industries.'

Focusing instead on the value added created by the slave trade itself, several points are worth noting. First, the British slave trade increased from around 15,000 slaves per year on average in the first decade of the eighteenth century to *c.* 40,000 slaves per annum on average a century later, when the British slave trade was abolished. True, the prices of slaves also increased so that the value of those arriving in the Americas on British ships rose substantially. However, the concurrent increase in the cost of slaves acquired in Africa, at almost the same rate as their landed cost in the Americas, resulted in an average annual real growth rate of only 1.2 per cent. 'As a consequence, the value added involved in trading slaves was comparatively small, and only increased marginally relative to British GDP over the period. Furthermore, fluctuations between years were substantial.'[29]

Taking account of forward and backward linkages arising from the slave trade, Rönnbäck analyses their economic impact in terms of three ascending levels of aggregation, with each estimate expressed as a percentage of British GDP. The most narrowly defined aggregate consists of manufactured exports to Africa, the trade in slaves across the Atlantic, and the exports of raw materials to Europe, which collectively created an annual average value-added equivalent of around 2.0 per cent of British GDP

[27] D. Eltis and S. Engerman, 'The Importance of Slavery and the Slave Trade to Industrializing Britain', *Journal of Economic History*, **60** (2000) 123–144, pp. 32–133.

[28] K. Rönnbäck, 'Sweet Business: Quantifying the Value Added in the British Colonial Sugar Trade in the eighteenth Century', *Revista de Historia Económica/Journal of Iberian and Latin American Economic History*, **32** (2014),223–245.

[29] K. Rönnbäck, "On the Economic Importance of the Slave Plantation Complex to the British Economy during the Eighteenth Century: A Value-added Approach," *Journal of Global History*, **13** (2018) 309–327, p. 319.

during the first decade of the eighteenth century, rising to around 5.2 per cent of British GDP a century later. Adding in total plantation production in the Americas, the corresponding estimates for the two sub-periods are 2.3 per cent and 7.6 per cent, respectively. With the further addition of industries dependent upon the American plantation complex, the estimated value added together increases to the equivalent of 3.1 per cent of British GDP during the first decade of the eighteenth century and 10.8 per cent a century later. Thus, the maximum contribution of the Atlantic Slave trade to the British economy amounts to *c.* 11 per cent of GDP.

Several important caveats apply concerning these estimates. First, value added is derived by subtracting prices received for slaves in the Caribbean from the prices paid by the shippers in Africa. For any single voyage, an accurate assessment of financial margins requires that the prices received should take account of inter alia voyage duration and slave mortality and morbidity. Even if the long-term trends resulted in shorter crossing times and reduced slave attrition rates, as appears to have been the case, they, nevertheless, remained critical inputs affecting the profitability of a given voyage. Given such risks, we would expect shippers to have diversified their cargoes to minimise potential losses, and evidence exists that such indeed occurred with its attendant favourable impact on voyage profitability. These additional cargoes included gold coins and bullion, initially from West Africa, and subsequently Brazil, the latter acquired via exchanges between Portuguese and British traders in West Africa; other goods included ivory and wood dyes.[30]

Second, the value-added calculation corresponds to net profit, which by itself conveys little useful information concerning the viability of the trade. It is not just the fact of it being positive that matters but rather whether the residual covers, or more than covers, the investors' opportunity cost of capital; if not, it would discourage further financial commitments for undertaking subsequent ventures. The fact that slave trade survived for 150 years before it was abolished creates the strong presumption that investors achieved or exceeded their required rate of return, a view that conflicted with the traditional historiography of American plantation slavery. During the first forty years of the twentieth century, the reigning paradigm favoured the view that slavery was ultimately paternalistic, inefficient, and, accordingly, unprofitable. 'The dominating

[30] D. Eltis, F. Lewis and K. McIntyre, "Accounting for the Traffic in Africans: Transport Costs on Slaving Voyages," *Journal of Economic History*, 70 (2010) 940–963, p. 962.

consideration with masters and mistresses was not that of great profit, but that of comfortable living in pleasant surroundings, with a consciousness of important duties well performed.'[31] In a later publication Phillips asserted categorically that by 'the close of the (eighteen) fifties it is fairly certain that no slave holders but those few whose plantations lay in the most advantageous parts of the cotton and sugar districts and whose managerial ability was exceptionally great were earning anything beyond what would cover their maintenance and carrying charges.'[32] It was Eric William's classic 1940 study that first drew attention to the fact that slavery must have been profitable, so much so, he concluded, that profits from the trade financed the Industrial Revolution.[33]

William's initial contention was affirmed in numerous subsequent studies, which, however, rejected the inferences he asserted followed from it. It is now widely accepted that the transatlantic slave trade was profitable, although some of the more extravagant claims concerning restrictions on entry and the super-normal profits they produced are dubious; the evidence now suggests that 8–10 per cent was the norm.[34] This is not to deny that returns on individual voyages were exceptionally high, only that a balanced assessment of overall industry profitability must take account of the considerable losses many voyages incurred, as may be seen from the published accounts of merchants that participated in the slave trade. For example, the account books for the Liverpool merchant William Davenport provide information on the profits made on the sixty-two ventures he invested in. They show that 'losses were made on at least one out of every three of these ventures. But profits of over 20 per cent were made in twenty-five instances; and in seven ventures profits averaged over 50 per cent. Highly profitable voyages were not uncommon, therefore, and in a

[31] U. Phillips, "The Slave Labor Problem in the Charleston District," *Political Science Quarterly*, **22** (1907) 416–439, p. 437.

[32] U. Phillips, *American Negro Slavery* (New York, NY: Appleton-Century, 1936), p. 391.

[33] E. Williams, *Capitalism and Slavery* (Chapel Hill, NC: University of North Carolina Press, 1944).

[34] D. Richardson, "Profitability in the Bristol-Liverpool Slave Trade," *Revue française d'histoire d'outre-mer*, **62** (1975) 301–308; K. Morgan, *Slavery, Atlantic Trade and the British Economy, 1660–1800* (Cambridge, U.K: Cambridge University Press, 2000), pp. 36–44. The same was true for the French slave trade, although recent research suggests that it may have had more to do with market restrictions than the trades' inherent profitability. G. Daudin, "Profitability of Slave and Long-Distance Trading in Context: The Case of Eighteenth Century France," *Journal of Economic History*, **64** (2004) 144–171, p. 167.

trade of this sort merchants may well have come to expect and even to depend upon the occasional financial killing.'[35]

Davenport's accounts also underline the financial downside of the slave trade. After numerous legal wrangles for money owed from previous voyages, in 1792, Davenport finally wrote off debts outstanding from four previous voyages, his personal losses totalling £1600, a considerable sum considering that his profits from the twenty-two voyages made between 1772 and 1774 amounted to £1700.[36] Note that the total return on the £96,000 invested in 110 ventures between 1757 and 1785 amounted to just under 11 per cent, more or less in line with overall industry returns. This compares with British lending rates in the eighteenth century of 4–5 per cent, although the premium could be justified in terms of the higher risks associated with the slave trade, a conclusion confirmed by the large differences in Davenport's annual returns over the nearly thirty years he was engaged in such trade.

The Royal African Company was the first of two joint stock companies awarded the right to trade along the West Coast of Africa; the Company's charter was granted in 1660, the shareholders included the Royal (Stuart) family and City of London Merchants, and was the principal supplier of slaves to Britain's American colonies. Trading rights were restricted to the territories specified in the Charter which ended at the Cape of Good Hope, where those of the East India Company began. The monopoly lasted until 1698, after which all Englishmen were conceded the right to trade in slaves. The Royal African Company became insolvent in the 1720s when its ports, settlements, and factories in Africa were transferred to the

[35] D. Richardson, "Profits in the Liverpool Slave Trade: The Accounts of William Davenport, 1757–1784," in R. Anstey and P. Hair (Eds.), *Liverpool, The African Slave Trade, and Abolition: Essays to Illustrate Current Knowledge and Research*. Vol. 2 (Liverpool, UK: Historic Society of Lancashire and Cheshire, 1989), p. 77. These results, seemingly, cannot automatically be applied to other nationalities that participated in the slave trade. 'Liverpool merchants at least seem to have been managing the trade relatively successfully, for recent evidence suggests that Continental traders were making markedly lower profits and even incurring losses in the second half of the eighteenth century. As slave traders of all nationalities faced certain common problems, this apparent discrepancy in profit margins would seem to indicate that Liverpool traders were better placed than their Continental counterparts to deal with some if not all of these problems.' Ricardson, 'Profitability in the Bristol-Liverpool Slave Trade,' p. 308.

[36] N. Radburn, "Keeping 'the wheel in motion': Trans-Atlantic Credit Terms, Slave Prices, and the Geography of Slavery in the British Americas, 1755–1807," *Journal of Economic History*, 75 (2015) 660–689, p. 678.

Company of Merchants Trading to Africa, which was incorporated by an Act of Parliament in 1750; it was abolished in 1821 and its assets became Crown property. The Merchants' Company had directors in all the major British ports, with Bristol furnishing the largest quota of ships, estimated at 237 in 1755. Jamaica was the largest single market for slaves, and an estimated 610,000 were imported between 1700 and 1786; the trade still flourished in 1763, when about 150 ships sailed yearly from British ports to Africa with capacity for nearly 40,000 slaves.

The second, the South Sea Company, was founded in 1711 as a joint stock company whose principal *raison d'etre* was to consolidate and reduce the cost of Britain's national debt, in effect replicating the example of the Bank of England, created fifteen years earlier and for the same purpose. In 1713, as part of the Treaty of Utrecht, Britain secured the right to supply slaves to Spanish America, a prerogative formerly enjoyed by France; the quid pro quo was that Spain would gain access to all the British forts along the West Coast of Africa, then controlled by the Royal African Company. The contract, or *asiento*, was then assigned by the British government to the South Sea Company conditional upon the latter taking on *c.* £9.5 million, a substantial portion, of Britain's national debt.

The contract granting the monopoly was perceived to be of enormous commercial and financial benefit to Britain as it opened up trade with Spain's rich South American colonies, which extended from the Orinoco River down to Tierra del Fuego. Slaves constituted the Company's principal cargo and were urgently needed to address Spain's colonial manpower problems.[37] The *asiento* granted the Company the right to transport 4800 slaves annually to the Indies and was to last for thirty years, subsequently extended by a further four years. A duty of 33 1/3 pesos was to be levied on each of the first 4000 slaves landed, with the remaining 800 duty-free. It would appear, however, that the payment of duties and taxes by the Company to the Spanish Crown 'were never prompt or accurate.'[38] During the first twenty-five years of the contract permission could be obtained to import more than 4800 slaves if needed; in the last five years, by contrast, 4800 was the maximum number that could be shipped annually.[39]

[37] H. Paul, "The South Sea Company's Slaving Activities," University of Southampton Discussion Papers in Economics and Econometrics, No. 0924, p. 3.

[38] N. Hunt, "Contraband, Free Ports, and British Merchants in the Caribbean World, 1739–1772," *Diacronie*, **13** (2013) 1–12, p. 5.

[39] Document 18: 'Project for the Asiento for Negroes between England and Spain,' in E. Donnan (Ed.), *Documents Illustrative of the History of the Slave Trade to America*. Vol. II. The Eighteenth Century (Washington, D. C.: Carnegie Institution of Washington, 1931), p. 16–21.

In addition to slaves, there was scope to export manufactured goods, above all, textiles, to the region that would have represented an additional source of revenue for the Company. The contribution of these legal and extra-legal exports to Company revenues—the extent of which is suggested by the number of Company vessels that docked at Spanish ports—remains a matter of dispute. At the time of the assignment, 'Spain was basically an agricultural country that failed to supply its own industrial needs, let alone those of its colonies. It has been estimated that by the end of the seventeenth century Spain supplied only 5 per cent of the merchandise that was sent on the fleets to America, with the remaining 95 per cent of the cargo consisting of European manufactured goods and luxury items from the Far East. In effect she had become an intermediary between the raw materials and bullion from her colonies in America and the export trade of the rest of Europe.'[40]

According to John Plowes, the Company's Secretary and Chief Accountant, 'beginning with the first permission ship in 1715, the company had carried on a large contraband trade. No ship of this class … had gone to the Indies that had not borne, besides its legitimate cargo, a surplus of contraband goods, while, at the same time, the negro packet-boats had also consistently engaged in illicit trade. Bribes, on a large scale, to the Spanish officials at the American ports had made the illegal commerce possible.'[41] Apart from the few examples cited by Plowes, Brown makes no attempt to estimate the contribution of the contraband trade to the Company's bottom line, although contemporary reports suggest it was considerable. Sevillian merchants, for example, complained in the 1730s that British traders had so thoroughly dominated the sale of textiles that they were effectively crowded out from the region.[42] How much of this trade was accounted for by the South Sea Company is a matter of dispute. Sorsby claims 'undoubtedly the illicit trade was profitable to some

[40] V. Sorsby, *British Trade with Spanish America Under the Asiento, 1713–1740* (doctoral dissertation, Faculty of Arts, University College, London, November 1975), pp. 25–26.

[41] V. Brown, "The South Sea Company and Contraband Trade," *American Historical Review*, **31** (1926), 662–678, p. 665.

[42] Thomas, *Atlantic Slave Trade*, p. 246. Britain was not the only country engaged in the contraband trade; Dutch and other European merchants were likewise involved.

directors and most factors and Company ships' officers; it is doubtful if much benefit accrued to Company stockholders.'[43]

That the potential may not have been realised is indicated by the actual number of slaves shipped by the South Sea Company under the *asiento*. According to Helen Paul, the total number of slaves transported on these voyages amounted to 34,000, with a mortality rate of *c*. 12 per cent, virtually identical to estimates compiled sixty years later and based upon records kept by ships' surgeons.[44] Paul interprets the latter estimate as evidence the Company sought to efficiently manage the transatlantic crossing to maximise revenues. However, the fact that many of the slaves delivered to Spanish ports were sourced in the Caribbean, Jamaica, in particular, suggests the hypothesis is doubtful.[45] The exact scale of this re-export trade is unknown, but figures presented by Stephen Fuller, agent for Jamaica, to the Board of Trade in 1778 suggest that some 28,000 slaves, equivalent to roughly one-eighth of the slaves imported at the island, were re-exported from Jamaica to other colonies during the third quarter of the eighteenth century. At the same time, it is clear that the level of re-exports fluctuated considerably from year to year, varying from less than 5 per cent of slave imports in 1762 to over 25 per cent of imports in 1760 and 1764. Although shipments of slaves from Jamaica to Spanish America after 1748 were well below previous levels, re-exports of slaves from several of the British islands in the eastern Caribbean seem to have expanded considerably during the 1750s and 1760s. The growth in re-exports of slaves from these islands may have been stimulated in part by trade with the Dutch colony of St Eustatius and the Spanish colonies of Cuba and Puerto Rico. But it seems to have depended mainly on shipments of slaves to the French

[43] Sorsby, *British Trade with Spanish America*, p. 260.

[44] R. Steckel and R. Jensen, "New Evidence on the Causes of Slave and Crew Mortality in the Atlantic Slave Trade," *Journal of Economic History*, **46** (1986) 57–77, p. 62, Table 3.

[45] G. Nelson, "Contraband Trade Under the Asiento, 1730–1739," *American Historical Review*, **51** (1945) 55–67, p. 57. Paul summarises her argument as follows: 'Large numbers of slaves were introduced to Spanish America after 1720. This evidence shows that the company was sufficiently well-organised to maintain its trade even after the upheaval of the Bubble period. It also implies that the Bubble itself was not as destructive to the economy as is sometimes thought. If the investors in the South Sea Company had been ruined by the crash, then there seems little reason why the company itself would have been able to continue. Its large-scale operations and the length of time it took to complete a trading cycle could only have been maintained if the home economy was able to support it.'

sugar colonies.[46] Paul's efficiency claim is further undermined by the fact that the minimum number of slaves authorised under the *asiento* amounted to 144,000, that is, more than four times the number transported, although her estimate appears to understate actual volumes; others have suggested the figure was closer to 66,000.[47] Even so, the higher estimate still amounts to less than one-half of those authorised.

Slave voyages were financed initially with either equity capital or maritime loans, the latter secured by bottomry loans or ship mortgages. The former constituted senior secured maritime liens, while providers of the latter were in effect residual claimants, that is, entitled to any funds that remained after all other claims against the vessel had been discharged. While these vehicles were acceptable for financing single voyages, they were unsuited for larger-scale operations given the sums required to develop local infrastructure and plantation production. This, in turn, led to the adoption of the joint stock company, which raised funds by spreading the risks across a relatively large number of investors. This option, in principle, served three broad interests: it provided for long-term financing, thus eliminating dependence on a single merchant or consortium of merchants for funding, spread the risks of loss, and created a highly liquid market in which company shares could be traded. These companies flourished in the first half of the seventeenth century, but before long, it became clear that too much capital was tied up in the start-up phase, which demanded continuing injections of new funds well beyond the initial investment horizon, most of which were financed out of exiting cash flows thus limiting potential dividend pay-outs. By the turn of the eighteenth century, 'as Caribbean plantations were becoming productive, private traders, sensing the coming payoffs, inherited their commercial contracts, shipping practices and credit arrangements.'[48]

Among the principal risks faced by merchants that invested in the slave trade, of greatest concern was loss of the vessel and its cargo, whether by seizure or natural disaster, prior to, during, or after the completion of the voyage; it is, however, the case that such losses were no greater than in

[46] D. Richardson (Ed.) *Bristol, Africa and the Eighteenth Century Slave Trade to America*. Vol. 3 The Years of Decline, 1746–1769 (Bristol Record Society, 1991), p. xxiv.

[47] W. Goetzmann, *Money Changes Everything* (Princeton, NJ: Princeton University Press, 2016), p. 337.

[48] 'Capital and Trade in Trade and Production,' J. Miller (Ed.) *The Princeton Companion to Atlantic History* (Princeton, N, J. and Oxford, UK: Princeton University Press, 2004), p. 149.

other segments of the seaborne trade[49] and, in any event, could be insured against. One estimate places the insurable risks in English foreign trade at £20.3 million in 1720, of which only *c.* 10 per cent was underwritten by the then two leading marine insurers.[50] John concludes these data signify that a large part of coastal and international shipping proceeded without cover, most likely reflecting a lack of capacity. In any event, he avers it is not until 'the beginning of the nineteenth century that the first reasonably accurate account of the volume of business is available.'[51] Other scholars have instead focused on merchant account books and arrive at a different conclusion, finding that merchants routinely arranged insurance to cover potential losses, and considerably earlier than John indicated.[52]

The following, extracted from a policy underwritten in 1729 by Royal Assurance, one of the principal British maritime insurers, provides an indication of the type of coverages available to slave traders. The document specifically relates to an enquiry made by the insurer to its legal counsel as to whether a particular exclusion applied. The enquiry thus provides insights into a number of specific features of slave trade coverage, the risks insurers were willing to cover, and those considered unacceptable. The document, first, confirms that human freight was insured at that time. Also, the insured was required to confirm that the underside of the vessel was sheathed in copper. And, finally, the insured agreed to assume all liability for losses incident upon slave insurrection or prohibited trade.

> A policy of insurance was made on Ship and Goods at and from London to the Coast of Africa and thence to Carolina upon interest with the following warranty: The Assured hath agreed to warrant the ship sheathed, to take upon himself all Averages arising by Death and Insurrection of Negroes and all Loss and Damage by prohibited trade'. The ship proceeded to Africa, and the Master disposed of the outward-bound cargo in purchasing Negroes, a few Elephant's teeth, and some Gold Dust, and having finished the trade there, departed for Carolina, but before he got off the Coast, the Negroes

[49] 'With a loss rate of 6.5 percent between 1760 and 1810, a period covering war and peace, British slaving voyages were no more risky than general foreign trades during war years. In fact, as we have seen, more British slave ships were lost on the legs of the triangular route without slave cargoes than with,' R. Pearson and D. Richardson, "Insuring the Transatlantic Slave Trade," *Journal of Economic History*, **79** (2019) 417–446, p. 442.

[50] A. John, "The London Assurance Company and the Marine Insurance Market of the Eighteenth Century," *Economica*, **25** (1958) 126–141, p. 127.

[51] Ibid.

[52] Richardson, 'William Davenport Accounts,' p. 71.

made an insurrection, killed two of the mariners, and the Ship taking fire, the Master and rest of the mariners quitted her and got away in the boat, the Negroes ran the ship ashore and made their escape by leaping overboard and swimming to land, as is supposed, and the Ship was beat to pieces and totally lost with other goods on board.[53]

Taken at face value, copper sheathing should have had a profound impact on shipping economics and, by extension, the profitability of the transatlantic slave trade. The high take-up rate among slave traders has been explained in terms of two main influences: sheathing increased a given vessel's longevity by as much as 50 per cent; it resulted in shorter transatlantic crossings, reducing voyage times by *c.* 16 per cent, which in terms of the slave trade, allegedly contributed to a significant decrease of *c.* 50 per cent in slave mortality during the Middle Passage relative to uncoppered vessels.[54] Solar and Rönnback estimate the benefits from prolonging ship life in isolation made copper sheathing a profitable investment, 'but hardly a compelling one, particularly since the cost of the ship probably accounted for no more than a quarter to a third of the total outfitting costs of a slave voyage. The icing on the cake for slave traders was the reduction in death rates.'[55] In this regard they appear to confirm Eltis' hypothesis proposed decades earlier that the decline in slave mortality reflected 'general improvements in ship design and navigation' meaning, presumably, a decline in voyage length.[56]

The cost of sheathing the average slave ship was about £225 and would last for at least three voyages. Hence, the gross cost per voyage was about £75; since copper replaced wooden sheathing, the net cost would have been around £60. An average slave ship would have embarked about 250 slaves in the 1770s, with an average mortality rate of 10–12 per cent (twenty-five to thirty slaves). Based upon their estimates of slave acquisition costs in coastal Africa and selling prices in the New World, Solar and Rönnback estimate that copper sheathing had only to reduce losses by two

[53] Cited in K. Cozens, "What Part did the London Marine Insurance Market Play in the Trans-Atlantic Slave Trade?" Typescript (October 2005).

[54] P. Solar and K. Rönnback, "Copper Sheathing and the British Slave Trade," *Economic History Review*, **68** (2015) 806–829. Their data cover the period from 1760–1807).

[55] Ibid., pp. 825–26.

[56] D. Eltis, "The Direction and Fluctuation of the Transatlantic Slave Trade, 1821–1843: A Revision of the 1845 Parliamentary Paper," in H. Gemery and J. Hogendorn (Eds.), *The Uncommon Market* (New York, NY: Academic Press, 1979.)

to four individuals per voyage in order to cover its cost. However, their empirical results indicate that copper sheathing would have resulted in a significantly larger reduction in mortality, of the order of 10–15 fewer deaths, 'in which case the investment in copper sheathing would have been recovered in a single voyage. These calculations indicate that longer-lived ships and lower death rates made copper sheathing a highly profitable investment for slave ship owners. Moreover, these calculations may understate the cost savings for two reasons. First, faster passages may have meant that captives arrived in the Americas in better condition and hence commanded better prices. Second, copper sheathing may also have influenced insurance costs because it helped maintain ships' structural integrity.'

Slave price data, however, fail to confirm the key prediction of their analysis, namely, that improved shipping economics should have narrowed the gap between purchase costs in Africa and realised prices in the Americas; indeed, the authors concede that on the available evidence the price differential nearly doubled between the 1770s and the early 1780s and the late 1780s and 1790s, that is, concurrent with the introduction of copper sheathing. Of course, other costs may have increased offsetting the efficiency gains resulting from copper sheathing, but these costs have yet to be identified leading the authors to conclude that the 'rise in the intercontinental price difference remains a puzzle.' One possibility is that the results are a statistical artefact, given that the introduction of sheathing coincided with the adoption of legislation that sets limits on crowding. 'Pre-1790 estimates are almost all in the area of a 15 percent loss. The estimates for the 1790s are generally in the area of a 10 per cent loss. ... Put together in this manner, the existing information leads to the conclusion that slave mortality, in terms of loss in transit per voyage, declined over time.'[57] If so, the correlation between the rise in the number of copper-clad vessels and time would be expected to be quite high, thus obscuring the statistical significance of the cladding variable.

This is not to say that sheathing was irrelevant, but previous research pointed to the fact that the increase in speed due to copper sheathing 'was probably fairly small compared to the gains from reduced repair time and a longer ship life.'[58] Copper cladding undoubtedly improved shipping economics, but not to the extent that it materially affected the cost-price

[57] R. Cohn, "Deaths of Slaves in the Middle Passage," *Journal of Economic History*, **45** (1985): 685–692, p. 687.

[58] Ibid., p. 691.

differential connected with transporting slaves across the Atlantic. The fact that unrelated shipping sectors likewise adopted the innovation underlines that its benefits were largely or entirely independent of a vessel's cargo. This is not to say that cladding contributed little or nothing to the profitability of the slave trade, only that its contribution should not be overstated; more realistically, its contribution was realised jointly with other concurrent developments that in all probability were of greater significance. The critical factors that contributed to reduced slave mortality should be sought not in marine innovation, but rather in terms of legislation designed to eliminate some of the worst abuses of the trade, above all, crowding that increased significantly the risk of spreading infection. Not all slave traders sought to maximise the number of slaves per ton of vessel capacity but, on the contrary, adhered to a ratio consistent with minimising losses. The following illustrates the different approaches followed by slave traders.

The usual maximum number of slaves carried by a slaver such as a vessel of the *Zong*'s *110 tons* size was around 250. The *Michael*, for example, a slaver of 132 tons going to Jamaica in 1781, embarked from Africa with 210 slaves and disembarked 195. Like the *Zong*, it left Africa with a crew of twenty. Seven crewmembers died or left *en route*. Its ratio of slaves to crew was 10.5 on departure and 15 on arrival. The average ratio of slaves to crew for ships going to Jamaica in 1781, excluding the *Zong*, was 8.91 when ships left Africa and 10.18 when the ships arrived in Jamaica. The *Zong* had a ratio of slaves to crew of 23.15 (19 crew and 440 slaves) when they left São Tomé and an extraordinary 34.5 ratio (11 crew and 380 slaves) on 29 November. In addition, only one ship voyaging to Jamaica in 1781—the *Jane*, a vessel of 242 tons with 677 slaves, a ratio of 2.8 slaves per ton—was more crowded than the *Zong*, which had 2.26 slaves per ton. The standard slave-to-ton ratio in the British transatlantic slave trade prior to the passing of the Dolben Act in 1788 was 1.60.[59]

To test the reliability of the latter estimate, data covering a sample of voyages originating from the English port of Bristol were collected and analysed. While Bristol was one of the three leading ports out of which the slave trade was conducted, over the period sampled, it had yielded its preeminent position to Liverpool owing, according to some scholars, to the 'greater energy' and the 'superior business methods' of the northern

[59] T. Burnard, "A New Look at the *Zong* Case of 1783," *XVII-XVIII*, 76, (2019) [accessed at: https://journals.openedition.org/1718/1808], p. 9.

merchants who specialised in this trade. 'They trained their men better, paid lower wages, allowed more generous expenses and costs to their captains and factors than Bristol.'[60] The most significant implication of MacInnes' argument is that as the profitability of slave trading out of Bristol declined, the willingness of locals to invest in the trade diminished. Richardson, however, rejects the argument. 'The African trade continued to attract substantial levels of investment at Bristol after the War of Austrian Succession [1740–1748] and, on available evidence, yielded fairly satisfactory returns. Moreover, much of this investment was undertaken by groups of new merchants who not only invested regularly in the African trade but also took over the organisation and management of most of the voyages fitted out for the coast.'[61] While investment in the slave trade may in fact have been profitable, it leaves unexplained the reasons behind Liverpool's rise to first rank and why London in due course surpassed Bristol in terms of the total numbers shipped.[62]

Table 2.1 summarises three key parameters of the slave trade, namely, vessel tonnages, crewmen on the outward voyage, and the number of slaves transported. The data, including nearly sixty voyages in total, are shown for two sub-periods two decades apart. The fact that this period coincided with what Richardson describes as Bristol's 'years of decline' it seemed worthwhile to test whether this was the case and which aspects of the trade were most directly affected. Comparing the results for the two sub-periods, on all but the number of slaves transported the figures show little difference; indeed, the results of the statistical test shown in the last column indicates the observed differences cannot be considered statistically significant. By contrast, the results indicate that the volume of Africans transported between the two sub-periods declined by a quarter, while the statistical test confirms the difference is unlikely to have arisen by chance. Taken together the evidence appears to confirm Bristol's decline, perhaps connected with a more conservative and cautious approach to the

[60] C. MacInnes, *Bristol and the Slave Trade* (Bristol Branch of the Historical Society Association the University of Bristol, 1968), p. 7.

[61] D. Richardson, *Bristol, Africa, and the Eighteenth Century Slave Trade to America.* Volume 3: Years of Decline 1746–1769 (Bristol Record Society, 1991), p. xxxi.

[62] Between 1750 and 1807 slaves on ships transported in Liverpool-based vessels totalled 1.4 million, and the figures for Bristol and London from the seventeenth to early nineteenth centuries are 516,000, and 813,000, respectively. J. Moody, *The Persistence of Memory: Remembering Slavery in Liverpool, 'Slaving Capital of the World'* (Liverpool University Press, 2020) pp. 30–31.

Table 2.1 Vessel Tonnage, Outbound Crew, and Number of Slaves Landed, Bristol, 1746–1748 and 1766–1769

	1746–1748	*1766–1769*	*t-test for Differences in Means*
N	*(32)*	*(26)*	
Tons			
Mean	127.5	119.4	0.55 ($p = 0.58$)
Median	100.0	103.0	
Standard deviation	67.08	36.9	
Crew			
Mean	34.0	33.0	1.37 ($p = 0.18$)
Median	30.0	30.0	
Standard deviation	11.5	10.5	
No. of slaves			
Mean	303.9	233.5	3.22 (p = 0.002)
Median	285.0	235.5	
Standard deviation	99.9	86.1	

Source: Data are from D. Richardson, *Bristol, Africa, and the Eighteenth Century Slave Trade to America*. Volume 3: Years of Decline 1746–1769 (Bristol Record Society, 1991)

trade. The fact the numbers transported fell implies a reduction in both overcrowding—from 2.4 to 1.95 slaves per ton—which would appear consistent with a decline in revenues per ton. And while the risk of insurrection declined with the number of slaves per crewmen falling from 8.9 to 7.1, that too would be consistent with higher costs, and thus a further hit to revenues. In comparison with the estimates cited above, the slaves/ton ratio was above, and the slaves/crew ratio below, the industry averages.

One of the most notorious incidents relating to the slave trade, but which had wider ramifications, relates to events that occurred aboard the above-mentioned *Zong*, a corruption of the vessel's original Dutch name (*Zorg*).[63] The incident had significant ramifications for the slave trade and continues to attract scholarly and popular attention—including the recent production of a play that dramatises the events that occurred on board the vessel—underlining the special place it occupies in the history of the slave trade. Most importantly because of the notorious behaviour of the captain and the ship's crew, but equally important on account of the light it sheds on the nature of marine insurance as provided in the late eighteenth

[63] A precis of the incident is given in *2 Douglas, 233: Gregson v. Gilbert*, Thursday, 22d May, 1783, p. 629. Commonwealth Legal Information Institute, English Reports Decisions 1783.

century, the fact it created pressures to regulate the slave trade, while '"galvaniz[ing]" the anti-slavery movement from being a minor campaign by a set of marginal figures infected by evangelical enthusiasm to becoming the most significant moral campaign in British history.'[64]

The result was two sets of proceedings, one before the King's Bench and a second parallel case in the Court of Exchequer. In the first instance, the owners were granted damages in which the losses were allowed, the jury having found the slaves were jettisoned in connection with an onboard insurrection. The Syndicate was awarded £3660 for the loss of 122 Africans insured at £30 each. But in an appeal hearing before Lord Mansfield (who had also presided in the first hearing) and two other judges, this judgement was overturned mainly on the grounds that the ship's Captain, Luke Collingwood, failed to act responsibly in the face of a possible insurrection, while several claims adduced at the first trial were shown to be inaccurate. The key point was that if indeed there was the risk of an insurrection, the actions taken by Collingwood and his crew failed to protect the vessel from shipboard revolt; on the contrary, their actions placed the ship and the crew in great danger.

Five years after the incident Parliament enacted the first legislation regulating the slave trade. The resulting legislation, the *Slave Trade Act of 1788* (also known as the Dolben Act, after its principal proponent), mandated, inter alia, that ships up to a maximum of 207 tons burthen could transport 1.67 slaves per ton, above which only 1 slave per ton could be carried[65]; it also required that every slave ship to carry at least one qualified surgeon, who must be able to prove that he had passed a recognised examination.[66] The ratio formalised in the legislation, at 1.67, was slightly higher than the generally accepted industry average, while the health requirement likewise acknowledged what was fast becoming standard practice among slave traders. Together, these standards, which while well short of abolitionist demands, would undoubtedly have been satisfactory to those engaged in this activity. The provisions of the 1788 Act applied for one year only, meaning that Parliament had to renew the Act annually. The statutes of 1790, 1794, and 1799, which continued and/or modified

[64] Burnard, *A New Look*, p. 18.

[65] Prior to 1788, slaves were commonly packed into ships at ööates over two slaves per ton.

[66] J. Webster, "The *Zong* in the Context of the Eighteenth-Century Slave Trade," The Journal of Legal History, **28** (2007):285–298, P. 288, fn. 12, p. 290, fn. 26.

the Dolben Act, contained clauses specifically prohibiting losses due to throwing overboard, ill treatment, or natural death. 'That under such Policies of Assurance so made or to be made, no Loss or Damage shall hereafter be recoverable on Account of the Mortality of Slaves by natural Death or ill Treatment, or against Loss by throwing overboard of Slaves on any Account whatsoever.' This provision, it is now widely accepted, was enacted against the backdrop of *Zong* hearings.

While there seems to be a general sense that the original legislation and its subsequent amendments was triggered by the actions taken onboard the *Zong*, it is equally likely the new regulations were adopted in the interests of the insurers, for the simple reason that the rapid and sustained growth of Britain's maritime supremacy depended upon the availability of marine insurance.[67] In other words, the official measures were meant to eliminate opportunistic behaviour on the part of vessel owners to jettison slaves that owing to their condition or disposition threatened the voyages' revenue potential. Insurers' obligations in respect of slave trading were set out concisely in 1781 by John Weskett: 'The insurer takes upon him the risques (sic) of the loss, capture, and death of slaves, or any other unavoidable accident to them: but natural death is always understood to be excepted:—by natural death is meant, not only when it happens by disease or sickness, but also when the captive destroys himself through despair, which often happens: but when slaves are killed, or thrown into the sea in order to quell an insurrection on their part, then the insurers must answer.'[68]

Two situations can be envisaged that justify jettisoning slaves, but which entail different financial outcomes. In the first instance, to eliminate the spread of disease slaves that had, or exhibited symptoms of, infectious diseases could be jettisoned, especially in circumstances where there was a grave risk to the vessel and its crew, in which case compensation would be at the general average; if, by contrast, the action was taken to supress a revolt, compensation would be significantly higher at the average realised sale price. Faced with these choices, the superior option would be to

[67] A recent study of the relationship between insurance and slavery in R. Pearson and D. Richardson, "Insuring the Transatlantic Slave Trade," *Journal of Economic History*, **79** (2019) 417–446.

[68] Cited in J. Oldham (2007) "Insurance Litigation Involving the Zong and Other British Slave Ships, 1780–1807," *Journal of Legal History*, **28** (2007) 299–318, p. 303.

justify jettisoning as a response to insurrection. The plausibility this hypothesis is suggested by the fact that slave insurrections were reportedly more common in the second than in the first half of the eighteenth century, with an even bigger increase in the last quarter of the century. Unless, however, there was a fundamental shift in the way the trade was conducted, for which there is little evidence, the observed increase in the incidence of insurrection would be unexpected.

There are two difficulties with this explanation. First, the evidence for Bristol in the second half the eighteenth century indicates that shipowners appear to have adopted practices that *reduced* the risk of a revolt (Table 5.2, *supra*). And for another, there is a marked difference in the experience of American and English slavers. Surviving records show that, 'Rhode Island vessels experienced only seventeen slave revolts from 1730 to 1807, one every four and a half years, or about one every fifty-five voyages,' but, by contrast, 'British slavers sustained a revolt about once every two years.'[69] More recently Krikler proposes that the responsibilities of physicians expanded from their original purpose, to ensure that only healthy slaves who could survive the Atlantic crossing were acquired in Africa, to determining which were most at risk at sea. 'In the slave trade, medical expertise became yoked to the fateful decision of whether or not to accord commodity value to the captive. Where the surgeons decided to deny commodity value to a captive in the trade, he or she suffered "commercial death", which was all too often followed by death itself.'[70]

Among other things, Krikler notes that the captain of the *Zong* was a physician and thus was well placed to differentiate healthy from sick slaves, thus converting an uninsurable loss to a general average loss, that is, the sacrifice of parts of a ship's cargo for the benefit of the whole. While it appears to be the case that the judges of the Court of Exchequer overturned the original jury award, it is possible, as some authors aver, that a number of other ships' captains in collusion with the ships' physicians acted similarly; others may have been even bolder, claiming insurrection, thus converting a natural loss to an even more profitable alternative. The

[69] J. Coughtry, *The Notorious Triangle: Rhode Island and the African Slave Trade, 1700–1807* (Philadelphia, PA: Temple University Press, 1981), p. 150.

[70] J. Krikler, "A Chain of Murder in the Slave Trade: A Wider Context of the *Zong* Massacre," *International Review of Social History*, 57 (2012) 393–415, p. 393.

fact that the *Zong* case was the first of its kind to be adjudicated must raise doubts as to the validity of the assertion.[71] It may be the case that other British captains did jettison live slaves, in which case the syndicate that financed the *Zong* would have been the first to make a claim, either as a test case or with the intention of making full recovery. As noted above, the Dolben Act of 1788 and subsequent amendments addressed the issue directly by outlawing the jettisoning of slaves.

Other important risks of the slave trade were concisely summarised by Edward Corrie, an eighteenth-century Liverpool merchant, as *The Purchase*, *The Mortality*, *The Market*, and *The Remittance*.[72] The first encompasses the possibility that a satisfactory volume of slaves might not be procurable on a given voyage, the success of which largely depended upon the range and acceptability of the goods offered in the exchange; as John Roberts, a Rhode Island merchant put it, 'The secret of the African trade lies mostly on the choice of a good proper cargo and managing the same cleverly on the coast.'[73] Things weren't quite that simple as different African markets demanded specific types of goods, so that vessels trading along the West African coast would have to have the appropriate mix in terms of assortment and quality if trading were to take place.[74] Royal Africa Company data for selected years of the last quarter of the seventeenth century indicate the principal goods bartered for slaves were textiles (61 per cent, of which *c.* one-third were produced in the East Indies), metal and metal wares (21 per cent), and armaments, gunpowder, firearms and knives (6.5 per cent).[75] The relative importance of the goods sold by

[71] 'While the brutalities of the slave trade cannot be overstated the jettison of living slaves from the *Zong* was clearly, even by contemporary standards, a most unusual event.' J. Webster, "The Zong in the Context of the Eighteenth Century Slave Trade," *Journal of Legal History*, **28** (2007) 285–298, p. 292.

[72] Cited in S. Haggerty, "Risk and Risk Management in the Liverpool Slave Trade," *Business History*, **51** (2009) 817–834, p. 819. The author correctly describes the first three as physical hazards, the fourth, remittances, as a moral hazard.

[73] Cited in A. Ruderman, "Intra-European Trade in Atlantic Africa and the African Atlantic," *William and Mary Quarterly*, 77 (2020) 211–244, p. 211.

[74] S. Behrendt, "Markets, Transaction Cycles, and Profits: Merchant Decision Making in the British Slave Trade," *William and Mary Quarterly*, **58** (2001) 171–204, p. 172.

[75] N. Zahedieh, 'Capital and the Colonies,' p. 249, Table 6.2. See also A. Alpern, "What Africans Got for Their Slaves: A Master List of European Trade Goods," *History in Africa*, **22** (1995), 5–43. On guns and gunpowder, see G. White, "Firearms in Africa: An Introduction," Journal of African History, 12 (1971)173–184, and W. Whatley, "The Gun-Slave Hypothesis and the eighteenth Century British Slave Trade," *Explorations in Economic*

the Royal African Company over the following half century was little changed: textiles still accounted for more than half of traded goods followed by metal and firearms (11 per cent each), and cowry shells (7 per cent).[76]

The account books of William Davenport not only confirm the types of exports suitable for barter on the West African coast but, like most other financial aspects of the slave trade, could be procured on generous credit terms. 'The length of credit on offer differed from one supplier to another and also fluctuated over time. But it would appear that during the second half of the eighteenth-century Bristol and Liverpool slave-traders normally expected and usually succeeded in obtaining twelve months' credit, particularly from suppliers of some of the major categories of trade goods such as East India and Manchester textiles, guns and liquor.'[77] Other risks faced at the port of embarkation included variable loading rates and ocean crossing times, and provisioning difficulties arising from these uncertainties.

Corrie's second category of risk related to the high crew and slave morbidity rates. While it is known that mortality rates declined over the course of the eighteenth century,[78] they nevertheless remained high in comparison with similar transatlantic voyages undertaken for other purposes (free and indentured immigrants, the movement of British troops and transportation of convicts). Considerable attention focuses on slave mortality particularly during the Middle Passage, although in reality this phase accounted for a relatively modest fraction of slave attrition rates, a fact

History, **67** (2018) 80–104. The weapons sold were not very good or reliable nor is it clear as to what use firearms were put. Nineteenth-century European observers reported that the natives used guns, inter alia, 'for show and had not been fired for years … to fire salutes "which they did as frequently as their supply of ammunition would warrant." In tribal warfare their noise was a deterrent, and this gave these ancient muzzle-loaders a value far beyond their effectiveness as weapons.' R. Beachy, "The Arms Trade in East Africa in the Late Nineteenth Century," *Journal of African History*, **3** (1962) 451–467, p. 452. It would appear moreover, that Arab traders were among the first to exchange weapons for slaves.

[76] R. Ronnbäck "The Business of Barter on the Pre-colonial Gold Coast," *Economic History of Developing Regions*, **35** (2020) 123–142 p. 129, Fig. 1.

[77] D. Richardson, 'William Davenport Accounts,' p. 72. See also S. Behrendt, "Markets, Transaction Cycles, and Profits: Merchant Decision Making in the British Slave Trade," *William and Mary Quarterly*, **58** (2001), 171–204.

[78] On comparative mortality rates of slaves and non-slave transatlantic voyages see H. Klein, S. Engerman, R. Haines and R. Shlomowitz, "Transoceanic Mortality: The Slave Trade in Comparative Perspective," *William and Mary Quarterly*, **58** (2001) 93–118.

conceded by even the most ardent early nineteenth-century abolitionists. Figures compiled by William Wilberforce, for example, implied that the share of losses attributable the Middle Passage amounted to one-quarter of the total, while Thomas Buxton in a later and more detailed assessment lowered the percentage to one-fifth.[79] Recent research indicates that contemporary estimates such as these were uniformly too high, by as much as a third or a half, and possibly a reflection of the fact that both were compiled by known abolitionists.[80]

Apart from general supply and demand conditions at the time of disembarkation, prices received for individual slaves depended upon personal characteristics, such as sex, age, temperament, health, physical condition, skill level, and so forth; prices received for the principal regional crops, likewise affected slave valuations. Generally speaking, male slaves, ceteris paribus, attracted higher prices than female slaves, even in North America, where reproductive potential was valued more highly than in Britain's Caribbean colonies. Payment could take various forms, specie, produce, or credit, the latter, the most common mode of settlement, typically in the form of bills of exchange, and without which the trade would almost

[79] The Wilberforce estimate is cited in Klein, et al. 'Transoceanic Voyages,' p. 97. Buxton's figures are from T. Buxton, *The African Slave Trade and its Remedy* (London, UK: John Murray, 1839), Chapter 2, 'Mortality.' Buxton includes in his enumeration Islamic slave trading which he estimates to have amounted c. 50,000 souls, with an attrition rate of 50 per cent. On Arab slave trading up to the end of the nineteenth century see "Mohammedanism and Slave-Trade in Africa," *Science*, **12** (Dec. 28, 1888), 325–326 and also "The Internal Slave Trade of Africa," *Scientific American*, **76** (Mar. 13, 1897) 168–169. On the history of Arab slave trading see B. Lewis, *Race and Slavery in the Middle East* (Oxford, UK and New York: Oxford University Press, 1990), especially Chapter 14, 'Myth and Reality,' which explores why historians appear more accepting of slavery among Western than Islamic countries. See also F. Cooper, "The Problem of Slavery in African Studies," *Journal of African History*, **20** (1979) 103–125, as an antidote to the fact that scholars 'have often refused to face the question of whether in Africa, as in most of the world, the concentration of wealth and power also meant exploration and subordination.'

[80] Manning concludes that crude mortality rates for the Middle Passage averaged c. 15 per cent per voyage. P. Manning, 'Migrations of Africans to the Americas: The Impact on Africans, Africa, and the New World', in Slave Trades, 1500–1800, in P. Manning (Ed.) Globalization of Forced Labour, p. 69. By contrast, Steckel and Jensen, whose analysis is based on a detailed study of surgeons' logs dating from the 1790s, lower the estimate by 11.5 per cent, although the lower percentage may be due to the different time periods covered as it is known that mortality rates declined post-1790 owing to legal, economic, technical, and organisational factors. R. Steckel and R. Jensen, "New Evidence on the Causes of Slave and Crew Mortality in the Atlantic Slave Trade," *Journal of Economic History*, **46** (1986) 57–77, p. 62, Table 3.

certainly have ground to a halt.[81] As defaults were not uncommon—'planters in the West Indies had a terrible reputation for not paying their debts, and eventually factors in the West Indies only worked on commission, in order to avoid becoming responsible for the debt'[82]—Edgar Corrie ranked his fourth risk as the most serious of all: while the first three could impair the profitability of a voyage, he averred, remittance risk exposed 'the entire capital of the Merchant.'[83]

With a bill of exchange an American sugar planter instructed his merchant, agent, or banker in England, to whom his production had been consigned for sale, to use the proceeds from selling the sugar to pay the merchant who had originally financed goods sent from Europe on credit to the American planter. Bills of exchange served the interests of all the principal participants involved in the transaction. 'Planters needed credit to buy slaves before putting them to work for the next round of staple crop production; they could then afford to pay for these newly acquired laborers after the crop harvest. Increasingly, colonial factors became key middlemen by assuming the burden of debt; they received credit from

[81] 'Without these credit outflows, a slave trade of the scale that the British attained in the eighteenth century was inconceivable, even with the evident growth of demand for slave-produced goods such as sugar.' R. Pearson and D. Richardson, Social Capital, Institutional Innovation and Atlantic Trade Before 1800," *Business History*, **50** (2008) 765—780, p. 769. Also N Radburn, "Keeping "the wheel in motion": Trans-Atlantic Credit Terms, Slave Prices, and the Geography of Slavery in the British Americas, 1755–1807," *Journal of Economic History*, **75** (2015) 660–689.

[82] S. Haggerty, "Risk and Risk Management in the Liverpool Slave Trade," *Business History*, **51** (2009) 817–834, p. 823. 'In the late seventeenth century the Royal African Company experienced difficulties with remittances for slave sales. It was owed £170,000 by West Indian planters in 1690 and had to borrow on bond in England to cover this and other costs. In other words, the company agreed to pay, through a formal legal instrument, the sums it owed to creditors by a specific date or on demand. By 1708–10, this bonded debt had not been discharged; it amounted to between £300,000 and £400,000.' K. Morgan, "Remittance Procedures in the Eighteenth-Century British Slave Trade," *Business History Review*, **79** (2005) 715–749, p. 719. By the late eighteenth century only those with established credit were eligible to participate in slave transactions. 'Rich, creditworthy planters, through their standing with the factor, could access the highest-priced slaves, while poor planters with no credit would be excluded at the door to the sale or left to choose from sickly, old, or adolescent captives. Through the scramble sale, factors quickly sold entire shiploads of slaves and simultaneously rewarded favored purchasers within their networks.' N. Radburn, "Guinea Factors, Slave Sales, and the Profits of the Transatlantic Slave Trade in Late Eighteenth-Century Jamaica: The Case of John Tailyour," *William and Mary Quarterly*, **72** (2015) 243–286, p. 272.

[83] Cited in Radburn, 'Transatlantic Credit Terms,' p. 672.

their British merchant principals, extended credit to planters, and benefited from the commissions they earned on slave sales. British merchants favoured the new arrangements in remittance procedures, because institutional arrangements were put in place to limit the vagaries of dependence on personal trust in business. The guarantors of the bills of exchange supported the changing remittance practices, which assured them regular business and commissions.'[84]

[84] K. Morgan, "Remittance Procedures in the Eighteenth-Century British Slave Trade," *Business History Review*, 79 (2005) 715–749, p. 747.

CHAPTER 3

The Slave Trade and Britain's Industrial Revolution

What was the significance of the transatlantic slave trade to Britain's economy and its contribution to the rise of the Industrial Revolution? It has already been noted that the slave trade overall generated an appropriate return for those involved in it, although it does not follow from this, as Eric Williams claimed, that such profits 'fertilized the entire (British) productive system.'[1] For William's argument to be valid it must be shown that the profits from slave trading were large in relation to British capital outlays and, if so, contributed to the expansion of investment rather than merely redistributing existing industrial assets. The evidence, however, suggests that the sums involved were not all that great in relation either to total investment expenditure or GDP. 'Even on the most favourable assumptions ... the profits of the slave trade, had they all been invested in

[1] Williams, 'Capitalism,' p. 105. Williams saw capitalism as having contributed to both the rise of capitalism and its destruction. 'The capitalists had first encouraged West Indian slavery and then helped to destroy it. When British capitalism depended on the West Indies, they ignored slavery or defended it. When British capitalism found the West Indian monopoly a nuisance, they destroyed West Indian slavery as a first step in the destruction of West Indian monopoly.' 'But elsewhere it is mercantilism that was responsible for the rise and decline of slavery' (p. 169) 'The very vested interests which had been built up by the slave system now turned and destroyed that system .... The rise and fall of mercantilism is the rise and fall of slavery' (p. 136).

G. Pollio, *The Rise and Fall of Britain's North American Empire*,
https://doi.org/10.1007/978-3-031-07484-4_3

Britain, would have contributed no more than 3 percent of capital formation in 1770.'[2]

It is necessary to set against this moderate estimate the expenses incurred to support Britain's island colonies to arrive at a balanced assessment of the contribution of the transatlantic slave trade to the metropolitan economy. Caribbean output became increasingly uncompetitive as production shifted to the larger islands and thus had to be subsidised by consumers via the imposition of tariffs on lower-cost, non-British supplies, while the costs of administering and protecting the sugar islands were paid for by the British taxpayer. If properly costed these expenditures would likely have offset most or all of the private gains generated by the slave trade. It would thus appear that British policy towards its Caribbean colonies was driven less by the requirements of the prevailing, but increasingly challenged, mercantilist ethos, then by a desire to increase state revenues[3] and serve the interests of plantation owners and their supporters in Parliament.[4] While the number of parliamentarians with a direct or indirect

[2] J. Mokyr, "Editor's Introduction: The New Economic History and the Industrial Revolution, in J. Mokyr (Ed.) *The British Industrial Revolution: An Economic Perspective* (New York, NY: Routledge, 1998), p. 49, fn. 77. In an earlier study Engerman estimated the contribution of slave trading profits to British capital expenditure for the years 1688–1770 from 2.4 per cent to 10.8 per cent, and its contribution to British GDP a negligible 0.5 per cent or less. S. Engerman, "The Slave Trade and British Capital Formation in the Eighteenth Century: A Comment on the Williams Thesis," *Business History Review*, **46** (1972)430–443, pp. 439–440. Solow commenting on Engerman's estimates accepts that he 'never claims that they measure anything but an upper limit on what the slave trade could have contributed to British growth. On the evidence of his figures, the contribution *could have been* enormous.' B. Solow, "Caribbean slavery and British growth: The Eric Williams hypothesis." *Journal of Development Economics*, 17 (1985)99–115, pp. 105–106. Solow's position is favourably assessed by W. Darilty, Jr., "British Industry and the West Indies Plantations," *Social Science History*, 14 (1990) 117–149.

[3] 'In the fifteen years after the accession of William III to the English throne, the English tariff structure was transformed from a generally low-level, fiscal system into a moderately high-level system which, though still fiscal in its purposes, had become in practice protective; and which was then endlessly and minutely modified in ways that added marginally to this protective element.' R. Davis, "The Rise of Protection in England, 1689–1786," *Economic History Review*, **19** (1966) 306–317, p. 307.

[4] 'As the English islands lost their comparative advantage in sugar production to the larger islands, the prosperity of the vested West Indian interests, resting as it did on protective tariffs that kept sugar British sugar prices substantially higher than prices elsewhere in Europe, depended upon its political position. The extent of the sugar interests, reaching from the planters to the ports and into the manufacturing districts, combined with wealthy planters' ability to purchase seats in House of Commons, preserved the interests and supported slav-

connection to the West Indies is contentious, it has been estimated that as many as forty to fifty members in any one session of the House of Commons could be regarded as being supportive of the interests of the Caribbean plantations.[5]

Adam Smith was among the first to argue that Britain would have been much better off without its empire. 'To found a great empire for the sole purpose of raising up a people of customers, may at first sight appear a project fit only for a nation of shopkeepers. It is, however, a project altogether unfit for a nation of shopkeepers; but extremely fit for a nation whose government is influenced by shopkeepers' (WN: IV: 7). Later research confirmed the accuracy of Smith's assessment.

> Two groups reaped most of the long-term gains from this cruel trade; African and Arab traders and European consumers of tropical produce. For Africa the slave trade engendered private profits and heavy social losses-a horrifying example of 'the development of underdevelopment'. And if Europeans had been compelled to pay a 'free market price' for their tropical imports (that is to say a price which reflected the real cost of attracting and maintaining 'free' labour in the New World) then the prices of sugar, tobacco, spices, cotton, indigo, coffee, and other produce would have been far higher. The terms of trade would have swung massively against them and their real incomes would have diminished. By how much remains to be calculated. But with small ratios of plantation imports to national income and a relatively elastic demand for tropical produce, the fall in real income (which would have followed from a hypothetical British edict abolishing the slave trade, let us say in i607, rather than two centuries later) could not have made that much difference to the levels of wealth and income achieved in Western Europe by 1807. Though the consumption loss would certainly exceed the production loss.[6]

In this connection, it is important to differentiate the motives driving development between Britain's Island plantations and mainland colonies,

ery in the islands throughout the eighteenth century.' K. Harley, "Slavery, the British Atlantic Economy, and The Industrial Revolution," in A. Leonard and D. Pretel (Eds.) *The Caribbean and the Atlantic Word Economy* (Basingstoke, UK: Palgrave Macmillan, 2015).

[5] A. O'Shaughnessy, "The Formation of a Commercial Lobby: The West India Interest, British Colonial Policy and the American Revolution," *Historical Journal*, **40** (1997) 71–95, pp. 72–74.

[6] P. O'Brien, "European Economic Development: The Contribution of the Periphery," *Economic History Review*, **35** (1982) 1–18, p. 9.

as the former were developed as investment opportunities, and the latter as a place of permanent settlement. Concerning the former,

> many of the West Indian planters, including some of the biggest, were absentee landlords, at least for a large part of their lives. They left their estates in the hands of managers, content if their revenues did not decrease, and lived as country gentlemen in Britain. Even if they resided in the islands, they invariably sent their children to be educated in Britain. They formed no attachments with the West Indies which could not be broken. Britain was not to them the mother country, as it was to the North Americans; it was their home, and if business forced them to return to the islands they did so unwillingly. For these reasons it is to be expected that the number of West Indians sitting in the British Parliament will be higher than the number of North Americans.[7]

These absentees were a crucial element in the West India Interest: 'the West India planters living in Britain, whose numbers, according to contemporary sources, continued to grow throughout the eighteenth century, although modern historians still lack precise calculations of their size.'[8] What is known is they constituted a powerful lobby that brought together planters, merchants, and politicians whose main purpose was to support policies aimed at advancing the interests of its members in the West Indies, and large numbers of the Interest's supporters were members of Parliament. John Brooke, the author of the relevant section of the *History of Parliament*, concluded that the 'group was never as large as contemporaries seem to have imagined. On an average there were never more than about a dozen West Indians in the House at any time,' an estimate derived by counting the number of members with a direct West Indian connection returned at general or by-elections between 1754 and 1790. Andrew O'Shaughnessy, by contrast, maintains that such estimates grossly understate the number of House of Commons members that could be counted on at any time to vote in favour of West Indian interests.[9]

The situation in North America was fundamentally different from that of the West Indies, not only in respect of settlement patterns but also

[7] J. Brooke, *The History of Parliament*, 1754–1790. Section III: The Members, "West Indians and North Americans" (accessed at: www.historyofparliamentonline.org/volume/1754-1790/survey/iii-members).

[8] O'Shaughnessy, 'The West India Interest,' p. 72.

[9] Ibid.

because mainland colonists never attained anything comparable to the parliamentary influence of the Caribbean planters. Again, according to John Brooke, 'the North Americans who sat in the House (of Commons) were too few to present the American case effectively, and their long residence in Britain had isolated them to some extent from American opinion. The service officers and colonial governors who had been in America saw matters from the point of view of British authority, and the merchants trading with America were concerned mainly for their trade. The only men who could speak authoritatively for the Americans were the colonial agents, and they did not carry sufficient weight to impress the British Government and Parliament.'[10]

The southern mainland colonies were, in many respects, mirror images of the Caribbean Island economies producing a staple crop for export under the plantation system using slave labour. But it is equally true that southern planters, unlike their island counterparts, were not absentee proprietors; moreover, slaves never constituted a majority of the population, while a sizeable white yeomanry that practised mixed agriculture existed alongside the plantation system. As to the other American colonies, New England and the Middle Atlantic settlements never cultivated cash crops and only a few products other than raw materials vital to the British economy. By contrast, the North American colonies maintained close commercial relations with the sugar islands, the revenues from which financed the purchase of manufactured goods from the mother country. The West Indies were an important outlet for American goods, above all, those originating in New England and the Middle Atlantic regions, accounting for one-half of their combined exports.[11] To place these figures in perspective the value of mainland exports to the West Indies amounted to more than three times the value of the goods shipped to Great Britain.[12]

The importance of the West Indian trade to the New England and Middle Atlantic colonies was thus considerable, amounting on average to *c.* £1 million annually, the proceeds of which largely offset the latter's

[10] 'History of Parliament,' Members.

[11] J. Fernandez-Villaverde, "Regional Economics of Colonial America," slide presentation at the University of Pennsylvania, Philadelphia, April 2020. These figures are based on average exports in values in pounds sterling for the years 1768–1772. Exports from the Upper and Lower South were also large in value terms, but accounted for a much smaller share of total regional exports.

[12] H. Bell, "The West India Trade Before the American Revolution," *American Historical Review*, **22** (1917) 272–287.

commercial deficit with Great Britain. Both, accordingly, suffered from disruptions incident upon the outbreak of the American War for Independence. In the first instance, the war led to widespread hunger, as the West Indian islands depended overwhelmingly on mainland North America for their food supplies.[13] The British government hoped that such trade being mutually beneficial would not be adversely affected by the rising political tensions. 'Yet, despite this awareness of the need to maintain close intercolonial commercial ties, Parliament, in response to mainland restrictions on imperial trade, adopted an insensitive and coercive policy. It closed the port of Boston in 1774; it then passed two restraining acts and enacted the Prohibitory Act in December 1775. The enforcement of the Prohibitory Act early in January 1776 terminated all commercial intercourse between the mainland and West Indian colonies, except for an illegal trade.'[14] The loss of the West Indian trade likewise imposed substantial costs on the American Republic, acknowledged by, among others, James Madison, the fourth American president, who lamented the fact that 'the Revolution has robbed us of our trade with the West Indies, the only one which yielded us a favourable balance without opening any other channels to compensate for it … In every point of view the trade of this country is in a deplorable condition.'[15]

[13] 'In the 1770s the British West Indies received from the mainland colonies approximately one third of their dried fish; almost all of their pickled fish; seven eighths of their oats; almost three quarters of their corn; nearly all of their peas, beans, butter, cheese and onions; half of their flour; quarter of their rice; five sixths of their pine, oak, and cedar boards; over half of their slaves; nearly all of their hoops; most of their horses, sheep, hogs, and poultry; and almost all of their soap and candles.' S. Carrington, "The American Revolution and the British West Indies' Economy," *Journal of Interdisciplinary History*, **17** (1987) 823–850, p. 823.

[14] Ibid., p. 824.

[15] Cited in D, Irwin, *Clashing Over Commerce: A History of US Trade Policy* (Chicago, IL and London, UK: University of Chicago Press, 2017), p. 51.

CHAPTER 4

Economic Impact of Slavery

If Britain had never participated in the slave trade, would things have been any different? Harley, for example, concludes that 'in the absence of slavery, the northern settlements would have found alternative goods to sell into the Atlantic economy and their growth, and their demand for British manufactures, seems unlikely to have been stifled,'[1] certainly a reasonable counterfactual as it would have opened up new pathways for American manufacturing. A plausible scenario of how this might have played out was described by Alexander Cluny on the eve of the American War for Independence, his intention being to suggest to Englishmen ways to improve the then-strained 'Situation of Affairs, between Great Britain and her American colonies.' 'Let the inhabitants of these Colonies, I say, be properly encouraged to raise Flax and hemp, to tan the Hides of their Cattle, to spin the Wool of their sheep, &c. &c. And work them up into the most immediate Necessaries; and they will then be able to apply the price of their Exports, which now goes to purchase those Necessaries, to the purchase of other Articles, less necessary, but of greater Price and Profit to the Vendors; and not only this, they will also exert their industry

[1] Harley, 'Slavery, and The British Atlantic Economy,' p. 18.

G. Pollio, *The Rise and Fall of Britain's North American Empire*,
https://doi.org/10.1007/978-3-031-07484-4_4

to provide still more for the Exportation, as soon as they become acquainted with the Enjoyments thus procured for them.'[2]

The industries identified by Cluny as viable options were not selected arbitrarily, as his choices closely match those that were previously identified and opposed by the British Board of Trade. The point is well illustrated by the affray created over prospective colonial production of woollen goods. 'The preamble of the woollen act of 1699 expressed the view 'that "great Quantities of … Manufactures … have of late been made and are daily increasing in the Kingdom of Ireland and in the English Plantations in America and are exported from thence to Foreigne Marketts (*sic*) heretofore supplyed (*sic*) from England which will inevitably sink the Value of Lands and tend to the ruine of the Trade and Woollen Manufactures of this Realm" … Time after time (the Board of Trade) lamented that the New England colonies "do turn the course of trade to the promoting and incouraging (*sic*) woollen and other Manufactures proper to England, instead of applying their thoughts and endeavours to the Production of such Commodities as are fit to be encouraged in those parts, according to the first design and intention of such settlements."'

Three years later the Board further complained that English cloth workers were being enticed to the colonies by high wages, where they became engaged in manufacturing, not only for their immediate neighbours but also for the southern plantations. So far advanced were some of the colonial products that they equalled British goods in quality.[3] Other colonial manufactures banned by the Board of Trade included sail-cloth, leather shoes, and wrought iron, all regarded as being 'against the advantage of England.' Nor were the southern colonies exempt from such attention as, rather remarkably, the Board of Trade regarded the planting of cotton and flax in Virginia as being contrary to England's interests, and the colony's Governor, accordingly, was instructed to discourage its cultivation.[4]

[2] A. Cluny, *The American Traveller, or, Observations on the Present State, Culture and Commerce of the British Colonies in America, and the Further improvements of which They are Capable* (London: E and C Dilley, 1769), p. 71.

[3] C. Nettles, "The Menace of Colonial Manufacturing 1690–1720," *New England Quarterly*, **4** (1931) 230–269, pp. 233–234. By the end of the seventeenth century, 'English woollens made up about a third of the exports shipped to the northern plantations. The Board of Trade considered the woollen manufacture "the most substantial branch of the trade of this Kingdom." Because of their expanding population and their severe climate, the New England colonies offered a splendid prospect of future markets.'

[4] Ibid., p. 236.

This may very well have been the way things would have turned out, but to some scholars, the counterfactual does not support the conclusion that the slave trade was not all that important and that things would have been little different had it never existed. Mokyr, for example, while denigrating the significance of the West Indies, emphasises the important nexus between slavery in the southern mainland colonies, the rapid expansion of cotton cultivation it supported, and the growth and development of the Lancashire textile industries.[5] Other scholars, by contrast, without denying the importance of textiles to the rise of Britain's industrialisation, assert that it was just one of several expanding industrial sectors, and thus should not be accorded greater significance than any other. 'Although the history of the cotton textile industry deserves the attention it receives, it is far from providing the key to understanding the modern growth process.'[6]

The opposite, and more extreme, view goes even further, regarding slavery as essential for the emergence of modern industrial capitalism, or as Beckert recently expressed it, 'the beating heart of this new system was slavery.'[7] The 'New History of Capitalism' (NHC), as it has been described, represents, as its name implies, a revival of interest in the origins of Western capitalism, above all, in the United States. Given its aims, it is rather surprising the NHC fails to provide a definition of the central concern of its research programme, namely, capitalism; indeed, one of its leading advocates has gone so far as to commend the field's 'disavowal of theoretical definitions.'[8] Its content, however, is more polemical than analytical, and its conclusions, although widely acclaimed, are blighted by the authors' reluctance to engage with the results of cliometric research and its

[5] 'Simply put, without U.S. slave labour it is hard to see how the elastic supply of raw cotton would have been secured. Certain processes in the cotton industry could be mechanized, including some concerned with the production of the raw material (using, for example, the cotton gin). But the planting and picking of cotton in the fields of the southern United States remained a manual process, and as the demand for cotton increased, U.S. slave plantations rapidly switched to cotton. Without U.S. slavery, the British cotton industry would have run into a severe bottleneck. It is here and not in the consequences of eighteenth-century triangular trade that slavery truly "mattered" for the Industrial Revolution.' Mokyr, 'Introduction,' p. 50.

[6] C. Harley, "Prices and Profits in Cotton Textiles during the Industrial Revolution," University of Oxford, Discussion Papers in Economic and Social History, 81 (May 2010), p. 29.

[7] S. Beckert, *Empire of Cotton: A Global History* (Penguin Random House, 2014), p. 37. A. Olmstead and P. Rhode, "Cotton, Slavery, and the New History of Capitalism," *Explorations in Economic History*, **67** (2018) 1–17.

[8] S. Rockman, "What Makes the History of Capitalism Newsworthy?" *Journal of the Early Republic* **34**, (2014), 439–466, p. 444.

contributors' generally cavalier use of documentary and literary sources. As Herbert Klein recently commented, 'there have recently appeared studies on slavery and capitalism by US historians that virtually ignore all this accepted research. This is a rather shocking indication of the growing divide between history and economics, just at a time when other research areas have been deeply enriched by their study of economics.'[9] In short, the NHC literature, which focuses on *why* history should matter, fails to establish the far more important question of *whether* it matters.

It is possible, as many scholars aver, that slavery overall may have been less efficient than free labour which, if correct, suggests that it may have retarded regional and national economic growth. Several channels through which the system of slave labour could have impaired efficiency or imposed additional costs (or both) on southern planters have been identified by historians, but most, however, do not stand up to close scrutiny. Consider, for example, what is a fairly common rigidity attributed to slavery. 'When a Southern planter wanted to expand operations, he could do so, simply by buying more laborers, a fact that distinguished him from the Northern farmer. But having bought his laborers, he had them from then on, twenty-four hours a day, seven days a week, fifty-two weeks a year. He could not lay them off, as a Northern factory owner could, when orders fell, and unless he was very lucky, he could not even hire them out temporarily when he had no present use for them. All he could do was sell them but if he would shortly need them back again, this was clearly not a viable option'.[10]

[9] H. Klein, "Living with History as a Social Science," *The Americas*, **73** (2016) 291–301, p. 295. For a detailed critique of its methodology and findings see: A. Olmstead and P. Rhode, "Cotton, Slavery, and the New History of Capitalism," *Explorations in Economic History*, **67** (2018) 1–17. See also J. Clegg, "Capitalism and Slavery," *Critical Historical Studies*, **2** (2015) 281–304. NHC owes a debt, first of all, to Karl Marx: who wrote in 1847 'without slavery you have no cotton; without cotton you have no modern industry ... cause slavery to disappear and you will have wiped America off the map of nations.' K. Marx, *The Poverty of Philosophy*, (1848), Chapter Two: The Metaphysics of Political Economy, Fourth Observation. Marx's views on southern slavery were much influenced by the classical economists, above all, J. E. Cairnes. Temperley, 'Capitalism, Slavery, and Ideology,' p. 112. NHC also incorporates ideas originating with Karl Polanyi, above all, the interaction between the state and markets, that unfettered markets are inherently unstable and pose 'great perils to society.' E, Hilt, "Economic History, Historical Analysis, and the "New History of Capitalism," *Journal of Economic History*, 77 (2017) 511–536.

[10] R. Gallman, "Slavery and Southn Economic Growth," *Southern Economic Journal*, **45** (1979) 1007–1022, p. 1020.

Yet, the truth is the exact opposite. Strong demand for cotton did, of course, encourage the purchase of additional slaves, but a rental market also existed that enabled planters to hire in additional workers as needed or to hire out slaves that were surplus to immediate labour requirements. Nor were slaves used exclusively as field hands. They could be and were employed in industrial enterprises in both menial and skilled capacities and offered contractors greater flexibility in their employment. Because slaves worked longer hours, often in gangs, and not paid by the hour, they, unlike whites, could be transferred from one task to the next until their hire was ended or renegotiated with the slave owner.[11]

Among the 'basic facts' routinely cited in support of the importance of slavery to American economic development are that 'slave grown cotton was the most valuable export made in America' and 'that the capital stored in slaves exceeded the combined value of all the nation's railroads and factories.'[12] It is true that cotton production and exports rose steadily over the course of the nineteenth century and accounted for the largest share of total merchandise exports. But cotton was not exported until 1784, and in that year, only ten bags were shipped to England. Thereafter production continued to increase, as did the proportion exported, rising from 16 per cent in 1800 to a peak of 61 per cent in 1870.[13] However, as total

[11] Claudius Crozet reporting the conditions of the work under his charge, December 28, 1854. Archives, The Library of Virginia, Richmond, VA, Virginia Board of Public Works, Entry 125 "Blue Ridge Railroad." On the use of slaves in the development of the southern railway system see A Marrs, *Railroads in the Old South: Pursuing Progress in a Slave Society* (Baltimore, MD: Johns Hopkins University Press, 2009), p. 58.

[12] S. Beckert and S. Rockman, "Introduction," in Beckert and Rockman (Eds.) *Slavery's Capitalism* (Philadelphia, PA.: University of Pennsylvania Press, p. 1. This conclusion is contradicted by numerous studies that demonstrate that southern planters were as farsighted as their northern counterparts and, accordingly, managed their estates in a progressive commercial manner. 'Surviving plantation records confirm that the planters carefully tuned the purchase of slaves to their needs, and were keen to avoid creating a wasteful mix of labour and capital. They also confirm the fact that planters were keen to introduce new machinery as well as to experiment with new crops such as cotton and new varieties of sugarcane. With slave prices rising, the planters also attempted to increase the natality, and decrease the mortality, of their slave populations by spending more plantation money on providing better food, housing, and medical care.' P. Emmer, "The Big Disappointment. The Economic Consequences of the Abolition of Slavery in the Caribbean, 1833–1888," *History in Focus* (accessed at: https://archives.history.ac.uk/history-in-focus/Slavery/articles/emmer.html#4t.

[13] "Cotton Financing," *Federal Reserve Bulletin* (Washington, DC: Government Printing Office, May 1923), p. 566

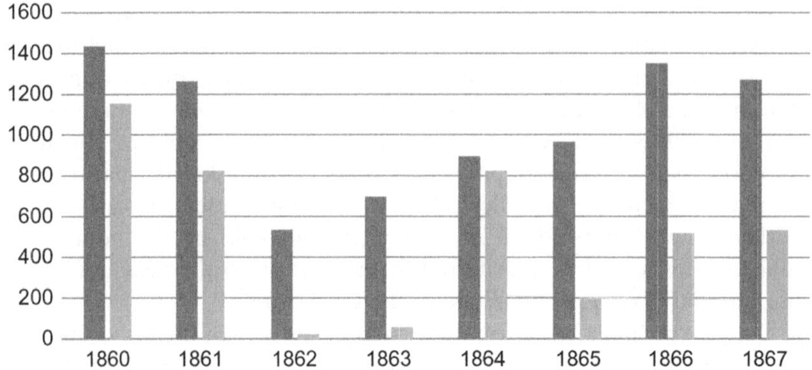

Chart 4.1 British cotton imports, total and from the United States, 1860–1867 (1000 pounds) (Notes: Blue bars: Total British cotton imports; Brown line: Imports from the United States. Source: John Pender and Co., *Statistics of Trade of the UK with Foreign Countries from 1840* (London: Simkin Marshall, 1869), *Historical Statistics of the United States (HSUS)*)

merchandise exports historically amounted to less than 10 per cent of American GDP, the contribution of the cotton trade to the national economy was negligible. Even if these numbers are augmented to take account of marine and rail tonnage directly linked to, and the employment dependent upon, the cotton trade, it would still be an exaggeration to claim that cotton dominated the American economy (Charts 4.1 and 4.2).[14]

The second stylised 'fact' is not only ambiguous, in that the year to which it relates is unstated, but also of questionable relevance. There are two dimensions to this issue. The first is whether the investment in slaves

[14]'In the decade before the Civil War, more than 2000 U.S. merchant ships, totalling 1,100,000 registered tons, and 55,000 seamen were employed in the coastal navigation that brought cotton from Southern ports to New York. Another 800,000 tons of American shipping and 40,000 seamen were employed in the transoceanic cotton trade. Even the fast New York to Liverpool passenger packets relied upon cotton to fill their cargo holds on the eastbound voyage across the Atlantic. Without cotton outbound ships would have had to cross the ocean empty, other American exports being insufficient to fill the cargo space that on westbound crossings was taken up by British manufactured goods.' K. Boodry, *The Common Thread: Slavery, Cotton and Atlantic Finance from the Louisiana Purchase to Reconstruction*, (Doctoral dissertation, Harvard University, 2014), p. 181. British estimates indicate that cargoes were brought to, and carried from, (British) ports under the American flag in 1860 to the extent of nearly 23 million tons (2734,38I tons). J. Golver, "Tonnage Statistics of the Decade 1860–70," *Journal of the Statistical Society of London*, **35** (1872), 218–230, p. 219.

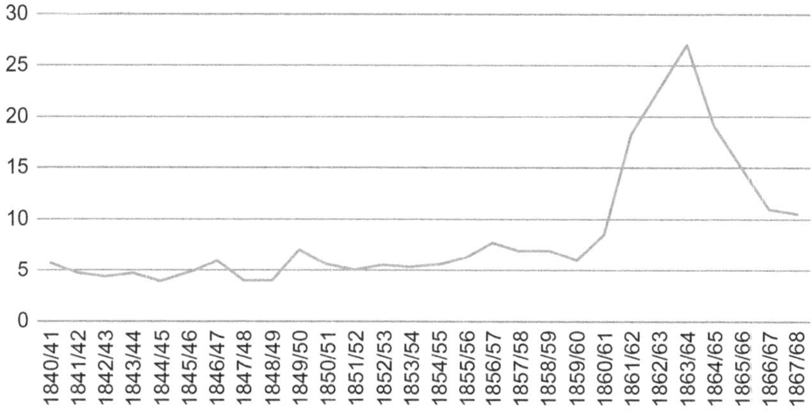

Chart 4.2 US Middling Uplands cotton prices, Liverpool, 1840/1841–1867/1868 (pence per lb). (Source: J. Watkins, *King Cotton: A Historical and Statistical Review, 1790 to 1908* (New York: J. L. Watkins and Sons, 1908), p. 30)

was economically rational, that is, among the various investment opportunities available to plantation owners, did investment in slaves generate returns that covered or more than covered their opportunity cost of capital.[15] The fact that until the start of the Civil War, the prices paid for slaves continued to rise reflects plantation owners' optimism concerning the continuing profitability of slavery and by extension its viability. The second dimension likewise has two distinct components. The first has to do with the perception that southern planters favoured investments in cotton over industry. To underline the point, John Fountain expressed what may have been the view of many southerners when he wrote that planting cotton was 'the "safest and best," as manufactories are liable to greater

[15] Implicit in this discussion is that returns to slaveholding, at 10 per cent, were below those that could be earned on alternative investments. It is difficult to verify the accuracy of such claims since comparisons should be made among asset classes of similar risk. A definitive comparison would have to make risk adjustments to both the returns to slaveholding and banking. But the unadjusted figures confirm Fogel and Engerman's claim that the rates of return earned by slave holders were equal to or higher than the rates that could have been earned with alternatives. H. Bodenhorn and H. Rockoff, "Regional Interest Rates in Antebellum America," in C. Goldin and H. Rockoff (Eds.) *Strategic Factors in Nineteenth Century American Economic History: A Volume to Honor Robert W. Fogel* (Chicago, IL: University of Chicago Press, 1991), pp. 1818–182.

dangers, and frequently have to be maintained at a loss. When not in operation the machinery soon injures.' Assuming this perception to be widely shared, historians have concluded that the refusal to diversify their investment portfolios confirms planter irrationality, in consequence of which other aspects of the southern economy, such as mechanisation, suffered; it also curtailed immigration.

Carole Scott, by contrast, not only challenges that conclusion but provides compelling reasons why the refusal to do so was in fact economically rational.

> That the South's economic choices were reasonable would not have surprised Adam Smith ... He expected that rational, self-interested regions operating in a free trade environment like that which existed within the United States would specialize so as to maximize the value of their joint output because this would benefit each of them. If trade was not free, as was true of trade between the United States and the rest of the world, this would not be the case. America's trade restrictions—tariffs on imported manufactured goods—were designed to promote domestic manufacturing. ... Because they had no such protection from their northern competitors, southern mills did not thrive and come to dominate the industry until the twentieth century, when rising wages in the North and declining opportunity costs in the South because farm incomes had plummeted drove the industry South.[16]

Such views likewise ignore other positive aspects of the slave labour system, but which individually or collectively do not amount to proof of its centrality to American economic development. These additional benefits include the fact that slavery 'had something akin to a "multiplier effect" due to southern banks' willingness to accept slaves as leverage for other investments ... the need for support industries like factoring, ginning, railroads, and a bustling steamship industry. A vibrant domestic slave trade also infused capital into slave-exporting eastern regions.'[17] Even if

[16] C. Scott, "Why the Cotton Textile Industry Did Not Develop in the South," *Agricultural History*, **68** (1994), 105–121, pp. 108–109. Perhaps not the entire explanation, but one that does not rely upon either the importance of slavery or the lack of southern financial sophistication. Scott is also the source of Fountain's quote. Tariffs were at the heart of North-South tensions, as the high tariffs of the 1830s limited cotton exports to the detriment of southern profit causing some southern states to threaten secession.

[17] B. Schoen, "The Political Economies of Secession," *Journal of the History of Economic Thought*, **37** (2015) 203–219, p. 205 and the references cited therein. On slaves as collateral

these and other benefits are factored into the equation—such as the fact that northern textile mills were important consumers of cotton, and the bulk transported abroad was handled by New York factors and financiers—it hardly alters the conclusion.

There is a second channel through which investment concentration may have impeded the development of southern industry that follows directly from finance theory, but as it ultimately is an empirical question, it must be decided on that basis. The hypothesis depends upon demonstrating that the lack of diversification resulting from the concentration of southern wealth, coupled with the risks intrinsic to the widespread use of slave labour, would have raised the cost of capital to southerners compared with rates applicable to comparable projects in the North. If these additional costs were not offset by official subsidies, the higher cost of capital would have resulted in a smaller volume of capital projects, such as the development of railroads,[18] which expanded rapidly in the first half of the nineteenth century, albeit at a much faster rate in the North than in South. On the eve of the Civil War, for example, the South accounted for only *c.* 30 per cent of national railroad mileage.

Notwithstanding the practice of subsidisation was common across the early Republic, the fact is southern dependence on public guarantees, at *c.* 60 per cent, was well above the 25–30 per cent national average. These differences have been attributed, in addition to the lack of southern interest in investments other than in slaves, to local bank preferences that favoured the cotton trade over infrastructure development,[19] the lack of

see B. Martin, "Slavery's Invisible Engine: Mortgaging Human Property," *Journal of Southern History*, 76 (2010) 817–866. 'Although 61 percent of the 735 mortgages sampled in the colonial period did not use slaves as collateral, the remaining 39 percent, those that did use humans as all or part of the collateral, raised 66 percent of the cash and credit. There was a similar pattern in the national era. Of the 8105 mortgages examined, the 41 percent that included slaves as all or a portion the col. lateral raised 63 percent of the capital,' pp. 821–822. On the relationship between the greater liquidity of slave assets compared with land and its relationship to business development see F. González, G. Marshall and S. Naidu (2016): "Start-Up Nation? Slave Wealth and Entrepreneurship in Civil War Maryland," NBER Working Paper 22,483 (August.

[18] M. Yanochik, M. Thornton and B. Ewing, "Railroad Construction and Antebellum Slave Prices," *Social Science Quarterly*, **84** (2003) 723–737, p. 728. See also J. Ely, Jr. and M. Underwood, "Review: Railroads in the Old South: Pursuing Progress in a Slave Society by Aaron W. Marrs," *Virginia Magazine of History and Biography*, **117** (2009) 295–297.

[19] 'Simply put, cotton looked like a much better bet than the development of regional infrastructure,' Boodry, 'Common Thread,' p. 9.

regional financing options, or to geographic advantages that privileged the North over the South. It is known with respect to railroads,[20] returns to investors in, say, Pennsylvania, were well above those earned in Virginia,[21] although whether this resulted from the different ways each was financed has yet to be determined. It could be that the shift from state to private financing of railroad projects that followed the widespread defaults that occurred in the late 1830s might explain the disparity in financial results.[22] Pennsylvania defaulted on its debts in 1842 and subsequently amended its constitution in ways that reduced the state's role in infrastructure investment[23]; other states did likewise, but Virginia never followed suit and

[20] The impact of the antebellum transportation revolution on sectional division is analysed in J. Binder, "The Transportation Revolution and Antebellum Sectional Disagreement," *Social Science History*, **35** (2011) 19–57.

[21] J. Majewski, "Who Financed the Transportation Revolution? Regional Divergence and Internal Improvements in Antebellum Pennsylvania and Virginia," *Journal of Economic History*, **56** (1996) 763–788, pp. 781–782. The author attributes differences in profitability to the fact the 'population density of the Old Dominion in 1860 was only 24 persons (free and slave) per square mile, compared to 64 persons per square mile for the Keystone state. Given that per capita incomes were significantly higher in Pennsylvania, railroads there were able to carry substantially more traffic. The direct rate of return of Virginia's railroads … was simply too low to attract investors who could not capture the local, indirect benefits of the railroads.'

[22] J. Larson, *Internal Improvement: National Public Works and the Promise of Popular Government in the Early United States* (Chapel Hill, NC and London: University of North Carolina Press, 2001). 'Amid the wreckage of so many state treasuries, state-chartered banks, and public works programs, private capitalists and smart politicians understandably turned (albeit sometimes grudgingly) toward the relatively untried liberal course of private enterprise (p. 220) … (constituents) hurled themselves at the traders of bonds rather than pay taxes or invest their own savings in developing their own communities' (p. 224).

[23] Pennsylvania's outstanding debts amounted to $36.4 million, four-fifths of which was transportation related. Virginia's debts amounted to $7.0 million, 90 was related to transportation. W. English, "Understanding the Costs of Sovereign Default: American State Debts in the 1840's," *American Economic Review*, **86** (1996) 259–275, p. 262, Table 1. See also A. Grinath, J. Wallis, and R. Sylla, "Debt, Default, and Revenue Structure: The American State Debt Crisis in the Early 1840s," NBER Historical Working Paper No. 97 (March 1997) and J. Wallis, R. Sylla and A. Grinath, "Sovereign Debt and Repudiation: The Emerging Debt Crisis in US States, 1839–1843," NBER Working Paper 10,753 (September 2004). Pereira, et al. argue that the low effective state tax rates that prevailed in the antebellum period meant that railroad investments were not self-financing, and contributed in part to high levels of public indebtedness which, when aggravated by depressed economic conditions in the late 1830s, led many states to default. R. Pereira, A. Pereira, and W. Hausman, "Railroad Infrastructure Investments and Economic Development in the Antebellum United States," *Journal of Economic Development*, **42** (2017) 1–16. On the impact of usury ceilings

continued with public funding of the state's railroad investment programme.[24] The higher returns earned post-1840 appear to have resulted from the fact that northern investments were increasingly dictated by economic considerations, as measured by prospective returns, in contrast to the South where politics appears to have been the more critical input. Given the underdevelopment of the early Republic's financial markets, much of the financing was provided either directly or indirectly by foreign investors. Indeed, bonds issued by several states were denominated and payable in foreign currency to facilitate their placement,[25] and there is no evidence that international investors discriminated against debt issued by slave states, as might be expected given their monoculture economy and relatively more limited tax base. Foreign investors did add premia to issues that defaulted, such as those of Pennsylvania and Indiana, but spreads narrowed once a state resumed payments.[26]

As should now be clear, the main difficulty with the NHC project is that it reverses the direction of causation, assuming it was slavery that

on bank loan rates see H. Bodenhorn and H. Rockoff, "Regional Interest Rates in Antebellum America," in Claudia Goldin and Hugh Rockoff (Eds.) *Strategic Factors in Nineteenth Century American Economic History: A Volume to Honor Robert W. Fogel* (Chicago, IL: University of Chicago Press, 1992).

[24] 'In the 1840s state constitutions created explicit procedures for authorizing government borrowing. State and local governments were required to identify the purpose of the debt issue; raise current taxes by an amount sufficient to service the debt; and hold a public referendum to authorize the tax increase. Procedural limitations did not cap the amount of debt a state could issue. They required state and local governments to raise taxes before they borrowed and made those taxes irrevocable until the debt had been repaid,' J. Wallis, Constitutions, Corporations, and Corruption: American States and Constitutional Change, 1842 to 1852," *Journal of Economic History*, **65** (2005) 211–256, p. 271. See also C. Thies, "The American Railroad Network During the Early nineteenth Century: Private versus Public Enterprise," *Cato Journal*, **22** (2002) 229–261 and M. Reed, "Government Investment and Economic Growth: Louisiana's Ante Bellum Railroads," *Journal of Southern History*, **28** (1962) 183–201.

[25] English, 'Costs of Sovereign Debt,' p. 261. Nearly half of Maryland's debt was denominated in pounds sterling and payable in London; two-thirds of the Georgia's debt was likewise denominated in pounds and payable in London, as was over 70 per cent of the debt of Mississippi, and more than 90 per cent of the debt of Louisiana.

[26] Investment took the form of equity or convertible bonds, but either way, the issues required full official backing. This applied equally to northern and southern investments. 'A very few railways, such as certain early southern lines, were able to issue stock, but the returns were guaranteed by cities such as Charleston and Savannah.' B. Eichengreen, *Financing Infrastructure in Developing Countries: Lessons from the Railway Age*. Washington, D.C.: World Bank Group, 1995), p. 82.

drove the capitalist revolution, when in fact it was the Industrial Revolution that encouraged the expansion of slavery. Prior to the Industrial Revolution, the English textile industry was based on wool and hemp, and flax/linen. The bulk of cotton textile imports were sourced through the East India Company, and while Indian imports were subject to a tariff, labour cost differences were so vast—weekly wage rates between 1680 and 1820 were four to six times higher in Lancashire than India[27]—the impost did virtually nothing to improve England's competitive position.

If labour costs were all that mattered, India's comparative cost advantage in the production of textiles should have persisted indefinitely. Even after the establishment of the East India Company, India remained a major exporter of cloth; as noted *supra* in the late eighteenth century Indian textiles were included among the goods traded for slaves in West Africa. CIF prices for Indian textiles until the late eighteenth century were, accordingly, lower than British FOB prices, thus providing a quantitative measure of the former's competitive margin. Thereafter the balance began to shift increasingly in Britain's favour, the main cause of which was the introduction of new inventions that raised productivity leading, in turn, to a decline in unit labour costs; lower capital and cotton import costs further enhanced Britain's competitive advantage. Between 1750 and 1820 fob prices shifted from 2:1 in favour of India to 0.53:1 in favour of England.[28]

[27] S. Broadberry and B. Gupta, "Lancashire, India, and Shifting Competitive Advantage in Cotton Textiles, 1700–1850: The Neglected Role of Factor Prices," *Economic History Review*, **62** (2009) 279–305, p. p. 293, Table 9.B.

[28] Ibid. It should be noted that in 1700 Parliament enacted the first Calico Act, described as 'An Act for the more effectual employing the Poor, by encouraging the Manufactures of this Kingdom.' The Act applied only to Great Britain; whatever impact it may have had on domestic production—it is generally accepted that these Acts contributed to the development of the local cotton industry—it should perhaps be seen more broadly as an attempt at reconciling two broadly conflicted objectives. The first, to protect the domestic market, the second, to minimise the harm to the East India Company, the main supplier of Indian calicoes. After all, '[l]arge numbers of its directors sat in the Commons from i66o to I774 and numerous members of the House came onto its payroll over those year.' P. O'Brien, T. Griffiths and P. Hunt, "Political Components of the Industrial Revolution: Parliament and the English Cotton Textile Industry, 1660–1774," *Economic History Review*, **44** (1991) 395–423, p. 398. On evasion see K. Chaudhuri, *The Trading World of Asia and the English East India Company, 1660–1760* (Cambridge: Cambridge University Press, 1978). On the colonial impact see J. Eacott, "Making an Imperial Compromise: The Calico Acts, the Atlantic Colonies, and the Structure of the British Empire," *William and Mary Quarterly*, **69** (2012) 731–762 and.

Thus, the technical advances that created the Industrial Revolution antedated the expansion of cotton cultivation. Moreover, it seems reasonable to suppose that even in the absence of slave labour, improved seed varieties planted in the more fertile south-western soils of Alabama and Mississippi would have improved yields, thus accommodating British industrial demand.[29] Potential constraints associated with the absence of slave labour could have resulted in a less favourable price trajectory that might have hindered the growth of British textile production.[30] However, to the extent the declining price trend that actually occurred was reversed, it may very well have accelerated the expansion of cotton production in regions that otherwise developed more slowly; these would include the West Indies, Brazil, India, and Egypt.[31] While southern production dropped in the immediate aftermath of the Civil War, thereafter output rose sharply, implying that output produced using coerced labour could

[29] 'Technological changes revolutionized southern cotton production in the 60 years preceding the Civil War. The amount of cotton a typical slave picked per day increased about 2.3 percent per year due, primarily, to the introduction and perfection of superior cotton varieties' A. Olmstead and P. Rhode, "Biological Innovation and Productivity Growth in the Antebellum Cotton Economy," *Journal of Economic History*, **68** (2008) 1123–1171. Note that production and slave prices continued to rise notwithstanding that real cotton prices stagnated or declined in real terms. Rising slave productivity is the only way these trends can be reconciled.

[30] Labour could have been reallocated from industrial to agricultural production, although in the absence of slaves it most likely would have pushed up agricultural wages and retarded the development of southern industry. On southern industry see F. Batemen and T. Weiss, "Comparative Regional Development in Antebellum Manufacturing," *Journal of Economic History*, **35** (1975)182–208, and T. Huertas, "Damnifying Growth in the Antebellum South," *Journal of Economic History*, **39** (1979) 87–100.

[31] English imports of cotton rose by 40 per cent between 1861 and 1864 and accounted for two-thirds of total cotton imports in the latter year. F. Logan, "India–Britain's Substitute for American Cotton, 1861–1865." *Journal of Southern History*, **24** (1958) 472–480, pp. 475–476. Egyptian exports rose from 60 million lbs in 1861 to 82 million in 1862, 1289 million in 1863, 1736 million lbs in 1864, and 2507 in 1865. The cumulative value of cotton exports between 1862 and 1864 amounted to $152.7 million. A. Hale, Consul General, Alexandria to Secretary of State, Wm. Seward, (Feb. 24, 1865) "Annual Report of Foreign Commerce," *Commercial Relations of the United States with Foreign Countries for the year ended September 30, 1864*, (Washington: D.C.: Government Printing Office, 1865), p. 670. As for India, during the four years of war, it furnished slightly over 55 per cent of the total raw cotton supply of England, with exports rising from 986,000 in 1861 to 1,398,000 (67 per cent of total cotton imports) in 1864. F. Logan, "India–Britain's Substitute for American Cotton, 1861–1865," *Journal of Southern History*, **24** (1958) 472–480, pp. 475–476.

equally have been produced under a system of share-cropping. Slavery, in short, was neither critical to the growth of American cotton production nor a constraint on regional economic development. A comparison with Brazil underlines the point. Since the two countries shared in common an economy based on slave labour, it would be expected the pattern of development would have been similar, yet 'even with slavery the South experienced a much greater degree of development than did Brazil.'[32]

Suppose for the sake of argument slavery had not been established in America, and that the volume of cotton produced under a non-slave production regime widely assumed to have been considerably lower, what would have been the impact of British industrial development and economic growth? To address this counterfactual, the most apposite comparison would be with the impact of the Civil War, which led to significantly reduced exports from southern US ports. The supply disruptions resulting from the war were caused in the first instance by the Confederacy's embargo on cotton shipments as a means of pressuring Great Britain into recognising the secessionist regime and, in the second, by the Union's blockade of Southern ports. 'One thing is certain,' averred the Confederate Vice President, Alexander Stephens, 'in some way or other it [the embargo or blockade] will be obliged to be raised, or there will be revolution in Europe—there will be starvation there.'[33] Many European merchants, manufacturers, and politicians believed likewise.[34]

The fact that Britain's cotton textile industry was already advanced at the time of Civil War could easily exaggerate the impact of the 'cotton famine,' especially in comparison with the outcome if the Britain's cotton textile industry were in its infancy and demand accordingly considerably lower. The dominant position of the United States in the international cotton market derived mainly from the staple's higher quality and lower production cost. The latter may, of course, have had something to do with

[32] R. Graham, "Slavery and Economic Development: Brazil and the United States South in the Nineteenth Century," *Comparative Studies in Society and History*, **23** (1981) 620–655, p. 621.

[33] Cited in J. Abbott, *History of the Civil War in America*, Vol. 1 (Springfield: Gurdon Bill, 1866), p. 158

[34] Any disruption of the close connection between slavery and cotton production might, as the *Bremer Handelsblatt* (11 October 1862) expressed it, 'destroy one of the essential conditions of mass production' of cotton textiles. S. Beckert, "Emancipation and Empire: Reconstructing the Worldwide Web of Cotton Production in the Age of the American Civil War," *American Historical Review*, **109** (2004) 1405–1438, p. 1405.

possible cost advantages connected with the use of slaves but, then again, the United States wasn't the only country to have used slave labour to produce cotton. Thus, the assumption that the American planation system generated labour cost savings compared with non-slave agricultural systems is questionable, largely because such arguments typically exclude the large upfront capital costs incurred by American slaveholders. The impact on British industrial development likewise depends upon questionable assumptions, above all, that the implied higher cost of cotton would *not* have stimulated technological improvements that enabled British textile manufacturers to substitute inferior grades of cotton for American supplies. But more important still even after abolition and the shift to sharecropping, America was able to recapture much of its pre-war share of the global cotton market, and at prices little different from those that prevailed prior to the Civil War.

Nothing better illustrates the perceived importance of the use of slave labour to historic developments in the international cotton market than an analysis appearing in the Bombay *Saturday Review* in the immediate aftermath of the American Civil War. According to the article, whatever advantages southern planters had previously enjoyed were lost because the handicaps imposed upon the region following the abolition of slavery were so severe that America neither could nor ever would recover its dominant global position. Three main reasons were cited in support of the conclusion: 'First, the initial effect of total abolition would be the exodus of large numbers of Negroes from the plantations; secondly, those remaining would not work half as efficiently as under the old system; and thirdly, such labour as was obtained from them would be at a much greater cost than before the war. Under these circumstances … there was no question but that for many years the United States would be able to produce not more than two million bales, or approximately half the number it did before 1861.' The author concluded that India would furnish the bulk of the additional supply needed by the English and European cotton mills.[35]

[35]Cited in F. Logan, "India's Loss of the British Cotton Market after 1865," *Journal of Southern History*, **31** (1965), 40–50, p. 48. This perspective was not unique. Writing in the early days of the Civil War (23 August 1862) *The Economist* concluded, that 'however and whenever this wretched and ruinous war may terminate, the ordinary routine of agricultural labor and the ordinary channels of transmission will have been so grievously disturbed that, for some time to come and perhaps for ever, the production of cotton in the Southern States will be smaller and costlier than it has been.' Even American officials concluded that as a result of the Civil War, the market for cotton had changed and that prices would never again

There is no question that American cotton exports contributed to the growth of Britain's textile industry, but they were not the only factor nor should it be assumed that but for US exports textile output would have grown more slowly, adversely affecting British economic development. In the 1850s the United States supplied 70 per cent of the industry's requirements, with Britain's second largest supplier, India, accounting for barely one-fifth of the imports. During the Civil War years, US exports accounted for less than 40 per cent of pre-war exports. Initial losses were made good mainly by India, Brazil, and Egypt, the large export increases induced by significantly higher prices.[36] By 1865, total imports had recovered to *c*. 80 per cent of the 1860 level, with non-Southern supplies accounting for *c*. 85 per cent of the total.[37] It is thus possible, indeed, very likely, that non-American supplies of cotton could have easily accommodated rising demand in Britain's textile industry. Even if it is accepted that other countries could have made good the assumed lower level of southern exports, two other considerations suggest that industry growth would not have proceeded as it actually did. For one thing, the price increases necessary to elicit a similar supply response from non-American suppliers would have significantly increased industry production costs. And for another, Indian supplies, the principal alternative to American exports, were grossly inferior to that of the other cotton-exporting countries, nor was there much prospect of any genuine improvement in the quality of its output.[38]

revert to pre-war levels, that is, to 5–10 pence paid for the least desirable types of cotton on the Liverpool exchange in 1858–1860. Hale to Seward (April 1, 1866) in 'Commercial Relations of the United States ... for the year ended September 30, 1866,' p. 436.

[36] The impact of the 'cotton famine' resulting from the Civil War is best indicated by the growth of Egyptian exports which increased steadily from 600,000 quintals (1 quintal = 100 lbs) in 1861 to 820,000 quintals in 1862, 1,287,000 quintals in 1863, 1736,000 quintals in 186,422, and 2507,000 quintals in 1865. Y. Salama, "The Impact of Cash Crops on Egyptian Economic Transformation—Cotton as A Model 1842–1863." *Academic Letters* (2021), p. 6.

[37] G. Wright, "Cotton Competition and the Post-Bellum Recovery of the American South," *Journal of Economic History*, **34** (1974) 610–635, p. 611, Table 1.

[38] 'In the decades following Appomattox, this world had given way to a global empire of cotton structured by multiple and powerful states and their colonies and worked by non-slave labor. Sharecroppers, tenant farmers, and peasants, often highly indebted to local merchants, produced most of the global cotton, a significant fraction of which was grown outside the American South, in such places as India, Egypt, West Africa, Turkmenistan, and Brazil. The American Civil War was pivotal in these transformations.' Beckert, 'Emancipation and Empire,' p. 1405. Central to Beckert's argument that developments in India, Brazil, Egypt, and elsewhere were part of a pre-planned and intentional global strategic economic plan that succeeded can easily be dismissed. There is no evidence to suggest a coordinated global

> Manchester never had liked "Surat", or Indian, cotton. It was short-staple, ill-prepared, ill-cleaned, and even adulterated with such foreign substances as mud, leaves, and stones. Laborers complained that it required more work for poorer results; calico printers said it destroyed their patterns; tradesmen and consumers grumbled at the coarseness of the product. ... Inadequate transportation from the interior of India to the seaboard, as well as a long and expensive voyage around the Cape of Good Hope or overland through Egypt to Europe, materially increased the cost of this inferior raw material. The Indian output was inadequate to meet the demand created by the cotton famine, and the yield per acre was so small that an area six times as great would have been required to produce a given quantity in India as in Egypt. To remedy all of these deficiencies would have necessitated: first, extensive governmental investments in transportation, irrigation, and experimentation; second, extensive private investments, principally by English cotton manufacturers, in plantation lands and in machinery for cultivating, ginning, cleaning, and pressing the crop. ... His Majesty's Government refused for fiscal reasons to undertake far-reaching projects of transportation and irrigation; it even objected to the appointment of a Royal Commission of Investigation, on the ground that it was not the function of the Government to undertake the supply of any article or to divert capital investments from the channels in which they would normally flow. All that could be hoped for from Lord Palmerston and his colleagues, therefore, was cordial cooperation with the Cotton Supply Association. But private capital declined to be drawn in where the Government refused to tread. Manchester interests were fearful that the eventual return of the American crop would seriously depreciate investments in Indian plantations.[39]

With little scope for improving Indian cotton exports, for many scholars that all but ruled out the possibility that Britain's textile industry could have grown at anywhere near the rate it had achieved historically. There

effort, while post-Civil War the United States recovered its previous historic share of the global cotton market. True, Egypt remained a major cotton exporter, while Indian production continued to rise, albeit its share of the global market actually declined by one-half between 1860 and 1910. And, finally, in Brazil, cotton almost immediately after the end of the Civil War ceased to be of any great significance .... The history of cotton developments after the Civil War is easily explained by the same forces that shaped market developments pre-war. There is no need to invoke an imperialist capitalist conspiracy to explain market developments. For an alternative view see R. Calhoun, *Seeds of Destruction: The Globalization of Cotton as a Result of the American Civil War* (doctoral dissertation: Kansas State University, 2012).

[39] E. Earle, "Egyptian Cotton and the American Civil War," *Political Science Quarterly*, **41** (1926) 520–545, pp. 527–528.

are thus two significant dimensions to this conclusion. The first is that it ruled out technological innovations that would have enabled British manufacturers to utilise the inferior Indian supplies, and the second, by hobbling Britain's most dynamic industrial sector, it would have severely undermined the country's subsequent economic development, and England, very likely, would not have emerged as the world's first industrial nation.

As to the first point, it was noted long ago that the supply shock associated with the American Civil War encouraged the British cotton industry to seek ways to overcome the difficulties created by the substitution of Indian for American supplies, and therefore there is no reason to suppose that things would have been any different had they existed in much smaller quantities or not at all. 'The shortage of American cotton compelled employers to re-equip their mills in order to spin Surat [Indian cotton], and especially to improve their preparatory processes ... The reorganization of the preparatory processes entailed such an extensive investment of capital that it amounted almost to the creation of a new industry.'[40] Farnie's conclusion is supported by a recent econometric study that confirms the 'cotton famine' generated what has been termed 'directed technical change.' The fact that the main alternative source of supply, Indian cotton, differed in important ways from the American variety encouraged the adoption of technology that addressed these differences. The success of these initiatives is best indicated by the fact the relative Indian/US price of cotton rose—in some years exceeded—the average level observed in the pre-war period, notwithstanding the substantial increase in the relative supply of Indian to US cotton.[41]

Against this backdrop, there is still the question of whether more limited supplies of lower-grade cotton typically supplied in the quantities required by British cotton mills would have resulted in a slower rate of industry growth with the knock-on effect of reducing overall British economic growth. McCloskey has grappled with this issue and came to the conclusion that the role of the cotton industry was nowhere near as decisive as traditional historiography assumes. In other words, the supply of American cotton and its contribution, in conjunction with other factors,

[40] D. Farnie, *The English Cotton Industry and the World Market 1815–1896* (Oxford: Clarendon Press, 1979), pp. 152–153.

[41] W. Hanlon, "Necessity is the Mother of Invention: Input Supplies and Directed Technical Change," *Econometrica*, **83** (2015) 67–100.

to Great Britain's industrial revolution was not all that critical; the latter would have occurred even if the contribution was one-half, the figure McCloskey uses, its actual outcome. 'The resources of labour and capital go into other industries, albeit ones with lower productivity change than the amazing cotton textiles. Since cotton was not the only industry experiencing productivity change even in the classic period of the early Industrial Revolution ... The dynamic effect sounds promising. In quantitative terms, though, a cotton textiles industry counterfactually smaller (if foreign trade were shrunk) does not kill off growth. It's another popular explanation that doesn't work very well.'[42]

A final point is worth considering, namely, the importance of cotton to American economic growth. To NHC historians, such as Edward Baptist, 'more than $600 million, or almost half of the economic activity in the United States in 1836, derived directly or indirectly from cotton produced by the million odd slaves—6 percent of the total US population—who in that year toiled in labour camps on slavery's frontier.'[43] A recent study by Thomas Piketty appears to provide support for Baptist's argument. Not only does he treat slaves as capital, but in so doing 'demonstrates' that the value of slaves equalled that of land resources.[44] Not everyone, however, agrees with Piketty's estimates, while many economists question the legitimacy of the approach. Early supporters of the concept include Anderson and Gallman: 'Those scholars who have referred to slaves as "capitalized labor" have grasped an important truth. To own a slave was to have access to his entire labor and to be responsible for his full maintenance. Thus a slave was a form of capital; specifically, "fixed" capital (as opposed to "cir-

[42] D. McCloskey, *Bourgeois Dignity* (Chicago, IL: University of Chicago Press, 2010), pp. 217–220 (Chapter 25).

[43] E. Baptist, *The Half Has Never Been Told: Slavery and the Making of American Capitalism* (New York: NY: Basic Books, 2014). The gross errors incorporated in his estimate are summarised in B. Hansen, 'The Back of Ed Baptist's Envelope,' 30 October 2014. 'Baptist is simply pulling numbers out of thin air, or a hat, or wherever it is that he gets them. Back of the envelope calculations tend to involve simplifying assumptions. Baptist seems to understand the term to mean that he can just make things up. The only reference provided is to Table 4.1. Table 4.1 does not provide, as one might assume, information about shipping and insurance. It does not even have any information at all for the year 1836. (accessed at: http://bradleyahansen.blogspot.com/2014/10/the-back-of-ed-baptistsenvelope.html#:~:text=A%20central%20claim%20of%20the,impact%20of%20slave%20produced%20cotton.

[44] T. Piketty, *Capital in the Twenty-First Century*, A. Goldhammer (Tr). (Cambridge, MA: Harvard University. Press, 2014).

culating" capital, such as inventories). One could analytically regard labour in the same way as a capital asset, but the fact is that nobody counts the present value of returns to human capital as "wealth."'[45] Even Piketty is ambivalent, including slaves as wealth in an Appendix to Chapter 4 of his text, but excluding them in his detailed discussion of US capital stock.[46]

Baptist's estimate of the overwhelming importance of slavery to American economic activity like many others presented in his study have been described as 'flawed beyond repair.'[47] Economists that have studied the issue reduce the estimate from 50 per cent to *c.* 6 per cent, admittedly a not insignificant figure, but a far cry from the importance attached by NHC historians. Hansen's estimate is built up along the following lines. On the eve of the Civil War, cotton accounted for about 35 per cent of the value of crops produced, but because crop production was only about 51 per cent of agricultural output, cotton only accounted for about 17.8 per cent ($0.35 \times 0.51 = 0.178$) of agricultural production. The more relevant issue, however, is cotton's importance to the broader economy. Given that agriculture accounted for 56 per cent of commodity output in 1859 and cotton accounted for 17.8 per cent of agricultural output, cotton would have accounted for about 9.9 ($0.178 \times 0.56 = 0.099$) per cent of commodity output. However, given that commodity output represented 59 per cent of all output, cotton would have accounted for about 5.8 per cent ($0.099 \times 0.59 = 0.058$) of total output. The same exercise for 1850 yields an estimate of about 4.8 per cent. Comparing the cotton values derived above with estimates of nominal GDP, cotton equals 4.95 per cent of GDP in 1860 and 4.57 in 1850. 'Even after cotton's rapid expansion

[45] R. Anderson and R. Gallman, "Slaves as Fixed Capital: Slave Labor and Southern Economic Development," *Journal of American History*, **64** (1977), pp. 24–46.

[46] This point was first made by the blogger Pseudoerasmus. "Piketty and Slave Wealth," 1 October 2014 (accessed at: https://pseudoerasmus.com/2014/10/01/piketty-slave-wealth/).

[47] A. Olmstead, in Roundtable Review of Baptist, *The Half Has Never Been Told: Slavery and the Making of American Capitalism*,' *Journal of Economic History*, 75 (2015) 919–931, p. 919. Wright goes further writing that Beckert fully acknowledges these post-emancipation developments but fails to grasp their significance in terms of his own argument. In fact, Wright avers, their significance 'undermine(s) the previous 300 pages of his book.' Wright, 'Slavery and Anglo-American Capitalism,' p. 20.

during the first sixty years of the nineteenth century, it accounted for less than 6 percent of GDP.'[48]

A final question arises: who benefitted from slavery? The most obvious answer would be the slave owners, but that would be wrong. Some did, some didn't: slaveholders and others who bought slaves when prices were low would have earned spectacular returns. By contrast, investors and speculators who bought when slave prices were high may not have fully amortised their investments. Framed within the traditional microeconomic framework, the benefits of slavery were distributed De Long concludes as follows: 'British manufacturers gained, the landlords of Manchester gained, and British workers pulled into the booming textile factories gained too. But the British textile-processing industry (and the American cotton-growing industry) were nearly competitive. And competitive industries do not capture economic surplus—they pass it along, forward to consumers and backward to the owners (in this case, initial slaveholders) of the factors of production.'[49]

[48] These figures and the sources upon which they are based is discussed in B. Hansen, "Was Slavery Central to American Economic Development?" 11 June 2018 (accessed at: http://bradleyahansen.blogspot.com/2018/06/was-slavery-central-to-american.html).

[49] B. de Long, "Who Benefited From North American Slavery?," (accessed at: https://delong.typepad.com/113_F07/20070910_cuibono.pdf).

CHAPTER 5

Industry

Whether or not the mainland colonies could have developed a manufacturing industry is debatable. What is known is that in an age when *laissez faire* policies were being adopted elsewhere, the new Republic opted to protect the domestic textile industry by imposing tariffs on imported goods. While such protection has been justified on infant-industry arguments, the more salient point is that the adoption of tariffs underlines the lack of confidence in the development of an indigenous industry in the face of international competition. Harley is correct to claim that the northern settlements could have produced and traded a wide range of goods within the Atlantic economy, many of which qualitatively were comparable to British-made goods, but for the fact their development was stifled by the Board of Trade as constituting a threat to British commercial interests.

The alternative perspective takes a dimmer view of colonial manufacturing prospects, albeit without rejecting outright its quantitative insignificance. 'Although manufacturing industry made more progress than mercantilists would have liked (especially in New England), the colonies remained heavily dependent on the mother country for complex capital goods and higher quality consumer items, as well as vast range of miscellaneous manufactures.'[1] The reasons include the small size of the colonial market, the lack of capital, and mercantilist legislation that discouraged

[1] Zahedieh, 'Capital and Colonies,' p. 262, and Table 6.5, p. 263.

G. Pollio, *The Rise and Fall of Britain's North American Empire*,
https://doi.org/10.1007/978-3-031-07484-4_5

the development of industries that constituted a threat to British manufactures. Notwithstanding 'these restrictive acts were not always enforced, they nevertheless created a climate in which colonial manufacturing might be silently tolerated but not openly enumerated.'[2] Other factors thought to have contributed to the lack of industrial development were that the vast majority of settlers, perhaps as many as four-fifths of the workforce, were engaged in agriculture; indeed, it was the prospect of farming their own land that had attracted many settlers to North America. It is also true that many immigrants lacked the skills necessary to develop a large-scale manufacturing industry.

British policy towards the development of colonial industry was shaped by two broad considerations: where industries were vital towards meeting British needs, they were encouraged by inter alia the payment of bounties; where colonial industries competed, either directly or potentially, with British industry, they were discouraged or prohibited. The policy of paying bounties, although well established within a mercantilist framework, naturally attracted support from favoured industries and resentment among industries that did not. The principal industrial sectors that benefitted from British financial support included naval stores, lumber, cooperage materials made of white oak, and indigo. The scheme was structured in such a way as to ensure forward planning so that England could count on a steady supply of the subsidised outputs. Support was initially limited to a few years only but was abandoned after 1765, which fixed the payment of bounties for as long as twenty years. The total sums expended by the British government for bounties of colonial products was considerable and extended over nearly three-quarters of a century, having attained their highest level just prior to the Revolution; between 1761 and 1776, the

[2] S. Smith, "The Market for Manufactures in the Thirteen Continental Colonies, 1698–1776," *Economic History Review*, **51** (1998) 676–708, p. 676. Adam Smith noted that the 'liberality of England, however, towards the trade of her colonies has been confined chiefly to what concerns the market for their produce, either in its rude state, or in what be called the very first stage of its manufacture. The more advanced or more refined manufactures even if the produce, the merchants and manufacturers of Great Britain choose to reserve to themselves, and have prevailed upon the legislature to prevent their establishment in the colonies, sometimes by high duties, and sometimes by absolute prohibition' (WN:IV:vii;2, On Colonies).

amounts expended on bounties cost the British Exchequer an estimated *c.* £200,000.[3]

Iron and shipping were two of the premier manufacturing industries that developed in the American colonies. Iron ore was known to have existed in Virginia as early as the late sixteenth century. In a book published by Thomas Hariot (or Harriot), a participant in Sir Walter Ralegh's first attempt to establish a colony in 'Virginia,' he noted that 'yron' could be found among the various natural resources discovered in 'many places of the country. I knowe nothing to the contrarie, but that it maie bee allowed for a good marchantable commoditie, considering there the small charge for the labour and feeding of men: the infinite store of wood: the want of wood and deerenesse thereof in England: & the necessity of ballasting of shippes.'[4]

Virginia's iron industry developed only after the discovery of Jamestown, when in 1619 investors organised as the Southampton Adventures established an ironworks at Falling Creek, upriver from the settlement, with an initial investment that totalled £4000. Production commenced the following year, with the archaeological evidence indicating the existence of a blast furnace, presumably intended to produce cast iron 'pigs' for export to England.[5] The facility was destroyed in 1622 following a Native American uprising, thus setting back the development of Virginia's iron industry by a century or more. Even so, on the eve of the Revolutionary War, Virginia's exports of pig iron to England amounted to 20,304 hundredweight.[6] In due course, the industry expanded from the Tidewater

[3] O. Dickerson, *The Navigation Acts and the American Revolution* (Philadelphia, PA: University of Pennsylvania Press, 1951), p. 49.

[4] T. Hariot, *A Briefe and True Report of the New Found Land of Virginia* (London: 1588), p. 13. University of Nebraska *Electronic Texts in American Studies*. 20.

[5] S. Walton, "Iron Beginnings in America," Penn State, *Medieval Technology and American History* (nd) [accessed at: https://www.engr.psu.edu/mtah/articles/pdf/iron_beginnings.pdf).

[6] *Historical statistics of the United States*, Series Z 326–330, p. 1185. Some idea of prices and quantities of iron shipped from the Tidewater region are itemised in Customs Report for exports to London and other British ports. A sample record of Virginia and Maryland (lumped together) for 1770 and 1771 are as follows: 1770: 512 tons of bar (or wrought) iron at 9½ to 10½ £ per ton and 1125 tons of pig (cast) iron at 18 to 20 shillings per ton. 1771: 654 tons of bar iron at 9–11 £ and 1857 tons of pig iron at 18–20 shillings per ton. H. Schenawolf, "Iron Forge in Colonial America," Revolutionary War Journal, September 2026 (accessed at: https://www.revolutionarywarjournal.com/iron-forge-in-colonial-america/).

region to south-central Pennsylvania through northern New Jersey, southern New York, and western Connecticut. By the time of the Revolution, very large furnaces existed in all these colonies (Table 5.1).

The growth of the colonial iron industry was officially encouraged as a way of reducing Britain's dependence on imported iron from Sweden, which prior to the development of the American industry supplied over 80 per cent of the amount required to build the Royal Navy and merchant fleet and for the production of armaments and household goods.[7] The rapid growth and geographic spread of the colonial iron industry soon attracted critical comment from the British government as the colonies were permitted, as set out in the Iron Act of 1750, to produce only pig iron and iron bar, which entered England duty-free, but were barred from producing finished wares by prohibiting the construction of any new slitting or rolling mills, tilt hammer forges, or steel furnaces. Judging by the widespread hostility the Act aroused, it seems fair to conclude the policy was successful in its goal of suppressing the manufacture of finished iron goods, while colonial production of basic iron and pig iron for export flourished under the Iron Act. The Act undoubtedly inhibited the development of an indigenous iron industry, but even so 'permitted the evolution of a more specialized trading relationship between the colonies and the mother country in which higher value items were imported and cheaper commodities produced at home.'[8] The available data fully support Smith's conclusion: at its peak, pig iron exports to England amounted to more than 5000 tons or 17 per cent of domestic production, implying that, apart from exports to other British regions, the bulk of the remainder was used to support local demand.[9]

Shipping was another major colonial industry—it was, in fact, mainland America's third largest industry—that likewise contributed positively to the colonial balance of payments. Some idea of the growth of the colonial shipbuilding industry is provided by Lord Sheffield, who reports that

[7] In 1740 the total quantity of iron produced in England was about 17,000 tons; at that time from 2000 to 3000 tons annually were regularly imported from the American colonies, F. Taussig, *Tariff History of the United States* Fifth Edition (New York and London: G. P. Putnam's Sons. Knickerbocker Press), p. 46, fn. 39.

[8] S. Smith, "The Market for Manufactures in the Thirteen Continental Colonies, 1698–1776," *Economic History Review*, New Series, 51 (1998) 676–708, p. 684.

[9] Export trade was even larger as it included exports to regions other than Great Britain, above all, Ireland and the West Indies. Non-English trade, including inter-regional trade, accounted for *c*. 25 per cent of total exports.

Table 5.1 Pig iron exports from the American colonies, 1768 and 1772 (hundredweight)

	1772					*1768*			
	Total	*Gt. Britain*	*Ireland*	*Cont. Colonies*	*W. Indies*	*Total*	*Gt Britain*	*Ireland*	*Cont. Colonies*
MA	1521	1301		220		2365	1360	370	635
RI	6325	1075		5250		5980	2310		3670
NY	26,755	15,585		11,170		23,795	14,960	40	8795
PA	9408	8840	160	8	400	21,896	21,676	220	
MD	33,405	27,215	150	6040		24,830	20,240	300	4290
VA	20,684	20,304	300		80	33,220	33,220		
Total	98,098	74,320	610	22,688	480	112,186	93,866	930	17,390

Source: *Historical Statistics of the United States*, Series Z 3341–337

American yards built a total 63,000 tons over the period 1769–1771, or an annual production of 21,000 compared with 4000 tons in 1700.[10] These figures were extracted by Sheffield from a report compiled by Thomas Irving, who at the time was the Inspector General of Imports and Exports of Great Britain. He claimed that while he was in office North American vessels had been consistently registered at two-thirds of their real tonnage. Sheffield appended Irving's reservation to the table published in *Observations*: 'The tonnage ... mentioned are registered tonnes, but one third ought to be added in order to know the real tonnage.' The validity of Irving's conclusion was tested by McCusker who concluded that his 'underestimate is precisely verified. This result not only supports Irving but considerably extends the scope of the practice about which he complained. Accepting these five cases (analysed by McCusker) as a random sample and even taking into account its small size, we are definitely able to conclude that a major reduction in the computed tonnage did occur as a standard practice in Philadelphia from 1740 to 1775. It is most likely that the reduction regularly approached one-third.'[11] In which case the average annual tonnage of vessels in the thirteen American colonies would more closely approximate to 30,000 tonnes.

Growth rates, moreover, appear to have increased significantly in the quarter century prior to the American Revolution, an acceleration most likely associated with the Seven Years War and the rapid growth of domestic commerce. At the start of the American Revolution, 30 per cent and 75 per cent of the vessels owned by British and American shippers, respectively, were colonial built. This implies that a considerable volume of industry finance must have been raised locally. McCusker has shown that for the period 1770–1775 local sources provided more than three-quarters of the capital invested in vessels built in Philadelphia, with less than an eighth provided by British and Irish investors; half a century earlier, the percentage amounted to less than 50 per cent of a much smaller

[10] John Lord Sheffield, *Observations on the Commerce of the United States*. Sixth Edition (London: J. Debrett, 1884), p. 96 table. It has been shown that while Lord Sheffield's data, compiled originally by Thomas Irving, Inspector General of Imports and Exports of North America, and Register of Shipping, accord well with other data for 1769 and 1770, but are understated for 1771 by as much as one-quarter. See W. Kelso, "Shipbuilding in Virginia, 1763–1774" (Master's thesis, College of William and Mary, 1964), Chapter 2.

[11] J. McCusker, "Colonial Tonnage Measurement: Five Philadelphia Merchant Ships as a Sample," *Journal of Economic History*, 27 (1967) 82–91, p. 90.

investment total (£12.305 versus £80,515).[12] In addition to exports, shipping income was the largest source of invisible earnings, being second only to tobacco exports and ahead of other major commodity exports such as bread and flour and rice. Shipping earnings averaged £610,00 for the period 1768–1770, accounted for *c.* three-quarters of total invisible income, and alone offset *c.* 40 per cent of the visible trade deficit.[13]

American shipbuilding increased *pari passu* with the rise in the triangular trade, and while it would be tempting to ascribe the increase to improvements in productivity, the reality is that industry growth derived mainly from better economic organisation and diminished external threats associated with pirates, privateering, and similar hazards, the best evidence for which is the decline in insurance rates.[14] On the eve of the American Revolution, British North American shipyards annually built a fleet totalling 40,000 measured tons and valued at £300,000. Of this total, around 18,600 tons was exported, resulting in a net surplus of more than £140,000 with the Atlantic world. The bulk (55 per cent) of colonial ship exports were produced in New England, the annual volume of sales varied between £122,000 and £181,000 depending upon the ships' operating life.[15] These data would seem to vindicate Alexander Hamilton's judgement as expressed in his *Report on Manufactures* that '[s]hips are no where (*sic*) built in greater perfection (Table 5.2).'

The success of New England shipbuilding attracted the attention of Sir Josiah Child, who concluded that it represented a great threat to Britain. 'Of all the American plantations, His Majesty has none so apt for the building of ships as New England; nor none comparably so qualified for

[12] J. McCusker, "Sources of Investment Capital in the Colonial Philadelphia Shipping Industry," *Journal of Economic History*, **32** (1972) 146–157, p. 154, Table 3. It might be supposed that, in Philadelphia as in Boston, many of the vessel built and outfitted were financed by joint ventures, with each partner's financial contribution proportional to their equity interest. 'Partnership agreements enabled merchants to gather the necessary capital to purchase a cargo, outfit a vessel, pay the captain and crew, and insure their risks,' S. Pitt, "Building and Outfitting Ships in Colonial Boston," *Early American Studies*, **13** (2015) 881–907. p. 883

[13] J. Shepherd and G. Walton, "Estimates of 'Invisible' Earnings in the Balance of Payments of the British North American Colonies, 1768–1772," *Journal of Economic History*, **29** (1969), 230–263, p. 250, Table 6.

[14] G. Walton, "Sources of Productivity Change in American Colonial Shipping, 1675–1775," *Economic History Review*, **20** (1967) 67–78, pp. 67 and 77.

[15] J. Price, "A Note on the Value of Colonial Exports of Shipping," *Journal of Economic History*, 36 (1976) 704–724, p. 721,

Table 5.2 Shibuilding in America's Thirteen Colonies, 1769–1771 (tonnage)

Colony	*1769*	*1770*	*1771*
New Hampshire	2452	3581	4991
Massachusetts	8013	7274	7704
Rhode Island	1428	2035	2148
Connecticut	1542	1522	1483
New York	955	960	1698
New Jersey	83	–	70
Pennsylvania	1469	2354	1307
Maryland	1344	1545	1645
Virginia	1269	1105	1673
North Carolina	607	125	141
Georgia	50	57	541
Total	19,212	20,558	23,401

Source: J. Holroyd, Lord Sheffield, *Observations on the Commerce of American States.* Sixth Edition (London: J. Debrett, 1784), p. 96

the breeding of seamen, not only by the natural industry of that people, principally by reason of their cod and mackerel fisheries, and in my opinion, there is nothing more prejudicial and in prospect more dangerous to any mother kingdom than the increase of shipping in her colonies, plantations or provinces.'[16] While Child exaggerated the risks, on one point he is certainly correct, namely, that even allowing for the full range of mercantilist trade and shipping policies adopted by England towards its North American colonies, over time it is clear the latter that got the better end of the bargain.

> As Englishmen residing in America, the colonists were able all along to have their share of shipping from which both Scotchmen and Irishmen had been excluded; the facilities, along the Atlantic sea-board, for shipbuilding were so great that there was some anxiety lest the business should be transferred from the old country altogether. The state of the trade at the out-ports was most unsatisfactory, in the time of James II; and in 1724, the Thames shipbuilders complained bitterly of the disadvantages under which they carried on their business. This was exactly a case where it might have been expected that Government would interfere to prevent the hostile competition of the colonies with an established home industry; but no steps were taken in the

[16] Josiah Child, *A New Discourse on Trade.* Fifth Edition (Glasgow: Robert and Andrew Foul, 1751), p. 162

> matter. American shipbuilding was allowed to develop under the stimulus it received from the opportunity of employment in English trade. This is all the more surprising as there would obviously have been special difficulty in obtaining the use of colonial ships for the purposes of naval warfare or transport.[17]

The growth of the domestic colonial shipping industry was encouraged precisely because of the shortage of local timber supplies that inhibited the further development of the British industry, while abundant timber supplies and lower wage costs in the colonies imply the latter industry enjoyed significant cost advantage over British shipbuilders. Contemporary estimates would appear to confirm the margin of difference was considerable, although such estimates vary widely. Joseph Goldenberg argued that costs per ton of built tonnage were £2–4 lower in Britain's colonies compared with home production.[18] Ralph Davis estimates the cost of building a fully fitted ship of 200 tons amounted to £8.18 s.6d in Britain as against £4.13 s.6d in New England, and £7.3 s.6d, indicating weighted average production costs well below those in Britain.[19] Jacob Price, by contrast, after reviewing the relevant data concludes that while production costs favoured the colonies the cost advantage difference was much narrower, closer to one-fifth.[20]

Production costs varied considerably across the thirteen colonies, with the result that shipbuilding contracts, even where local shipyards existed, were occasionally executed in neighbouring regions. Merchant consortia in Boston, the largest centre of colonial shipbuilding, often found it expedient for reasons of cost to bypass local shipyards in favour of having their vessels built in other colonies.[21] Indeed, notwithstanding the cost advantages enjoyed by colonial shipyards, on occasion, it was even more cost-effective to produce vessels in England than locally.[22]

[17] W. Cunningham, *The Growth of English Industry and Commerce* (Cambridge University Press, 1907) pp. 479–480.

[18] J. Goldenberg, *Shipbuilding in Colonial America* (Charlottesville, VA: University of Virginia Press, p. 95.

[19] Ralph Davis, *The Rise of the English Shipping Industry in the Seventeenth and Eighteenth Centuries* (London: Macmillan, 1962), p. 7, fn. 74. The data refer to 1784.

[20] Price, "Colonial Shipping Exports," pp. 719–721.

[21] Pitt, "Building and Outfitting Ships'.

[22] Goldenberg, 'Shipbuilding in Colonial America,' 722. Thomas Reynell's Journal provides detailed information on the costs associated with shipbuilding in Philadelphia, and the various trades involved in their construction. Journal entries for construction in 1729 for the

Apart from official restrictions, most colonial enterprises were conceived on a small scale and, even had they been permitted, would seemingly have constituted only a minimal threat to English interests. The larger question is that in the absence of official opposition could colonial industries have achieved the scale and efficiency needed to compete with British producers of comparable goods? The British Board of Trade thought they could, or at least had the potential to do so, while American statesmen concluded otherwise, regarding manufacturing as second best and could only flourish once the supply of land was exhausted, such as that occurred in Britain following widespread enclosure of agricultural lands to increase pastureland. Benjamin Franklin, in particular, advanced the thesis that an abundance of land would of necessity inhibit the development of local manufacturing industry. According to Franklin, 'No man, who can have a piece of land of his own, sufficient by his own labour to subsist his family in plenty, is poor enough to be a manufacturer ... Hence while there is land enough for our people there can never be manufactures to any amount or value.'[23]

Franklin's argument was underpinned by the conviction that the supply of new land would remain highly elastic, but local realities were already working in the opposite direction; increasing landless numbers should have, according to his analysis, stimulated the growth of domestic manufacturing industry.[24] Yet even in the 1790s the manufacture of cotton textiles was still inconsequential, there being no more than ten manufactories in the United States operating less than 2000 jenny spindles, compared with 2.4 million in England.[25]

Torrington indicates the principal costs were £487.7.0 (56 per cent) for building the vessel, £110.4.41/2 for iron work (13 per cent), and £22.18.81/2 for the ropemaker, £13.2.81/2 (3 per cent) for the ship chandler. H. Gillingham, Some Colonial Ships Built in Philadelphia Pennsylvania Magazine of History and Biography, 56 (1932), pp. 1160–161.

[23] B. Franklin, *The Works of Benjamin Franklin*. Vol. IV, Eighth Edition (Boston: Tappan and Dennett, 1844), p. 20.

[24] 'There are no colonies of which the progress has been more rapid than that of the English in North America ... Plenty of good land, and liberty to manage their own affairs their own way, seem to be the two great causes of the prosperity of all new colonies' A. Smith, [WN:VII:2]. A further significant consequence was that by 1774 the American colonies had the most equal distribution of income in the Western world and per-capita purchasing power of income that exceeded that in Great Britain. P. Lindert and J. Williamson, *Unequal Growth: American Incomes since 1650* (Princeton, NJ: Princeton University Press, 2013).

[25] ' J. Rosenbloom, "Path Dependence and the Origins of Cotton Textile Manufacturing in New England," NBER Working Paper No. 9182 (September 2002), p. 36, Table 1.

Even if it is accepted that the steady reduction in available land for individual cultivation may have been necessary, it was not a sufficient condition for the rise of the industry. The focus of much scholarly research is fixed understandably on New England, which was, and remained throughout the colonial and antebellum periods, the centre of American manufacturing industry. John Hekman, for example, rejects the traditional significance attached to water power and the availability of merchant capital as the key inputs responsible for the development and concentration of the cotton textile industry in New England, favouring instead the importance of localisation economies resulting from close proximity to the sources of technological change.[26] 'After experiencing a revolution in organization by entrepreneurs who came to it from the merchant trade, (the industry) was highly concentrated in south-eastern New England, where new innovations in management, toolmaking, and textile machinery building were occurring. These activities formed a highly productive and immobile agglomeration.'[27]

Claudia Goldin and Kenneth Sokoloff, by contrast, maintain that industrial development proceeds first in agricultural areas where the marginal products of women and children are low relative to those for adult men. 'The lower the relative productivity of females and children in the pre-industrial agricultural or traditional economy, the earlier will manufacturing evolve, the proportionately more will the relative wage for females and children increase, and the higher will be the ratio of manufactured to agricultural goods.'[28]

Goldin and Sokoloff's hypothesis appears to describe accurately the early stages of British industrial development, but several additional qualifications must be considered when applying it in an American context. The first part of their hypothesis appears well founded: the wages of females and children in the north-eastern United States were low

[26] J. Hekman, "The Product Cycle and New England Textiles," *Quarterly Journal of Economics*, **94** (1980) 697–717.

[27] Ibid., p. 716.

[28] C. Goldin and K, Sokoloff, "The Relative Productivity Hypothesis of Industrialization: The American Case, 1820 to 1850," *Quarterly Journal of Economics*, **99** (1984) 461–487, p. 462. They do concede that the increase in the relative price of manufactured goods resulting from the cessation of trade during the Napoleonic Wars and, possibly, the maintenance of a high relative price with the imposition of a tariff on manufactured goods. But it was only in the American Northeast, where the wages of females and boys relative to those of adult men were initially low, that this industrial development flourished.

compared with those of adult males as women outnumbered men in New England in contrast to the South where the opposite applied. However, the margin of regional difference was not all that great, being about 5 per cent either way, and while the ratio applied uniformly across New England and much of the South, in Virginia, which accounted for *c*. 30 per cent of the latter region's population, the ratio at 1.12 was actually higher than in any New England state.

Cultural factors may, of course, have discouraged women from working in industrial enterprises in the South, and notwithstanding clear evidence that women were employed in the New England textile industry in the antebellum period, little is known about industrial activity in the preceding century. However, the most likely scenario then was that the bulk of manufactured output was produced at home, as by-employment, and intended primarily to supplement family income. As to factory production, what is known is that as the scale of the operation increased, children provided a larger fraction of the workforce than women,[29] most likely a reflection of operational considerations, as the Arkwright technology required fewer adult operatives than did spinning mules.[30] Only in the smallest operations (one to five employees) did women predominate, suggesting these may have been family workshops where men concentrated on agricultural pursuits while women worked mainly at home.

Two other seemingly relevant factors were considered but dismissed by the authors as being of marginal importance. The first of these was the increase in the relative price of manufactured goods that resulted from trade disruptions caused by the Napoleonic Wars, and the second was the maintenance of a high relative price owing to the imposition of tariffs on imported manufactured goods. The first cause was transient, and thus could be dismissed as being of short run significance only; indeed, following the end of the War of 1812 cheap imported cloth flooded domestic markets shifting the political debate in favour of greater protection.[31] The

[29] Ibid., p. 753, Table 3. The figures are for the cotton textile industry.

[30] 'The first spinning mill in the U.S. based on the Arkwright technology employed a labour force consisting of 9 children between the ages of 4 and 10, and a single adult supervisor,' Rosenbloom, 'Path Dependence,' p. 31, fn. 13.

[31] The average tariff on dutiable imports rose from 25 per cent in 1815 to more than 60 per cent in the early 1830s. Thereafter, average rates declined to *c*. 20 per cent on the eve of the Civil War. The reduction in rates reflected both technological and political considerations. 'Declining transportation costs as a result of railroads gave the West a growing stake in export markets and hence an economic interest in low tariffs. The economic interests of

second, by contrast, described by the authors as being of 'possible' importance finds only mixed empirical support. Mark Bils and Knick Harley, for example, conclude that the American cotton textile industry could not have survived without official support.[32] Joshua Rosenbloom argues that tariff protection was essential to develop and perfect cotton production technology to preserve the industry's viability.[33] Douglas Irwin and Peter Temin, by contrast, argue that by 1830 the industry could have easily survived even without protectionist measures.[34]

both the South and the West aligned in favour of low tariffs, and together they controlled a clear majority of the seats in Congress.' D. Irwin, "Antebellum Tariff Politics: Regional Coalitions and Shifting Economic Interests," *Journal of Law & Economics*, **51** (2008) 715–741, p. 739. The irony is that one of the compromises agreed by the southern states at the 1787 Constitutional Convention, namely, support for a simple-majority congressional vote for commercial regulations in exchange for northern delegates agreeing to limitations on national slave import restrictions and an export tariff prohibition. Because of the greater weight of exports in the South than the North, the former's consistent opposition to tariff legislation was understandable, while its support for a shift from a two-thirds to a simple majority is inexplicable as it ultimately proved politically disadvantageous. 'For the nine House votes (between 1816 and 1860 on tariff legislation) the winning margin was less than two-thirds for all except the 1832 tariff vote. With a two-thirds voting rule, this means only one of the tariff acts would have been sent to the Senate. For the eight Senate votes, the winning margin was less than two-thirds for all except the 1816 and 1857 tariff votes. ... A decision by the southern framers not to trade the two-thirds congressional voting rule would have greatly influenced the historical path of American tariff policy.' B. Baack, R. McGuire and T. Van Cott, "Constitutional Agreement during the Drafting of the Constitution: A New Interpretation," *Journal of Legal Studies*, **38** (2009) 533–567, p. 558.

[32] M. Bils, "Tariff Protection and Production in the Early U.S. Cotton Textile Industry," *Journal of Economic History*, **44** (1984), 1033–1045; C. K.Harley "International Competitiveness of the Antebellum American Cotton Textile Industry." *Journal of Economic History*, **52** (1992) 559–84.

[33] Rosenbloom, 'Path Dependence.'

[34] D. Irwin and P. Temin," The Antebellum Tariff on Cotton Textiles Revisited,' *Journal of Economic History*, **61** (2001), 777–798. But see C. K. Harley, "The Antebellum Tariff: Different Products or Competing Sources? A Comment on Irwin and Temin," *Journal of Economic History*, **61** (2001) 799–805. That manufacturing continued to expand between 1830 and 1860 notwithstanding the steady decline in average US tariff rates over the period provides strong support for Irwin and Temin's thesis. The fact that tariffs were increased in the late 1850s need not imply a recrudescence of protectionist sentiment, but rather an increased need for revenue. P. Magness, "Morrill and the Missing Industries: Strategic Lobbying Behavior and the Tariff, 1858–1861," *Journal of the Early Republic*, **29** (2009) 287–329. The Morrill Tariff Act has been identified by some scholars as having directly contributed to southern secession, but the impact more likely was political than economic. The bulk of the increase was directed at goods exported by Britain; the South not only favoured free trade, but was committed to the principle. By offering Britain what was denied by the

Agriculture was the foremost sector of the American economy and remained so for many years thereafter. Even if it is accepted that manufacturing for the most part was carried out in modest-sized establishments, it is nevertheless true that a wide range of manufactured goods were produced, some, such and iron and steel and shipbuilding, capable of competing successfully with the same goods produced in England, proved to be of considerable importance during the ensuing War for Independence. For example, in the early stages of the War, American forces depended upon ammunition provided by France, while in its later stages, iron and steel foundries supplied upwards of three-quarters of the shells fired at Yorktown; even more remarkable is that logistics problems of coordinating munitions' deliveries from geographically dispersed foundries were addressed and overcome by the Department of the Commissary General of Military Stores created by the American Congress in December 1776.[35] It is not farfetched to regard, as one recent study has, that the DCGMS laid the groundwork for the transition of American manufacturing from small-scale artisanal craftwork to modern eighteenth-century manufacturing practices, upon which the Republic's subsequent industrial development depended.[36]

While no census of manufactures exists either prior to or immediately after the Revolutionary War, Alexander Hamilton noted that 'To all the arguments which are brought to evince the impracticability of success in manufacturing establishments in the United States, it might have been a sufficient answer to have referred to the experience of what has been already done. It is certain that several important branches have grown up and flourished with a rapidity which surprises: affording an encouraging assurance of success in future attempts: of these it may not be improper to

North, the South hoped to gain British support for the southern states. Such initiatives were successful up to a point. 'Although the Morrill Tariff and other Anglo-American fallouts ultimately failed to gain British recognition of the Confederacy, the British press had been quick to take up the South's free trade propaganda, a stance that at the time seemed to enhance the prospect of recognition.' M-W. Palen, "The Civil War's Forgotten Transatlantic Tariff Debate and the Confederacy's Free Trade Diplomacy," *Journal of the Civil War Era*, 3 (2013) 35–61, p. 54. After the battle of Gettysburg (July 1863), as there was no prospect of southern victory, Britain reconsidered its position, favouring abolition.

[35] F. Barna, "A Most Intricate Department: The Commissary General of Military Stores or Ordinance Department Under Benjamin Flower and Samuel Hogdon, 1777–1782," (Master's Thesis, University of Maryland, 1984), p. 97.

[36] R. Smith, *Manufacturing Independence: Industrial Innovation in the American Revolution* (Yardley, PA: Westholme Publishing, 2016).

enumerate the most considerable,'[37] followed by an enumeration of manufactures organised into seventeen broad categories, including sectors such as skins, iron, wood, flax, and hemp.

> Besides manufactories of these articles which are carried on as regular Trades, and have attained to a considerable degree of maturity, there is a vast scene of household manufacturing, which contributes more largely to the supply of the Community, than could be imagined … Neither does the above enumeration comprehend all the articles, that are manufactured as regular Trades. Many others occur, which are equally well established, but which not being of equal importance have been omitted. And there are many attempts still in their Infancy, which though attended with very favorable appearances, could not have been properly comprized in an enumeration of manufactories, already established. There are other articles also of great importance, which tho' strictly speaking manufactures are omitted, as being immediately connected with husbandry: such are flour, pot & pearl ash, Pitch, tar, turpentine and the like.

Hamilton goes on to note that a logical corollary of a State's desire to promote manufacturing industry would be to protect it from foreign competition, but rejects the argument as specious. 'It is not an unreasonable supposition, that measures, which serve to abridge the free competition of foreign Articles, have a tendency to occasion an enhancement of prices and it is not to be denied that such is the effect in a number of Cases; but the fact does not uniformly correspond with the theory. A reduction of prices has in several instances immediately succeeded the establishment of a domestic manufacture. Whether it be that foreign Manufacturers endeavour to suppla⟨nt⟩ by underselling our own, or whatever else be the cause, the effect has been such as is stated, and the reverse of what mig⟨ht⟩ have been expected.' As we shall see, Hamilton's views on the desirability or necessity for state protection of domestic industry had less to do with the benefits of free trade than the fiscal consequences that might follow from it. In the quarter of a century that followed the publication of Hamilton's Report, American industrial production rose at an average annual rate of *c.* 5 per cent.[38]

[37] "Alexander Hamilton's Final Version of the Report on the Subject of Manufactures, [5 December 1791]," *Founders Online,* National Archives, https://founders.archives.gov/documents/Hamilton/01-10-02-0001-0007. All subsequent references to Hamilton's *Report* are from this (unpaginated) source.

[38] J. Davis, "An Annual Index of U. S. Industrial Production, 1790–1915," Author(s): *Quarterly Journal of Economics,* **119** (2004) 1177–1215, p. 1189, Table 3.

CHAPTER 6

Land Values, Tenancy, and Private Ownership

Developments in the American farm sector are less equivocal than those in manufacturing: prior to independence, the rapid growth of the American population put increasing pressure on farm values, as lands to the west of the Appalachians were out of bounds prior to the French and Indian War, and remained so even afterwards as imperial land policy barred new settlements. The traditional policy of offering free grants of land to attract immigrants in the early colonial period obviously could not be sustained owing largely to demographic pressures, agricultural reorganisation, and rising speculative investment in land.[1] The white population of colonial America increased from an estimated 210 souls in 1610 to 2.3 million in 1775,[2] the impact of which on land values was evident as early as the last quarter of the seventeenth century. A study of farmland costs in colonial Maryland concluded that land prices rose 135 per cent over the last four

[1] Earle argues that the cultivation of tobacco transformed Tidewater agriculture and encouraged the substitution of free with slave labour. 'The efficient functioning of Chesapeake Island rotataion was contingent on a prpetuually bound labour force. Slaveray offered the perfect complement to and agrarian system tha demanded periodic clearance of the land. … Conversely, use of temporary servant labour was inefficient in this system since land improvement was perpetual and continued long after the expiration of the servant's contract.' C. Earle, *Geographical Inquiry and American Historical Problems* (Stanford, CA: Stanford University Press, 1992), p. 283.

[2] "Population in the Colonial and Continental Periods, 2 *Historical Statistics of the United States* (US Government Printing Office).

G. Pollio, *The Rise and Fall of Britain's North American Empire*,
https://doi.org/10.1007/978-3-031-07484-4_6

decades of the seventeenth century, attributed in part to population increases, the importance Maryland settlers attached to growing tobacco, and the presence of widespread waterways; speculation in land warrants was also a consideration.[3] Data for Anne Arundel county indicate that land prices in Maryland had likewise remained under pressure throughout the first half of the eighteenth century, with the cost per acre rising by a factor of 2.5 between the end of the seventeenth century and the middle of the eighteenth century.[4]

The same held true elsewhere. A German traveller who visited Pennsylvania in 1750 reported that land prices around Philadelphia were already high amounting to some 30–50 florins 'for an acre only a day's journey from the city, although the ground is still uncleared forest land. If a place is desired for a homestead, which is already in a habitable and cultivated condition … twice as much is asked for it as for uncultivated land, the price being about one hundred florins per acre.' He goes on to note that 'rich Englishmen have already bought up from the Indians all the remote land far and near where all is as yet wild and wooded in order to sell it again to the Europeans who are coming to the country. Our German people who emigrate there do not get land enough for nothing upon which to build a cottage. The price of land is increasing from year to year, especially because the English see that so many people, anxious to own farms or plantations, are coming to the country every year.'[5]

The logical consequence of rising land prices would be expected to have pushed more people into making their living, as Franklin argued, outside agriculture, but not imminently, as there was an abundance of land there being 'few great Proprietors of the Soil and few Tenants; most

[3] V. Wyckoff, "Land Prices in Seventeenth-Century Maryland," *American Economic Review*, **28** (1938) 82–88. The importance of speculative influences was equally evident in New York. 'In the Hudson Valley, landlords' virtual monopoly of arable land drove land prices so high that people of modest means were forced into tenancy.' T. Humphrey, "Conflicting Independence: Land Tenancy and the American Revolution," *Journal of the Early Republic*, **28** (2008) 159–182, p. 163.

[4] C. Earle, *The Evolution of a Tidewater Settlement System: All Hallow's Parish, Maryland, 1650–1783* (Chicago, IL: University of Chicago Department of Geography, 1975), p. 210.

[5] G. Mittleberger, *Journey to Pennsylvania, 1750–1754.* (Tr.) C. Eben. Philadelphia: J. J. McVBey, 1898), p. 118. After Britons, Germans were the next largest group of immigrants in colonial America, most of whom entered the colonies in Philadelphia and settled mainly in the Mid-Atlantic region. Pennsylvanians of German ancestry accounted for 50 to 60 per cent of Pennsylvania's population in 1760. F. Grubb, "German Immigration to Pennsylvania, 1709 to 1820," *Journal of Interdisciplinary History*, **20** (1990) 417–436.

People cultivate their own Lands, or follow some Handicraft or Merchandise.'[6] While conceding that tenancy occurred, Franklin regarded it as being of no great importance. His claims should, however, be regarded more as an advertisement meant to encourage British emigration than an accurate assessment of the true incidence of tenanting. In which case, the alternatives dismissed by Franklin, above all, tenanting, more accurately represented the options available to new immigrants. Of course tenanting should be viewed as an interim step towards eventually acquiring land of their own, but as this is an empirical issue it can only be determined with respect to the available data. Scholars who address this question typically rely on probate lists or tax registers at the county or regional level. These data, for various reasons, are not without their limitations but, above all, to a lack of consistency in the way tenancy is defined. Such shortcomings will of necessity affect the extent to which the resulting estimates can be generalised, and would appear to explain at least in part the wide regional disparities reported.

Tenancy percentages appear to have varied between 20 and 50 per cent, while secular trends are equally equivocal. Even a small sample of the evidence makes the point. Shammas claimed that nationally *c.* 30–50 per cent of the land was tenanted.[7] Main and Main assert it amounted to 17–26 per cent in New England.[8] Simler's study, covering pre-independence Pennsylvania, found the tenancy percentage varied between 30 and 50 per cent.[9] Sarson's analysis for the first three-quarters of the eighteenth century estimated the landless component of the free population of the Tidewater region had grown from a third to more than half over 75 years, and continued to increase post-independence.[10] The Mains, by contrast, find no secular trend over the course of the century. The opposite situation prevailed in upstate New York, where the major landlords had great

[6] *Works of Benjamin Franklin*, Vol. 2 (Philadelphia, PA: Childs and Peterson, 1840), p. 468.

[7] C. Shammas, "The Rise of the Colonial Tenant; Review of G. Stiverson, Poverty in a Land of Plenty: Tenancy in Eighteenth-Century Maryland" *Reviews in American History*, **6** (1978) 490–495, p. 490.

[8] G. Main and J. Main, "The Red Queen in New England?" *William and Mary Quarterly*, **56**. The Economy of British North America (1999) 121–150, p. 138.

[9] L. Simler, "Tenancy in Colonial Pennsylvania: The Case of Chester County," *William and Mary Quarterly*, **43** (1986) 542–569.

[10] S. Sarson, "Landlessness and Tenancy in Early National Prince George's County, Maryland," *William and Mary Quarterly*, **57** (2000) 569–598, p. 543.

difficulty recruiting tenants until the late colonial era because 'farmers could inherit, buy, or squat on land nearby.'[11]

Overall, it would be rash to accept at face value the implications that demographic, technological, and speculative pressures drastically altered the agrarian landscape. It is true that 'as dense settlement grew, the proportion of families owning land dropped, many landowners farmed too few acres to feed their families, tenancy rose, and the number of poor, landless men increased.' But, as Kulikoff goes on to note, we should not 'overstate the change. Two-thirds to three-quarters of farmers owned land during the last half of the century in eastern New England, Long Island, New Jersey, and Tidewater Virginia. The rest included children waiting to inherit land, recently arrived immigrants, artisans renting their shop and land, or young leaseholders accumulating money to buy land. Many young couples had no land, but just a sixth of farm operators remained tenants their entire lives.'[12]

Nor did the rising incidence of tenancy promote exploitive rental agreements; in fact, the opposite appears to have been the case, especially where owners sought to attract tenants to the vast tracts of uncultivated land they owned. Again, the evidence here is mixed and appears to reflect conditions specific to the regions studied. Humphrey, for example, notes that 'most of these tenants signed leases that provided them some measure of stability on the leasehold. Landlords' promises of long leases at relatively low rates lured prospective tenants into the backbreaking labour of turning the North American countryside into European-style farmland.' On Livingston Manor, most tenants signed leases for three years; on nearby Rensselaerswyck, most signed leases that lasted 'for ever,' although it is clear the Van Rensselaers never meant to relinquish their ownership of the land, reserving the right to re-enter leaseholds where tenants failed to fulfil their lease stipulations. Virginian landlords also offered term leases. The Fairfaxes, for example, usually granted leases for two or three years, but they usually required tenants to pay rent in sterling. Robert Carter offered similarly long leases before the 1750s but switched to shorter leases late in the colonial period to maximise income by increasing rent with each new tenant.[13]

[11] A. Kulikoff, *From British Peasant to American Farmer* (University of North Carolina Press, 2000), p. 212.

[12] Ibid., pp. 127–128.

[13] Humphrey, 'Conflicting Independence,' p. 165.

Likewise, Simler: 'Despite the rhetoric claiming that tenants were shiftless and landowners were tyrannical, in everyday life tenancy was widely seen as equitable and generally profitable. Landowners could pursue their economic and family strategies efficiently by renting to farm tenants who, for their part, gained the use of commercially valuable land at rates that were low relative to land prices.'[14] And, finally, 'up to the Revolution the tenants were able to grow good crops of tobacco and corn, pay their rents on time, and in the words of the landlord, "by their Industry they Injoy a comfortable tho mean life." The … tenants were also a stable group. Those taking up farms between 1721 and 1749 remained for a mean often years apiece, and some for more than thirty years. The (landlords) also supplied their tenants with goods, lent them money on occasion, purchased produce from them, and hired many for off-season labour.'[15] The general consensus now seems to be that 'while recent research has firmly established that widespread tenancy existed in colonial America, it is not so clear what it signifies. Should we assume that tenants were a deprived class and thus studied as a distinct social group? One interpretation so argues, although the most common viewpoint rejects both premises and maintains tenancy was a temporary state for most colonials, who in time moved on to become comfortably fixed freeholders.'[16] Later studies vindicate the accuracy of her conclusion.

The high cost of colonial labour, implicit in Franklin's analysis, would likewise have served as a disincentive to invest in manufacturing. Even if rising land prices had contributed to a reduction in labour costs, the most likely consequence would have been a reduction in British and foreign immigration. But even if immigration had continued unbated, it is unlikely British policy would have facilitated the rise of an American proletariat via either the development of new industries or unrestricted access to western lands. Since the ultimate objective of mercantilist policy was to ensure colonial developments contributed to the welfare of the metropolitan centre, there is no question British authorities would have enacted measures that thwarted local industrial development, albeit at the cost of further unrest and thus the necessity for an even larger military presence. Against this backdrop, it is obvious British trade laws, while they may have

[14] Simler, 'Tenancy in Colonial Pennsylvania,' p. 569.

[15] L. Walsh, "Land, Landlord, and Leaseholder: Estate Management and Tenant Fortunes in Southern Maryland, 1642–1820," *Agricultural History*, **59** (1985) 373–396, p. 386.

[16] Shammas, 'Rise of the Colonial Tenant,' p. 490.

inhibited local development, were offset by the countervailing benefits they created. Foremost among these were security, restrictions on foreign competition, subsidies, and minimal taxation.

The status quo could not, however, have been maintained indefinitely. Pressures against restrictive policies of whatever form, abetted by the growing *laissez faire* mentality in Britain, would have intensified, further undermining smooth and effective colonial administration. But it is worth bearing in mind the bifurcated structure of American society. One component consisted of 'a hard-driving commercial society composed of plantations and seaport towns,' the other an 'inland pastoral society.'[17] The former was deeply involved in trade, finance, and commerce, the other dependent largely on subsistence with only a casual involvement in the market economy. The first group was concerned with political and social arrangements, the latter more so with 'neighbourly reciprocity.' These differences help to explain the divergent responses that followed the shift from the benign to aggressive policies enacted by the British government after the conclusion of the French and Indian War.

[17] C. Shammas, "Consumer Behavior in Colonial America," *Social Science History*, 6 (1982) 67–86, p. 67.

PART III

The Politics and Economics of British Trade and Revenue Policies

CHAPTER 7

The End of Salutary Neglect

Largely as a result of the policy of 'salutary neglect,' the American colonies took an increasing share of overall British trade, and an even larger fraction of its luxury exports. In return they exported mostly high value, low-weight commodities such as tobacco, wheat flour, rice, and indigo,[1] and other basic goods, such as timber or charcoal, which owing to the progressive deforestation of the countryside were in short supply in England.[2]

Before the Seven Years War, as the French and Indian War is known in Britain, the English press and public took little notice of American affairs. Following the clamour occasioned by the passage of the Stamp Act, the American colonies became a matter of considerable interest and concern

[1] These items were the first, second, fourth, and fifth most valuable American exports. J. Price, "Economic Function and Growth of American Port Towns in the Eighteenth Century," *Perspectives in American History*, **8** (1974) 123–188, p. 161.

[2] 'Because of the depletion of her forests, which constituted perhaps the most important of her natural resources, she could no longer look for prosperity from the old industries that for centuries had been her mainstay. In the days when the Norman conquerors first set foot upon English soil the virgin woods, broken occasionally by fields and villages, had stretched in dense formation from the Scottish border to Sussex and Devonshire. But with the passage of five centuries a great change had been wrought. The growing population, the expansion of agriculture, the increasing use of wood for fuel, for shipbuilding, and for the construction of houses, had by the end of the Tudor period so denuded the forests that they no longer sufficed for the most pressing needs of the country.' T. Wertenbaker, *The Planters of Colonial Virginia* (New York, NY: Russell and Russell, 1959), p. 7.

G. Pollio, *The Rise and Fall of Britain's North American Empire*,
https://doi.org/10.1007/978-3-031-07484-4_7

as proven by Adam Smith's observation that 'the expectation of a rupture with the colonies has struck the people of Great Britain with more terror than they ever felt for a Spanish armada, or a French invasion' (WN:IV:4). The French and Indian War was, as noted, the turning point in British American relations, largely as a consequence of the amount of debt Britain had incurred to pay for it, and the enormous ongoing debt service charges the Exchequer faced. At the end of the War Britain was also obliged to station troops in America to police areas north of the St Lawrence River and in the western territories acquired from France; the annual outlay estimated at £200,000 or more. Britain expected its colonies would willingly contribute to what essentially amounted to their own defence, but in doing so, the government neither consulted Americans as to the number, types of troops needed, or where they were to be deployed, nor was willing to offer commissions to American officers who had performed respectably in the French and Indian Wars. Even more infuriating was the timing of the new measures coincided with the British army in America's failure to protect the colonial frontiers from the ravages inflicted by western Indians in an uprising (Pontiac's Rebellion) attributable largely to the incompetence of Britain's military leadership.

To accomplish its financial and military desiderata, the British government approved a number of fiscal initiatives to raise significant new sources of revenue from its American colonies, in keeping with the conviction that the income generated was 'in no degree to the sum which might be expected from them.' A Commission looking into the matter concluded the fiscal deficiency arose largely as the result of administrative and policy failures. More specifically, absentee politically appointed customs commissioners devolved responsibility for the collection of revenues to poorly paid and often incompetent subordinates, and to prohibitively high duties on goods then in strong demand in the American colonies. The Commission's recommendations regarding administrative shortcomings were to compel commissioners to reside at their respective stations; to discourage smuggling and maximise revenues, a remuneration scheme should be introduced whereby customs officers would be paid a 'poundage out of their respective remittances.' This could best be accomplished by lowering rates to levels that would discourage smuggling while increasing the customs take.[3]

[3] Ibid.

Molasses was singled out as the prime example of an overtaxed commodity, the exorbitant duty imposed in the Molasses Act of 1733, ostensibly designed to protect the mainland market from foreign competition but was, in reality, intended to prevent New England distillers from producing rum by importing lower-cost molasses supplies from the French and Dutch West Indies. That this was the Act's primary objective was widely acknowledged by contemporary observers. Governor Nicholson of South Carolina, for example, writing in 1720, noted that 'the New Englanders ... are setting up a trade for making rum which they do out of mollasses (sic) etc. from Surinam the French Islands and Cape Francois. ... I suppose they will endeavour to engross all the trade of mollasses from both the former places and also our Islands if so they will furnish all this Continent with rum and how prejudicial this affair will be.'[4] A duty, accordingly, was imposed on both molasses and sugar. The latter provoked hardly any reaction; the duty on molasses was another matter as the tax would have doubled the mainland price of rum, which given its widespread consumption throughout the North American colonies triggered universal condemnation.

The Act was, in practice, systematically evaded, the best indication being the aggregate revenues it generated amounted to £18,702 or £603 per year over the thirty-one years the Act was in force. As expected, it induced widespread smuggling which, as the Commissioners' Report pointed out, was facilitated by the venality of local customs officials. If it is assumed the same volume of molasses was imported after as before the Act's passage, the savings would have been smaller than the difference between the official 9d per gallon duty and the 3½d estimated to have actually been paid,[5] once proper account is taken of the cost of bribes and other expenses incurred to smuggle molasses into the colonies.[6] Some financial savings must have accrued to mainland merchants for the practice to have continued, although the gain cannot easily be quantified. Beer, for example, cites an official British report claiming the smuggling expense

[4] G. Ostrander, "The Colonial Molasses Trade," *Agricultural History*, **30** (1956) 77–84, p. 79. The Molasses Act imposed a prohibitive duty of 9d per gallon on the price on foreign rum, doubling its price, and five shillings per hundredweight on foreign sugar.

[5] Ibid., p. 81.

[6] 'Smuggling involved the use of bribes and go-betweens, as well as the risk of capture, particularly in the area of the British West Indies, and these conditions naturally discouraged the trade.' Ibid.

amounted to 1½d per gallon,[7] which together with the estimated 3½d tax reputedly paid, suggests a per gallon savings of *c.* 45 per cent over the legal import price.

Whatever the truth, the fact remains that the main costs of the Molasses Act were borne principally by the British government. In keeping with the Commissioners of Customs' recommendations, the government adopted the Sugar Act (1766), which incorporated all the provisions of the Molasses Act, only lowering the duty, while adopting measures meant to strengthen the means of its enforcement. The Act attempted to accomplish two main objectives, although the end result was to incite indignation and opposition, particularly among shipping and distilling interests, attributable principally to the greater risks stricter enforcement entailed. The Act's primary objectives were to protect the British West Indies from French and Dutch competition and to raise revenues, neither of which were accomplished owing to flaws inherent in its formulation; an Act designed to aid one group of British colonies at the expense of another was doomed to failure from the outset. Lower rates of duty reduced the degree of protection afforded to West Indian planters but were still too high to discourage smuggling. But perhaps the most contentious feature of the Sugar Act was the reduction in rates intended to convert a trade measure into an excise tax. The Molasses Act and its successor were thus the first of a series of parliamentary measures that progressively alienated the North Americans colonies.[8]

It was generally accepted that Parliament's right to tax required the consent of those being taxed, except only in cases involving the regulation of trade, the latter principle established as far back as the mid-fifteenth century. Americans were not represented in Parliament while the parliamentary distinction between direct and virtual representation that supposedly addressed the issue was rejected by the colonists; what was true for

[7] G. Beer, *British Colonial Policy, 1754–1765* (New York: Macmillan and Company, 1922), p. 280, fn. 1. Beer considers the estimate 'merely a surmise and is patently a gross exaggeration.'

[8] 'Although the Molasses Act was not primarily a revenue measure, it levied a substantial tax on imports into the colonies. Imperial centralists would later cite this Act as a precedent for taxing the colonies without their consent. American patriots would look back on the resulting smuggling as the beginning of the protest which undermined the legitimacy of imperial control in America.' I. Steele, "Metropolitan Administration of the Colonies, 1696–1775," in J. Green and J. Pole (Eds.), A Companion to the American Revolution (Oxford and Malden, MA.: Blackwell Publishers, 2000), p. 11.

Manchester, Liverpool, and Birmingham was unacceptable to Boston, New York, and Charleston. For Americans the 1707 Acts of Union with Scotland and England were the more relevant exemplar.[9] The two regions had roughly the same number of inhabitants in 1750: 1.3 million Scots[10] compared with 1.2 million (white) Americans.[11] Significantly fifteen out of the Act's twenty-five articles were concerned with economic matters. The principal concessions of immediate colonial interest included allowing Scots the right to continue to retain their own laws and court system, and absolved them from absorbing a share of England's public debt. From an American perspective, the most significant compromise was that the Acts provided for direct Scottish representation in the Commons on terms which, given the broad demographic, economic, and fiscal disparities between the two countries, was regarded, with typical British understatement, as 'not ungenerous.'[12] Although support for similar direct American representation in the Commons was favoured by a number of prominent Britons, including Lord Chapman, Thomas Pownall (former governor of Massachusetts and MP), and Adam Smith, nothing ever came of it. And while Scotland was exempt from certain taxes and debts previously incurred by the English government, Parliament was demanding the opposite from the American colonies.

Several prominent Americans and Englishmen not only raised the question but identified the quid pro quo for its realisation. Why then did most British statesmen resist the idea? Even when confronted with imminent rebellion, the best the British government could do, as in Lord North's 1775 *Conciliatory Proposal*, was to view the issue uniquely in terms of taxation, failing to grasp American colonists were demanding that issues of taxation ***and*** representation must be considered jointly. One strand of

[9] On the Acts of Union see J. Ford, "The Legal Provisions in the Acts of Union," *Cambridge Law Journal*, **66,** (2007), pp. 106–141.

[10] J. Kyd (Ed.), *Scottish Population Statistics including Websters Analysis of Population 1755* (Edinburgh: T. and A. Constable Limited, 1952), p. 8. The population of England and Wales at the same date amounted to *c.* 6.5 million.

[11] *Historical Statistics of the United States:* Population in the Colonial and Continental Periods, p. 8.

[12] 'According to calculations of 1706, the ratio of wealth as reflected in the yield from customs and excise was 36:1 in England's favour, in the yield from the land tax 41:1, Population was probably around 5:1 in England's favour. Parliamentary representation in the ratio of 11 or 12:1 was therefore not ungenerous.' T. Smout, "The Anglo-Scottish Union of 1707. I." The *Economic Background, Economic History Review*. New Series, **16** (1964), 455–467, p. 455, fn. 4.

thought that seeks to explain such myopia argues that the official British views were atavistic, regarding things much as they were in past times and accordingly unwilling to make any concession to current realities. Colonial representation was deemed 'neither in the nature and purpose of colonisation, nor the place and power of Parliament in the British constitution, were the same thing in the late sixteenth century they became in the eighteenth. The English colonial system, like the Venetian, Portuguese, and Spanish, began in quasi-feudal concessions to individuals or corporations who made the overseas ventures and succeeded or failed. It was conceived in relation to provinces and possessions that had still to be, and might never be, discovered or conquered or occupied; that might or might not be advantageous to acquire or hold. So the colony was "loosely" regarded as a fief held for the Crown, a dependent community and not an organic part of the state.'[13]

George Grenville, the British Prime Minister, although claiming a willingness to consider colonial representation in Parliament, was no enthusiastic supporter of the idea. 'Whether it would not be just and reasonable to grant to the Colonies Members of Parliament upon their petition to Parliament, for that purpose, in like manner as was done in the cases of Chester and Durham, is another question which, whenever such an application shall be properly made, will I hope be considered with every favourable disposition which their situation requires or admits of.'[14] Such assent was unlikely, as the incumbent government regarded Americans as 'capricious, easily misled by troublemakers such as Wilkesite or his counterparts in Boston. … Hand the Americans one concession, and they would ask for more until they won autonomy.'[15] Benjamin Labaree suggests that apart from considerations of the proper relationship between the metropolitan centre and its colonies, the government was equally sensitive to British public opinion. 'A study of British attitudes toward the colonists greatly enhances our understanding of British behaviour. The government's policy was shaped only in part by a set of rational beliefs about the proper relationship between colonies and mother country. Equally important was

[13] E. Benians, "Adam Smith's Project of and Empire," Volume 4, in J. Wood (Ed.) *Adam Smith Critical Assessments* (New York and London: Routledge, 1984), p. 29.

[14] Letter from Grenville to William Knox, 4 September 1768, cited in N. York, "Thomas Crowley's Proposal to Seat Americans in Parliament, 1765–1775," *Quaker History,* **91** (2002) 1–19, p. 15. fn. 16.

[15] N. Bunker, *An Empire on the Edge: How Britain Came to Fight America* (New York: Vintage Books, 2014).

the way in which Britons viewed the colonists as people. Their resentment of Americans as ungrateful and disloyal, their assumption of superiority, their righteous indignation, and their fear of American power all helped create an atmosphere in which violent measures became more acceptable than conciliation.'[16]

Such attitudes were reinforced by the fact that not only were taxes considerably lower in America than in England but that bounties paid at considerable cost to the Exchequer further reduced the fiscal burden. Bounties, however, were not a gift but rather a subsidy to encourage the production of goods, such as naval stores, timber, and iron, that were needed and in short supply in the mother country, as well as to keep northern industry dependent upon England.[17] Overall levels of taxation were in fact lower in the American colonies than in England and, generally speaking, were raised in response to military exigencies but, more significantly, only with a Parliamentary refunding commitment. Pitt 'encouraged the American colonies to aid the war effort with unprecedented promises of reimbursement for the provisions provided and expenses incurred. Eventually, Parliament fixed the sum of £50,000 sterling to reimburse the Carolinas and Virginia for expenditures "in defending his Majesty's rights and Possessions in North America."'[18] Indeed, many of the expedients adopted by individual colonies to help finance the Seven Years War greatly influenced state financial policies adopted during the Revolutionary War.

The Seven Years War was, prior to the later American Revolution and Napoleonic wars, Britain's most expensive eighteenth-century conflict, costing in total some £83 million, or two-fifths of the total amount spent on warfare up to the century's final quarter, and *c.* 50 per cent of total

[16] B. Labaree, "The Idea of American Independence: The British View, 1774–1776," *Proceedings of the Massachusetts Historical Society*, **82** (1970) 3–20, p. 20.

[17] L. Hacker, "Economic and Social Origins of the American Revolution," in Wahlke, 'Causes of the American Revolution,' p. 1. Hacker goes on note that in respect of iron, the policy was a failure, as the bulk of pigs and bars produced in New England were absorbed within the colonies.

[18] J. Maass, "All This Poor Province Could Do": North Carolina and the Seven Years' War, 1757–1762," *North Carolina Historical Review*, **79** (2002). 50–89, p. 51. The importance of Pitt's commitment is to be understood against the colony's prior reluctance to provide further financial support for the war owing in part to its then poor economic conditions and its remoteness from the seat of war. Maass goes on to note that a contemporary reported the importance of 'the divided state of this Province, and the ill state of the Revenue here' as well as the problems associated with 'paper Bills formerly and lately issued' (the colony had) 'neither Bullion nor Coin ... by which the Troops can be paid when they go out of the province.'

colonial outlays between 1740 and 1775.[19] Other British expenditure was minimal, with the cost of colonial administration that accounted for 7.3 per cent of total period outlays, and 9.3 per cent for Parliamentary reimbursements.[20] The contribution of the Americans towards the war, at £2.6 million, covered a meagre 3 per cent of the total cost, notwithstanding that the conflict posed a direct threat to them. At £818,000, Massachusetts was the largest single contributor, covering *c.* one-third of the total colonial amount raised, of which 45 per cent of the total was in due course reimbursed by Parliament. As a general matter, the amounts reimbursed varied considerably from colony to colony, ranging from zero (Maryland) to 89 per cent (Connecticut), with an overall reimbursement rate of 42 per cent.[21] As a result of these commitments, the total colonial debt, according to Charles Lloyd, author of the financial estimates for the Stamp Act, rose to £2.6 million pounds; however, by 1765 it was reduced by 70 per cent to £767,000, with the greater part of that amount liquidated by 1767.[22] In addition to borrowing, several colonies also raised local taxes.[23] True, not all proceeds were applied to cover military expenditure; other uses included the redemption of previously issued paper currency.

For some historians Britain's 1756 subsidy policy, by which Parliament reimbursed its American colonies with specie in direct proportion to the amounts they actually expended for the war worked with 'reasonable

[19] L. Neal, "Interpreting Power and Profit in Economic History: A Case Study of the Seven Years War," *Journal of Economic History*, 37 (1977), 20–35, p. 31, Table 6. Over the first three-quarters of the century, debt covered roughly one-third of British military expenditures, the Seven Years War percentage was somewhat higher (37 per cent), while the Revolutionary War, at 40 per cent, was higher still.

[20] J. Gwyn, "British Government Spending and the North American Colonies 1740–1775," in P. Marshall and J. Gwyn (Eds.) *The British Atlantic Empire before the American Revolution* (London and New York: Routledge, 2017), p. 77, Table 1. Gwyn points out that between 1740 and 1763 overall British spending in America amounted to an estimated £11.2 million while the estimated trade deficit with Britain was £10.7 million for a surplus of *c.* £520 or about £22,000 annually.

[21] E. Wicker, "Colonial Monetary Standards Contrasted: Evidence from the Seven Years' War," *Journal of Economic History,* **45** (1985) 869–884, p. 877, Table 3.

[22] O. Dickerson, "Were the navigation Acts Oppressive?" in Wahlke 'Causes of the American Revolution,' p. 34.

[23] Massachusetts and Connecticut were two of the leading contributors to the military effort; Georgia and Maryland, owing largely to their remoteness from the fighting, made the smallest contribution. L. Gipson, "The American Revolution as an Aftermath of the Great War for the Empire," in Wahlke. 'Causes of the American Revolution,' p. 44.

efficiency': it provided provincial troops in large numbers, probably stimulated a dramatic rise in colonial importations of British goods, helped to stabilise paper currencies, and encouraged hearty cooperation with the mother country—all this while respecting traditional colonial liberties. Thus, at an annual expense to Britain of £200,000 (later reduced to £133,000), the colonies raised about 20,000 provincials per year through 1762, paying about half the cost themselves. Yet by adopting the Stamp Act after the war, Britain in effect honoured the 'panicky demands of 1754–1757, not the solid achievements of 1758–1762.'

> Without major exception, London by-passed the lessons of victory to embrace projects stimulated by fear of defeat. With the Gallic Peril finally eliminated from North America, Britain espoused reforms once deemed necessary to meet that threat. In the process she alienated her mainland colonies-and thus revived the Gallic Peril. Yet after the war London regressed, almost without reflection or debate, to the attitudes of 1754-57, which in turn rested upon still earlier assumptions and demands that had never worked properly and which were, in any case, quite inadequate to the needs of the 1760s. Fiscal considerations alone probably cannot explain this choice. Direct taxation of the colonies promised to raise only about a fourth of the annual £400,000 needed to maintain ten thousand redcoats in America after 1763. Well-placed subsidies might have fielded as many provincials at less cost to Britain by stimulating a larger voluntary response from the colonies. ... Yet it remains quite remarkable that ... the subsidy option was never even considered. Apparently English leaders thought of subsidies not as acceptable instruments of policy, but as desperate wartime expedients justified only by a terrible emergency. Despite their conspicuous success, in other words, they could not compete as legitimate precedents with earlier failures or risky, untried suggestions.[24]

An important factor contributing to the reversal of previous fruitful British policies towards the American colonies was the gross disparity in tax rates between the two: according to Alvin Rabushka, British tax rates were between three and thirty times higher than those applying among its North American colonies.[25] The colonies, moreover, were largely debt

[24] J. Murrin, "The French and Indian War, the American Revolution, and the Counterfactual Hypothesis: Reflections on Lawrence Henry Gipson and John Shy," *Reviews in American History*, **1** (1973) 307–318, p. 315.

[25] A. Rabushka, *Taxation in Colonial America* (Princeton University Press, 2008), p. 711. Tax rates per adult white male varied considerably across the thirteen colonies, with South

free and judged in relation to the metropole were grossly undertaxed, while their vast expenditure on luxuries was proof that Americans could easily afford, and therefore should, assume more of the burden of paying for their own defence. As one British observer commented at the time, 'no people in the world live more comfortably than the Americans; indeed, if the truth were known, the colonies would soon depopulate the mother country.'[26]

Whether true or not, the fact is such views ignore the additional benefits that accrued to England in the aftermath of the French and Indian War. American imports of British goods, luxuries included, rose in both absolute terms and as a share of total British exports, confirmation that the elimination of the French presence in Canada and east of the Mississippi River added to overall British commerce. In 1761 British exports to its North American colonies totalled £1.7 million and accounted for 15 per cent of the total; ten years later the figure amounted to £4.2 million while the colonial share had risen to nearly 40 per cent. These facts did not escape London merchants, and even some English statesmen, who argued that increasing the burden of colonial taxation would adversely affect England's prosperity.

It was thus both the principle behind and the substance of British policy towards the colonies that Americans resented. They were denied a direct say in matters that directly affected them and faced the prospect of escalating financial demands. As British citizens Americans insisted upon the same rights as their fellow countrymen across the Atlantic. The sole concession they were prepared to make was that Parliament could legislate trade duties; internal taxes, by contrast, could only be imposed with colonial consent,[27] and as no Americans sat in the British Parliament, *ipso facto*

Carolina having the highest and New Hampshire the lowest per-capita rates. Data on individual colonies are as follows: South Carolina 10.94, Virginia 7.20, North Carolina 1.28, Massachusetts 10.70, Pennsylvania 6.62, Georgia 1.51, New Jersey 8.77, Rhode Island 3.51, Connecticut 1.01, New York 7.52, Maryland 1.91, New Hampshire 0.84. J. Greene, "The Seven Years' War and the American Revolution: The Causal Relationship Reconsidered," in Marshall and Gwyn, 'British Atlantic Empire,' p. 98.

[26] Cited in E. Hughes, "The English Stamp Act Duties, 1664–1764," *English Historical Review*, **56** (1941) 234–264, p. 259.

[27] 'A right to impose an internal tax on the colonies, without their consent for the single purpose of revenue, is denied, a right to regulate their trade without their consent is, admitted.' D. Dulany, *Considerations on the Propriety Imposing Taxes in the British Colonies, for the Purpose of Raising a Revenue, by Act of Parliament* (North America Printed; London: J. Almon, 1766), p. 47.

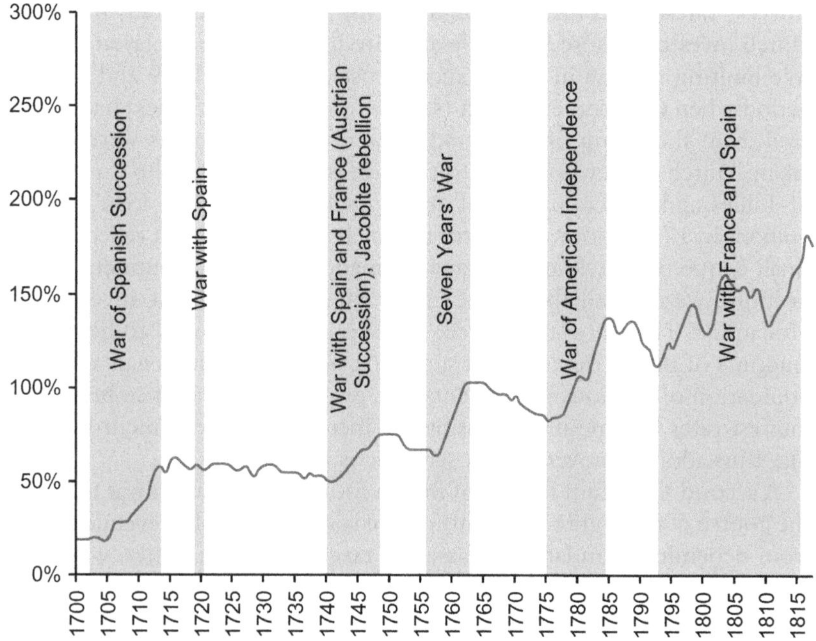

Chart 7.1 National debt of Great Britain, 1692–1815 (per cent of GDP) (Source: Bank of England, *A Millennium of Macroeconomic Data*, March 2017)

they would have to be approved by local Assemblies. Parliament exploited the fiscal distinction, and notwithstanding American aversion to any form of taxation, the customs duties were annually remitted. When Parliament via the Stamp Act sought to eradicate the distinction both as a way of raising revenue and asserting its supremacy in all matters pertaining to the colonies, it achieved neither, while the nonimportation movement that developed in response to its enactment vindicated those who opposed the government's hard-line approach. Americans, in short, had grown too powerful, too sophisticated, and too independent to remain second-class citizens.

Chart 7.1 illustrates the impact the way eighteenth-century wars were financed had on the size of the public debt, which rose from a negligible 15 per cent of GDP in 1700 to 100 per cent upon the conclusion of the French and Indian Wars, while debt service charges rose proportionately.

Interest rates, by contrast, showed hardly any increase at all, thanks to Dutch investors whose insatiable appetite for British debt played a major role limiting the rise in war financing costs. 'Between 1759 and 1762, a period when Government credit (supported by Pitt's victories) had recovered from the slump of 1755 and huge new commitments were undertaken, Dutch money poured into the Funds. The list of "The Proprietors of Tallies and Orders made out at the Exchequer" for the loan of eight millions in 1759, shows the extent to which the Government relied on this small clique of Dutch and Huguenot financiers, whose Continental connections were invaluable in reaching the wider circle of investors in Holland.'[28] Thereafter the Dutch, although they continued to hold large amounts of British debt, ceased supplying new funds and began a modest liquidation of previous investments, the principal consequence being that interest rates became more sensitive to increases in government borrowing, thus adding to overall debt service costs.

A second significant feature of British fiscal administration was that over the course of the eighteenth century, the sources of public revenue shifted from dependence on land and assessed taxes and excise duties, with each accounting for *c.* 40 per cent of total public revenues, to excise taxes, which during the 1760s contributed one-half of total government receipts.[29] Parliament's principal fiscal objective was thus to shift the financial burden more towards excises and stamp duties as a means of reducing land taxes. The American colonies were accordingly expected to pay their fair share of the total, above all, to cover Great Britain's increased North American expenditure. 'Appalled at the debt and taxation which resulted from the war, (Grenville) was genuinely interested in devising fiscal expedients as little burdensome but as fruitful of revenue as might be. In this spirit he proposed a more productive levying and a more efficient collection of the duties on American trade. At the suggestion for laying a stamp tax he hesitated. The resolution that was passed on the subject asserted a right and probability of action; it was a sort of trial balloon to test feeling in the colonies and at home' (Chart 7.2).[30]

[28] C. Wilson, Anglo-Dutch Commerce & Finance in the Eighteenth Century (Cambridge University Presse, 1941), p. 160. See also S. Oppers, "The Interest Rate Effect of Dutch Money in Eighteenth-Century Britain," *Journal of Economic History*, **53** (1993) 25–43.

[29] P. Brien and M. Keep, *The Public Finances: A Historical View* (House of Commons Library Briefing Paper No. 8265, 22 March 2018), p. 16.

[30] Laprade, 'The Stamp Act in British Politics,' p. 743. He goes on to note: 'Perhaps (Grenville's) mind was not yet made up beyond all peradventure of doubt, though he after-

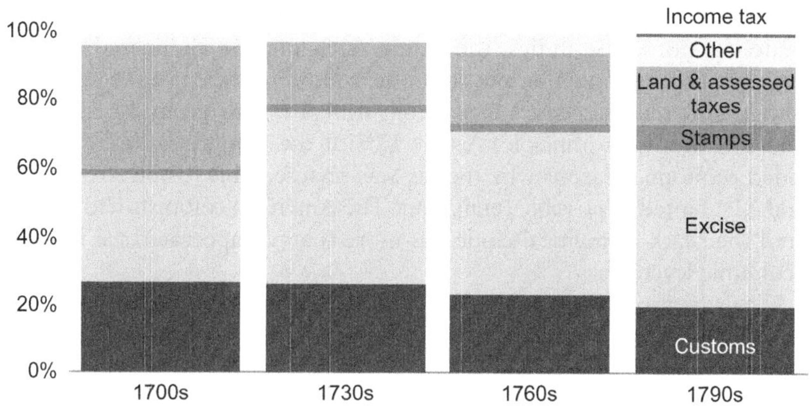

Chart 7.2 Public income sources during decades of the 1700 (per cent of total income). (Bank of England, *A Millennium of Macroeconomic Data*, V3.1, 2 March 2017)

Taxing Americans thus proved to be much more daunting than successive British governments envisaged. The extent of Parliamentary indifference to colonial input was manifest in the run up to passage of the 1765 Stamp Act. The British government was expected to solicit and take account of the views of American colonists in the formulation of the legislation, and although claiming a willingness to do so, did neither. The colonists' response was to convene a Congress held in New York City, the purpose of which was to draft and forward petitions to the king and Parliament setting out the reasons why they opposed the legislation. The delegates reiterated the principle they could only be taxed with their consent and broadened the scope of colonial rights in that regard. Whereas

ward came to feel so. Still he recalled a year later: "When I proposed to tax America, I asked the House, if any gentleman would object to the right; I repeatedly asked it, and no man would attempt to deny it." The members with mercantile connections, who realized and were disquieted by the probable consequences of the measure, may not have replied on this point, realizing the futility of their opposition. But the colonies had tried in vain to get consideration for petitions supporting their contention. ... However hesitant in launching it, once he had committed himself to the policy, Grenville made it a matter of unswerving conviction, and he was ever afterward quick to defend both its constitutionality and expediency.' Ibid., p. 744. On taxation policy in the period leading up to and including the Seven Years War see R. Browning," The Duke of Newcastle and the Financing of the Seven Years' War," *Journal of Economic History*, **31** (1971) 344–377.

previously it had been accepted that Parliament had the authority to enact trade but not excise duties, the Stamp Act Congress eliminated the distinction insisting now that the colonists' right to tax themselves was absolute in all circumstances.[31] Departing from the high ground of political and constitutional principle, Article IX[32] of the Congress' Resolves provided economic reasons why the tax was unacceptable, while Articles X[33] and XI[34] hinted at possible retaliation. The American colonists had discovered their lack of political clout was more than compensated for by their economic leverage.

Their petitions having failed to elicit the desired result,[35] the colonists opted instead for direct action in the form of nonimportation agreements, thus underlining their importance as consumers of British goods and could only be ignored at Britain's commercial peril. Having by these means secured repeal of the Stamp Act, nonimportation became the standard tactic by which American colonists challenged the policies of a Parliament determined to assert its supremacy in all matters affecting the interests of Great Britain but hesitant to accept that potent countervailing forces on the opposite side of the Atlantic were capable of frustrating its will. Hence, the inevitability of a war that no one wanted.

[31] It is worth noting here that the First Continental Congress (14 October 1774) in Resolve Number 4 declared that 'we cheerfully consent to the operation of such acts of the British parliament, as are bon fide, restrained to the regulation of our external commerce, for the purpose of securing the commercial advantages of the whole empire to the mother country and the commercial benefits of its respective members.' Avalon Project, *Declaration and Resolves of the First Continental Congress* (14 October 1774).

[32] 'The duties imposed by several late Acts of Parliament, from the peculiar circumstances of these colonies, will be extremely burthensome and grievous; and from the scarcity of specie, the payment of them absolutely impracticable.'

[33] 'As the profits of the trade of these colonies ultimately center in Great-Britain, to pay for the manufactures which they are obliged to take from thence, they eventually contribute very largely to all supplies granted there to the Crown.'

[34] 'The restrictions imposed by several late Acts of Parliament, on the trade of these colonies, will render them unable to purchase the manufactures of Great-Britain.'

[35] Apart from matters of principle, Parliament may have thought that the Resolves did not reflect unanimous colonial opinion as only nine of the thirteen colonies attended. For various reasons Virginia, Georgia, New Hampshire, and North Carolina did not attend. With the exception of New Hampshire, delegates from the other three states were barred by legislative manipulation from attending.

CHAPTER 8

Trade and Navigation Acts

For many scholars, English trade and trade policies, above all, the Navigation Acts, were considered major inputs into the rise of the nation's commercial supremacy. The measures contained in the Acts, designed in keeping with the then-prevailing mercantilist doctrine, stipulated that the import and export of goods could only proceed along the lines laid out by Parliament, that goods had to be shipped in English vessels, and anything coming to or from the European continent or its colonies had to travel first through English ports.[1]

The first Navigation Laws, which gave the emerging empire a formal structure and clear policy, were written in part by tobacco and sugar merchants determined to protect those trades from foreign competition, especially from Dutch merchants. While it is likely that Dutch activity in the English colonies of America has been greatly exaggerated, the English merchants had reason to worry. During the Dutch Revolt against the Habsburgs, English merchants had been able to take advantage of Dutch

[1] Max Weber traced the mercantilist doctrine back to one of England's 1440 Statutes of Employment that, inter alia, laid down the two essential propositions of the doctrine. 'The first that foreign merchants who brought goods to England must convert all the money which they received into English goods; the second that English merchants who had dealings abroad must bring back to England at least a part of proceeds in cash. On the basis of these two propositions developed gradually the whole system of mercantilism down to the navigation Acts 1651, with its elimination of the foreign shipping.' M Weber, *General Economic History*. (Tr.) Frank Knight. (Glencoe, IL: The Free Press, 1927) pp. 348–349.

G. Pollio, *The Rise and Fall of Britain's North American Empire*, https://doi.org/10.1007/978-3-031-07484-4_8

distractions to move into trade networks in the Baltic and the Levant. Once freed of Spanish control, the Dutch were able to use their commercial superiority to regain control of those trades previously lost to the English. Some English colonial merchants feared that the American trades might be next, so they turned to the state and enacted the Navigation Acts to protect their interests.[2]

It is widely conceded that the Trade and Navigation Acts had little impact on the colonial economy, a conclusion that reaches back generations. Oliver Dickerson long ago dismissed their importance with arguments that soon became the conventional wisdom. 'Were the navigation and trade laws so generally burdensome upon the colonies so as to interfere with their development and thus produce general poverty and distress? Again, the answer must be negative; just the opposite condition existed. The colonies were prosperous and wages of labour were admittedly higher in the continental colonies than elsewhere in the world.'[3] Later research confirmed the legislation was indeed benign,[4] being one of the most widely accepted propositions among American economic historians.[5] British economic historians likewise dismiss its significance. Despite being rooted in traditional mercantilist doctrine, it appears to have contributed little to the prosperity or development of the English economy. The Navigation Acts 'may have provided a nudge in the right direction, (but) it was not alone responsible for the commercial advances of the period. The seventeenth century state was too weak to enforce legislation which imposed a heavy cost on those in the commercial front line. As shown by the fate of other ambitious legislation, aspirations would have remained little more than wishful thinking without the accumulation of

[2] R. Menard, "Plantation Empire: How Sugar and Tobacco Planters Built Their Industries and Raised an Empire," *Agricultural History*, **81** (2007) 309–332, p. 311.

[3] O. Dickerson, "Were the navigation Acts Offensive?" in J. Wahlk (Ed.) *The Causes of the American Revolution* (Boston, MA: D. C. heath and Company, 1962), p. 33.

[4] M. Egnal and J. Ernst, "An Economic Interpretation of the American Revolution," *William and Mary Quarterly*. Third Series, **29** (1972) 3–32. Rabushka, Colonial Taxation' L. Sawers, "The Navigation Acts," *Economic History Review*. New Series, **45** (1992), 262–284.

[5] R. Whaples, "Where is There Consensus Among American Economic Historians? The Results of a Survey of Forty Propositions," *Journal of Economic History*, **55** (1995) 139–154, pp. 140, 145.

capital, skills and enterprise needed to make the Navigation system work at competitive cost.'[6]

The reality is the Navigation Acts also had little impact on the lives of most Americans. 'The Acts imposed heavy costs upon some colonists who, not coincidentally, led the struggle that would end those Acts. Others received benefits from the Acts, but the vast majority was untouched. Most colonists consumed, either directly or indirectly, few imported goods and sold little or nothing in export markets. Tea, for example, was a luxury that most colonists could not afford; the Tea Act for them was not a great grievance.[7] The Navigation Acts thus had little impact on their lives.'[8]

Included among the more significant reasons confirming their limited impact are that the geographic diversion was minor; the goods affected accounted for only a small percentage of the total American GDP; a general indifference to the economic burdens the Acts created, even among those hardest hit, above all, planters in Virginia and Maryland, who almost never mentioned these restraints in their list of grievances against Great Britain. However limited the impact these measures may have had on aggregate economic activity, the fact is that certain sectors were disproportionately affected. In other words, for a burden of a given overall magnitude, the social impact varied inversely with the percentage of the affected subset. Among those most directly affected were America's merchant elites; many others, by contrast, derived direct benefit from their implementation, as enumeration lowered, for example, the price of tobacco and rice in the colonies; competition from English and Scottish merchants and factors contributed to a further reduction in consumer prices; and

[6] N. Zahedieh, *The Capital and the Colonies* (Cambridge University Press, 2010), pp. 280–281.

[7] As the Act lowered the price of tea, it would be expected that consumers would have welcomed the measure. The fact that it granted the East India Company a monopoly on the supply of tea implied large financial losses for American importers and smugglers of tea. The special pleading aspect of reaction to the tea is confirmed by the fact that while the First Continental Congress demanded the repeal of thirteen Parliamentary Acts passed since 1763, significantly, the Tea Act, notwithstanding the kerfuffle it created, was not included among them.

[8] Sawers, 'Navigation Acts,' p. 279. Thomas concluded they amounted to 0.54 per cent of estimated per-capita colonial income. R. Thomas, "A Quantitative Approach to the Study of the Effects of British Imperial Policy upon Colonial Welfare: Some Preliminary Findings," *Journal of Economic History*, **25** (1965) 615–638. Using current (lower) per-capita income estimates, the net impact would increase somewhat to 0.065 pr cent, but without in any way altering Thomas' conclusion.

mandated subsidies applied to producers of more than two dozen different goods, including indigo, pitch, and turpentine.[9]

On the other hand, the enumeration provisions of the Navigation Acts, above all, those relating to tobacco imposed substantial burdens on certain segments of the colonial elite that formed the core of the patriot leadership. 'These provisions excluded the Northern merchants from the lucrative tobacco trade, reduced the cash incomes of the Southern planters, and forced them into a humiliating and precarious dependence on British merchants.'[10] Sawers estimates the income of tobacco producers would have increased by 'no less' than 16 per cent, and up to 35 per cent, if enumeration were ended.[11] Irwin, reaches the same conclusion, but drastically lowers the impact on planter incomes. 'Only a minority of the colonial population is believed to have actively supported independence in 1776, and this vocal and politically powerful minority may have been precisely those most affected by Britain's trade policies. In fact, about 90 percent of the economic burden of the Navigation Acts is believed to have fallen upon the southern colonies, particularly tobacco planters in Maryland and Virginia, and might have reduced the region's income by as much as 2.5 percent in 1770. It was not a coincidence that these planters strongly supported independence. Virginians believed, apparently with good reason, that freeing the tobacco trade from Britain's commercial regulations would make the crop much more profitable. Indeed, in the 1640s, Virginia's House of Burgesses petitioned for a "free export of their Tobacco to foreign Markets directly," but their request was rejected by the British Privy Council.'[12]

Chart 8.1 shows the trend in tobacco exports and prices, which raises serious questions as to how injurious the enumeration provisions of the Trade and Navigation Acts actually were. As the chart shows, British imports rose steadily. True, from 1700 onwards, volumes exhibit greater volatility, which appears to have induced corresponding fluctuations in selling prices. There is, of course, the possibility that incomes might have been higher in the absence of enumeration. But if the economics of

[9] For example, parliament authorised a bounty of 6d per lb of indigo in 1748, subsequently reduced to 4d in 1763. O. Dickinson, *The Navigation Acts and the American Revolution* (Philadelphia, PA: University of Pennsylvania Press;1974), p. 28.

[10] Sawers, 'Navigation Acts Revisited,' p. 270.

[11] Ibid., p. 283.

[12] D. Irwin. *Clashing over Commerce: A History of U.S. Trade Policy* (University of Chicago Press, 2017), pp. 36–37.

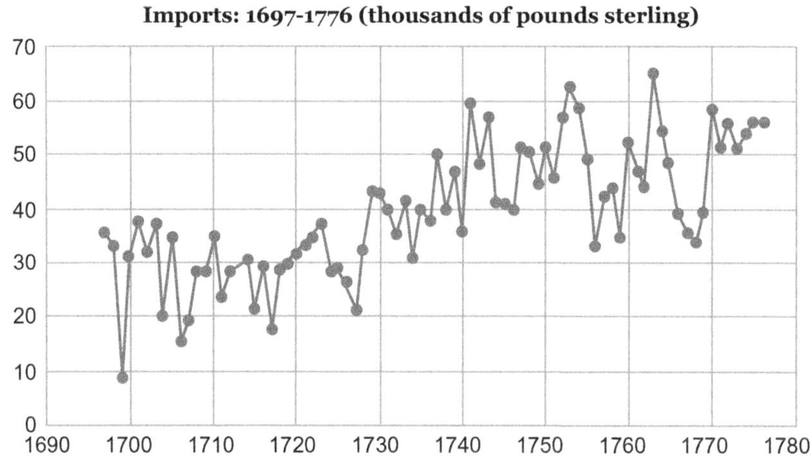

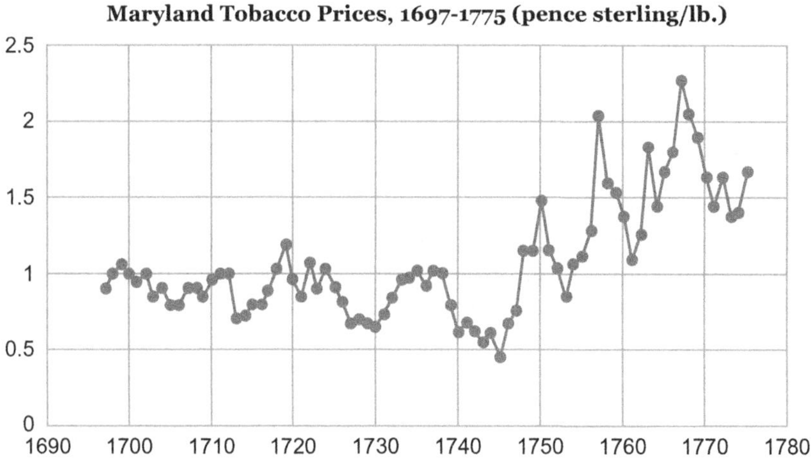

Chart 8.1 English imports of American Tobacco and Maryland Tobacco prices. Imports: 1697–1776 (thousands of pounds sterling). Maryland Tobacco prices, 1697–1775 (pence sterling/lb.). (Source: *Historical Statistics if the United States*, Chart A: Series Z 471–478; Chart B: Series Z 578–582)

tobacco production were so negative, a reduction, not secular increases, in production and export volumes would have been expected. The fact is production and productivity figures belie the hypothesis that enumeration undermined tobacco economics.[13] The data, in short, fully justify Dickerson's conclusion that 'any industry that enjoys an expansion of its total production of more than fifty per cent in five years (1767–1771) and holds that growth has at least the appearance of prosperity.'[14]

All these facts make clear that at worst the Navigation Acts had a neutral impact on trade and regional economic growth, and at best encouraged the development of southern agriculture. On the other hand, they clearly were structured to benefit British industry, which is to be expected given the mercantilist mentality that devised them, with colonial planters, above all, in Virginia and North Carolina, providing the raw materials which were then shipped, processed, and distributed throughout Great Britain and Europe, thus, ensuring that most of the added value accrued to British merchants and bankers, the latter providing the working capital needed to ensure continued trade expansion. As for the colonies, they benefitted from the combination of British protectionism and lax enforcement of the trade regulations. It is true that the impact of British customs charges resulted in the import price being multiples of the American farm gate price, the principal beneficiary being the Exchequer, again an outcome fully consistent with the then-prevailing economic doctrines.

But it is also true tobacco (and sugar) from foreign colonies sold at even higher rates, while English farmers were prohibited from growing tobacco. These policies gave colonial producers a virtual monopoly on the lucrative home market. Further, customs charges on both crops fell over the seventeenth century, so customs can hardly be blamed for forcing prices down. Duties, finally, on re-exported products were usually rebated, meaning that the tobacco and sugar of English colonial producers were competitive in the markets of Europe.[15] In this connection, tobacco duties were routinely evaded. Smuggling, as noted, was widespread on both sides of the Atlantic, with shipowners often arranging for the tobacco to be smuggled on board. 'Others arranged to ship tobacco in bulk rather than in hogsheads. Bulk packaging reduced the number of ships required to

[13] Productivity in the tobacco farming was evident from the industry's beginnings. Menard has shown that output per farm worker rose 2.4 times between 1619–1629 and 1680–1699, from 712 to 1710 pounds/worker. Rising productivity led to a corresponding decline in prices from 6½ d to 0.8 d between 1629 and 1699. R. Menard, *Economy and Society in Early Colonial Maryland* (New York: Garland, 1985), pp. 448–450, 462.

[14] Dickerson, 'Navigation Acts,' p. 25.

[15] R. Menard, "Plantation Empire: How Sugar and Tobacco Planters Built Their Industries and Raised an Empire," *Agricultural History*, **81** (2007) 309–332, p. 317.

transport tobacco by one-sixth, thus depriving the colony of port duties and lost business. A law passed in 1696, reflecting the political power of the planters, increased the size of a hogshead by one-fifth, which further diminished the revenue from export of hogsheads.'[16]

This is not to say that Americans were oblivious to some of the more palpable costs the Acts imposed on them, above all, the fact that Americans were paying higher prices for English imports, receiving lower prices for their exports, and that agency issues led British merchants to supply goods of inferior quality. In the first instance, John Adams argued that the Navigation Acts compelled Americans to sell goods to Britain 'at prices cheaper then we could get for them in foreign markets' and were 'obliged to take from Great Britain commodities that we could purchase cheaper elsewhere.'[17] The logic of his argument was clear: the Navigation Acts, by barring imports from other European countries such as Holland or France, reduced competition and in consequence consumer welfare, with smuggling becoming the main remedy by which such losses were minimised. Indeed, smuggling remained a major concern of the British government, and influenced the design of subsequent revenue acts.[18]

Tyler compiles a 'Who's Who' of Boston smugglers, which taken at face value suggests they were a tiny minority of the city's mercantile community: only 23 out of Boston's nearly 440 merchants can be documented to have engaged in smuggling.[19] There are several reasons for believing this list understates the number and importance of Boston merchants dealing in contraband merchandise. For one thing, the list is confined to merchants for whom 'written evidence' exists of their involvement with

[16] J. Fernandez-Villaverde, *Regional Economics of Colonial America* (accessed at: www.sas.upenn.edu/~jesusfv/PEEA_5_Regional_Economics_Colonial_America.pdf).

[17] John Adams, *The Works of John Adams*. Vol. 4 (Loshburg: Jazzybee Verlag Jurgen Beck, 2015), pp. 24–25.

[18] The latest research suggests that smuggling was a much smaller problem than contemporaries claimed and credited by historians. The standard text on the economy of colonial America reaches the conclusion that owing to the types of goods smuggled, typically low-volume, high-value goods, typically rum and brandy, was 'less of a problem than might be imagined.' Additionally, some European goods that were supposed to enter the colonies only by way of British ports found their way to major cities directly from their country of origin, Holland or France, for example, but again these exports were typically high value goods, which 'did not amount to any great value in any year.' J. McCusker and R. Menard, *The Economy of British America, 1607–1789* (Chapel Hill, NC: University of North Carolina Press, 1991), pp. 77, 78.

[19] Ibid., Appendix, pp. 253–277.

smuggling. Others, for example, find it odd that Thomas Hancock, 'uncle of John and the source of his mercantile fortune, is a documented smuggler, while John is not, but it is almost certain that the younger Hancock persisted in his uncle's business.'[20] And for another, it is not numbers that matter but rather the commercial importance and reputation of those mentioned. It is well known that many of those identified were among Boston's most prominent citizens, many of whom actively involved in the patriotic movement.

Further confirmation that prominent Bostonians were involved in smuggling is provided by the negative reaction of certain Boston merchants to the reduction in tea prices that followed the enactment of the 1773 Tea Act. The Act granted the East India Company the right to ship its tea directly to North America and to export tea from Britain duty-free, but which still was subject to the (reduced) tax imposed by the Townshend Acts. Opponents condemned the Act as a fiendish attempt by the British government to encourage colonial consumption by offering tea at an extremely low price as a way of getting Americans to pay the Townshend duties. The allegation, which may not have been meant seriously, was nevertheless dismissed on the grounds that Boston merchants had been paying the tax for several years, and that it was inconsistent to refuse to pay the tax on tea, and yet regularly remit the duty due on sugar, molasses, and wine.[21] A second element in the pro-government campaign against colonial

[20] E. Hinderbaker, *Boston's Massacre* (Cambridge, MA: Belknap Press of Harvard University Press, 2017), p. 59. Whether Hancock engaged in smuggling is an open question. The one incident in which he was accused and tried for smuggling, the seizure and sale of Hancock's ship the *Liberty*, was analysed years ago when it was concluded that Hancock was stitched up by British Revenue Racketeers. O. Dickerson, "John Hancock: Notorious Smuggler or Near Victim of British Revenue Racketeers?" *Mississippi Valley Historical Review*, **32** (1946) 517—540. Hancock was tried in an Admiralty Court, was defended by John Adams, and the case was eventually thrown out of court. Others have questioned the verdict. 'Hancock's innocence is open to question. His reported boasts that he would defy the Commissioners and the rumours that he had done so may be dismissed as the self-serving statements of interested royal officials, but there remains the fact that the Liberty was condemned for unloading cargo before entry. ... It seems unlikely that Hancock would have been so out of touch with his affairs as not to have been involved.' "Editorial Note," *Legal Papers of John Adams*. Vol. 2 Digital Edition (Massachusetts Historical Society (accessed at: http://www.masshist.org/publications/adams-papers/index.php/view/LJA02d042).

[21] B. Carp, "Did Dutch Smugglers Provoke the Boston Tea Party?" *Early American Studies*, **10**, Special Issue: Anglo-Dutch Revolutions (2012) 335–359, p. 350. Carp cites a source that attributes colonial smuggling to the East India Company. 'The East India Company had enjoyed a monopoly on tea and was hoarding it to prop up prices. "This, has

resistance to pay the tax on tea was to insist that the main source of such opposition derived from certain Boston merchants involved in smuggling Dutch tea. These charges appear to have been widely accepted, as confirmed by a conversation repeated by John Adams in which his interlocutor solemnly claimed that 'All the Bustle and Bombast about tea … (had) begun by about ½ doz. Holland tea smugglers who could not find so much profit in their trade, since the Nine Pence was taken off in England.'[22]

While the extent of smuggling may not have been all that important overall, tea was the principal exception. Holland was the chief source of illicit tea. Smuggling took place in every customs district, causing Peter Oliver, a Massachusetts Loyalist, to remark, 'in some of the Colonies it was notorious that the smuggled Teas were carted through the Streets at Noon Day.'[23] Several estimates exist as to the volume of tea smuggled into the colonies. Early accounts suggested that as much as one-half to three-quarters of the tea consumed in the colonies was illegally imported.[24] British government figures compiled in 1763 estimated the value of all smuggled goods, the bulk of which consisted of tea, at £700,000 annually. Hoh-Cheung and Mui, lastly, present estimates that vary between 4 and 7.5 million lbs.[25] Whatever the truth, the fact is so much tea was smuggled into the country that the price was often driven down to a point where legal importers had difficulty making sales at a profit. As John Kidd, a tea

occasioned all the smuggling of tea, that has been in the British dominions. If the East India Company had sold it as cheap as the Hollanders, and other nations … there would have then, been no temptation … to smuggle it." Indeed, since the passage of the Townshend duties, the "inconsiderable number" of people who had been legally importing tea from Great Britain were "chiefly of such who were always enemies to the nonimportation agreement, and strove to disconcert it." In other words, "A Citizen" (the source of the quote) explicitly linked smuggling with nonimportation, and the friends of government with legitimate traders.'

[22] Cited in Tyler, 'Smuggler and Patriots,' p. 196.

[23] B. Carp, "Dutch Smugglers,' p. 339. Smuggling was a well-organised and efficient operation, with those engaged in the trade even able to access marine insurance from Lloyd's of London at a 4 per cent premium. Also, Jensen, 'Maritime Commerce of Philadelphia,' p. 134: 'as you know that as all these goods that are shipped at Amsterdam are all counterband, you must pick out such Underwriters on whose honour you can depend upon for payment (notwithstanding that they are not Lawfull goods) in case of loss.' Hoh-Cheung and L. Mui "Smuggling and the British Tea Trade before 1784," *American Historical Review*, 74 (1968), pp. 44–73.

[24] R. Twining, "Observations on the Tea and Window Act and on the Tea Trade," (London: T. Cadell, 1784), p. 4.

[25] Hoh-Cheung and Mui, "Smuggling and the British Tea Trade," p. 44.

and spice merchant, wrote in 1755: 'we have had large quantities of Tea from Holland this year and still continue to have more, which will [e]ntirely ruin the trade of that article if a stop is not put to it by some means or other.'[26]

This result was hardly surprising because, as Adam Smith pointed out, strong demand for a highly taxed article would soon find a means of evading the additional charges[27]; tea, moreover, constituted the principal evidence Smith cited in support of his conclusion. The extent of tea smuggling was vast and involved not only the Dutch but other European countries as well, with the tea supplied by the latter regarded as superior to that smuggled by the Dutch.[28] 'Contemporaries reported that the Swedes "got the best tea" by contracting in advance with the silver they brought to China; the credit of the Danes "was tolerably well established at Canton"; and the French were willing to pay more than the English and thus obtained superior qualities. Only the Dutch had acquired a reputation for bringing to Europe "teas of the worst qualities," the refuse of all other nations; thus, "Dutch tea is become a name for all that are bad in quality and unfit for [British?] use."'[29] During much of this period the tax on tea varied between 80 and over 100 per cent of the original cost, thus providing the incentive which sustained smuggling, with the volumes involved a function of the availability of tax-free tea.[30]

Whether the extent of smuggling was significant enough to justify such action is debatable, but what is not is that some American merchants benefitted from smuggling, even to the French during the Seven Years War. To underline the point, on 27 May 1756, the King's Privy Council instructed colonial governors to 'hinder all correspondence between His Majesty's subjects and the subjects of the French King, and to prevent any of the Colonies and Plantations belonging to the enemy in America being

[26] Cited in H. Berg, *Merchants and Mercantile Life in Colonial Philadelphia, 1748–1763* (University of Iowa doctoral dissertation, August 1940), p. 98.

[27] 'The hope of evading such taxes by smuggling gives frequent occasion to forfeitures and other penalties which entirely ruin the smuggler; a person who, though no doubt highly blameable for violating the laws of his country, is frequently incapable of violating those of natural justice, and would have been, in every respect, an excellent citizen had not the laws of his country made that a crime which nature never meant to be so.' A. Smith WN: II:2.

[28] Estimates of tea imported by various European countries are given in R. Martin, *The Past and Present State of Tea Trade of England* (London: Parbury, Allen and Co., 1832), Chapter 2.

[29] Hoh-Cheung and Mui "Smuggling and the British Tea Trade," p. 48.

[30] Ibid., p. 45.

supplied, either by land or sea, from any of His majesty's Colony's with Provisions, or Warlike Stores of any kind.'[31] Smuggling, understandably, was condemned by the British government.[32] The fact that it provided goods to the country's enemies suggests that such behaviour must be counted among the reasons that encouraged Parliament to impose additional financial burdens on Americans. In other words, in addition to a pressing need for revenue, there was very likely a punitive element in the design and implementation of subsequent trade and revenue legislation. There is evidence the two were linked: in a letter from 1763, Lord Egremont writing to the colonial governors explicitly connected smuggling with financial pressures.[33]

The Townshend Acts supposedly addressed the issues of smuggling (and fraudulent entries at the customs) which, inter alia, dedicated a portion of the proceeds of the tax on tea to pay colonial officials' wages so as to ensure their loyalty to the Crown; previously they were paid by colonial legislatures. The Act also stripped colonial district courts of the right to

[31] Cited in Gipson, 'Coming of the American Revolution,' pp. 29–30.

[32] Adam Smith's insights (WN:V:2) into the reasons for smuggling and the reaction to its suppression are worth noting. 'Not many people are scrupulous about smuggling, when, without perjury, they can find any easy and safe opportunity of doing so. To pretend to have any scruple about buying smuggled goods ... would in most countries be regarded as one of those pedantick pieces of hypocrisy which ... [would] serve only to expose the person who affects to practise them to the suspicion of being a greater knave than most of his neighbours. By this indulgence of the publick, the smuggler is often encouraged to continue a trade which he is thus taught to consider as in some measure innocent; and when the severity of the revenue laws is ready to fall upon him, he is frequently disposed to defend with violence, what he has been accustomed to regard as his just property.'

[33] Smuggling is 'an iniquitous Practice;—a Practice carried on in contravention of many express and repeated Laws, tending not only to the Diminution and Impoverishment of the Publick Revenue, at a Time when this Nation is labouring under a heavy Debt incurred by the last war for the Protection of America; but also to expose every fair Trader to ... even Danger of Ruin by his not being able to carry his Commodities to market on an equal footing with those who fraudulently evade the Payment of the just dues and Customs,' cited in 'Coming of the American Revolution,' p. 28. While it is true the American colonies contributed financially to the cost of the Seven Years War, the amount was nugatory. 'Colonial war outlays amounted to 1.8 percent of those of Britain. The tax per adult white male in the colonies for the entire duration of the French and Indian War ranged from a low of £0.84 in New Hampshire to a high of £10.94 in South Carolina. ... Using the figure of £82,623,738 for British war expenditures for the twelve years 1755–66 inclusive puts annual war outlays at £6,885,312, more than four times total net colonial war expenditure. Using the population figure of 7,817,000 for 1760 puts per capita war outlays at £10.57 (£10 11 s. 4d.).' Rabushka, 'Taxation,' pp. 728–729.

adjudicate smuggling and customs cases, which upon passage of the Act would become the responsibility of British naval courts; because Admiralty courts were based on Roman rather than Common Law, this shift had the additional advantage of dispensing with juries comprising local citizens.[34] Parliament's final piece of tea legislation, the Tea Act of 1773, precipitated the Boston Tea Party, which continues to attract scholarly attention as to what ultimately caused the ruction, and the Parliamentary reaction in the form of the Intolerable Acts it provoked. Parliament dealt with England's American colonies as it had since 1764. The colonial response was equally predictable, as both smugglers and legitimate tea merchants were equally aggrieved by the Act's provisions, the former because lower prices reduced their margins, and the latter because of the way it was implemented privileged a handful of selected colonial merchants by granting them a trading advantage over their competitors, who further benefitted by having their increased margins boosted by earning an additional 6 per cent bonus.

As to agency risks associated with the Navigation Acts, George Washington writing to his London agent complained that many of the products shipped from Britain were 'mean in quality, but not in price, for in this they excel, indeed, far above any I have ever had.'[35] Washington may have been the Acts' most prominent critic, but was not alone in recognising the issue's significance. The editor of the *South-Carolina Gazette*, writing in October 1769, likewise noted that 'it is no secret that Her (England's) manufacturers and wholesale dealers, put off their worst goods this way, many of them making scruple to say, anything will do for America.' The *Gazette* goes on to identify the main source of the practice and the proposed remedy. 'This disadvantage to us, arises merely from Great Britain having an exclusive trade to her colonies. Were it otherwise, by our ports being freely open to all nations, she would then, soon find (it)

[34] 'With the establishment of peace in 1763, Britain saw vice-admiralty courts as a tool to strengthen customs enforcement, ensure that trade flowed to and from Britain in keeping with the trade acts, and support the collection of the several American taxes that were enacted during 1764–1767.' Rabushka, 'Taxation,' p. 739. The inefficiency of British customs administration is indicated by the fact that the 1733 Molasses Act generated annual revenues of £1800 as against annual enforcement costs of £7600. Estimates suggest that some 8 million gallons were traded so that at the prevailing rate of 6d per gallon the tax should have yielded £200,000. W. Nester, *The Struggle for Power in in Colonial America, 1607–1776* (Lanham: Lexington Book, 2017), p. 264.

[35] R. Dalzell and L. Dalzell, *George Washington's Mount Vernon: At Hone in Revolutionary America* (Oxford University Press), p. 56.

in her interest, to take the same care to please us, as well as with regard to the quality of her wares, as she is obliged to at the (where) she expects to meet any rival.'[36]

The timing of these and other similar complaints, the third year the Townshend Duties were in force, may not have been coincidental, but it does draw attention to the fact that anti-competitive imperial policies remained a continuing source of tension between Americans and Parliament. To underline the point, included among the twenty-seven grievances against the English King cited in the Declaration of Independence was 'cutting off our trade with the rest of the world.'[37] True, this was the only direct reference to the Navigation Acts, but other grievances allude obliquely to them, including reference to the increasing rigour of the administration of the Navigation Acts in the last years before 1776; another is mention of trial without jury, a reference to the fact Admiralty courts used to enforce the Navigation laws did not use juries.[38]

[36] Cited in T. Breen, *The Marketplace of Revolution* (Oxford University Press, 2004), p. 241. Contrast this with Menard's claim that 'true, the (Trade and Navigation Acts) forced colonists to purchase manufactured goods and commercial services from England, but these tended to be the best and least expensive available.' R. Menard, "Plantation Empire: How Sugar and Tobacco Planters Built Their Industries and Raised an Empire," *Agricultural History*, **81** (2007) 309–332, p. 315.

[37] Thomas Paine provided the context for the 'complaint,' writing that to a trading country, freedom of trade was 'of such importance, that the principal source of wealth depends on it; and it is impossible that any country can flourish ... whose commerce is ... fettered by laws of another .... A freedom from the restraints of the Acts of Navigation I foresee will produce ... immense additions to the wealth of this country.' T. Paine, *The Political Works of Thomas Paine* (Springfield: Peter Raynoids, 1826), p. 241.

[38] L. Sawers, "The Navigation Acts Revisited," *Economic History Review*. New Series, **45** (1992), pp. 262–284, p. 278.

CHAPTER 9

The Stamp Act

The most contentious legislation enacted by Parliament was the Stamp Act of 1765. Ostensibly meant to generate revenue for the Exchequer the proceeds of which were to be dedicated to defraying the military costs incurred by Britain on behalf of its North American colonies. This objective was stated in the Act's preamble: 'An act for granting and applying certain stamp duties, and other duties, in the British colonies and plantations in America, towards further defraying the expences (sic) of defending, protecting, and securing the same; and for amending such parts of the several acts of parliament relating to the trade and revenues of the said colonies and plantations, as direct the manner of determining and recovering the penalties and forfeitures therein mentioned.'[1]

The Stamp Act is accorded a special place in American history because, apart from its overt rejection of the colonists' argument that Parliament lacked the authority to impose excise taxes, it had much broader ramifications than any prior or subsequent revenue act. In addition to matters of principle, the American colonists felt a deep sense of betrayal which, according to Greene, arose 'out of the profound disjunction between how, on the basis of their performance during the Seven Years' War, they thought they deserved to be dealt with by the metropolis and the treatment actually accorded them, supplied the energy behind their intense

[1] Avalon Project, Parliament: The Stamp Act, March 22, 1765.

G. Pollio, *The Rise and Fall of Britain's North American Empire*,
https://doi.org/10.1007/978-3-031-07484-4_9

reaction to the Grenville programme in 1765–1766.'[2] There is no question the ultimate intent was to lay bare the fictional character that had long governed Parliament's fiscal relations with its American colonies. The key distinction was that Parliament lacked the authority to impose internal taxes; its writ ran only to the regulation of trade.

Up until 1764, Parliament respected the distinction by disguising patently revenue raising measures, such as the earlier Sugar Act, as trade legislation. With the Stamp Act, all pretence was abandoned. Referring to the Stamp Act in a letter to an American correspondent Thomas Whately, an adviser to the British Exchequer, regarded the Stamp Act legislation as being 'a great Measure on account of the important point it establishes, namely, the right of Parliament to lay an internal Tax upon the Colonies. We wonder here that it ever was doubted. There is not a single member of Parliament to be found that will dispute it, and the Proposition of a stamp duty seemed so reasonable when made last week to the House, that but 49 divided against it, when 245 were for it, and the Expediency only was debated; This puts an End to all Opposition to the principle of the Bill and now, the rates are the only Question.'[3] Whatley, of course, expressed the official view. Others, by contrast, while acknowledging the importance of principle, concluded that unless some alternative was implemented the potential financial consequences far outweighed any legislative or fiscal benefits that might derive from its enactment.[4]

This argument was most clearly advanced by John Temple who reported that the duties themselves were not the central issue; instead, matters of principle combined with economic interests were of far greater importance, and in the end would inflict harm on the British economy. '[T]he principal objections of the Americans to a Stamp Act do not arise so much from the nature of the Duties, or the manner of Collecting them as from the Consideration of their being *Taxed without their own Voice or Consent*, which they apprehend so nearly Effects their Essential &c Constitutional Rights as Englishmen and free born Subjects; that they think it must be as fatal to their Liberties as the draining off so much running Cash would be to their Trade, especially with Great Britain: And of Consequence the

[2] Greene, 'Seven Years' War and the American Revolution,' p, 101.

[3] Whately to John Temple, 9 February 1765. N. Stout, "The Missing Temple-Whately Papers," *Proceedings of the Massachusetts Historical Society*, Third Series, **104** (1992) 123–147.

[4] Laparade, Stamp Act in British Politics, p. 749.

Trade and Manufactures of Great Britain must be proportionably Effected so far as they depend upon American Consumptions.'[5] One would have imagined the same mistake would not be made twice, but subsequent legislation proves that was not the case. The government seemed unable or unwilling to address the conflict arising from its need to assert its right to impose internal taxes on the Americans and the threat it posed to British prosperity.

Parliament seemed equally myopic concerning the impact the Stamp Act would have on influential segments of American society. It offended those who were best placed to oppose the Act—merchants, newspaper publishers, and lawyers—and to mobilise supporters to their cause. Scholars continue to debate whether the law specifically targeted these occupations. But even if inadvertent, the result would have been the same as no act could have been better conceived to affect adversely the interests of members of the most influential professions that moulded public opinion.[6] 'Men representing all three of these vocations would lead the opposition to the Stamp Act and would succeed in making the case that the long reach of these taxes would impact all Americans. Moreover, these men were well positioned to gather support not just in the colonies, but among partners and allies in Great Britain as well.'[7] A final point worth noting is that the distinction between merchants and lawyers is not discreet as the two professions were frequently combined[8]; this, of course, would have reinforced opposition to the Act.

Stamp duties have a long history, being first introduced in England in 1694, and by the mid-eighteenth century, they were a well-established form of taxation.[9] Nor were they alien to the American colonies as both Massachusetts and New York had adopted their own stamp duties, in 1755 and 1756, respectively, in an attempt to generate revenues needed to strengthen military defences. 'There is little evidence that the stamp taxes levied by Massachusetts and New York were particularly unpopular, except perhaps in the sense that all taxes were unpopular. Far from being

[5] Nout, John Temple and Thomas Whately, p. 139 (letter dated 15 January 1765). Emphasis in the original.

[6] E. Surrency, "The Lawyer and the Revolution," *American Journal of Legal History*, **8** (1964) 125–135, p. 127.

[7] J. Mercantini (ed.) *The Stamp Act of 1765* (Peterborough, Ontario: Broadview Press, 2018), p. 12.

[8] E. Surrency, "The Lawyer and the Revolution," p. 126.

[9] On the history stamp acts in Great Britain see Hughes, 'English Stamp Act Duties.'

considered as a warning to the British government not to resort to such taxation, these colonial stamp acts and the absence of popular resistance to them may very well have encouraged George Grenville and his colleagues to extend the English Stamp Act to all the colonies in North America by parliamentary statute.'[10] In fact, stamp duties were considered a fairer form of taxation than the principal alternatives, as pointed out by James Delancey in 1766: 'I have thought of three of the following: a poll tax of ten shillings or more on every slave from fifteen to fifty years of age, an excise upon tea and a stamp duty. The first cannot be thought heavy, as none but persons of substance possess slaves, and the tax will fall equally according to men's abilities; the second is a tax upon a superfluity of pernicious consequence to the health and purses of the people, and therefore a proper object of a tax, and the third [the stamp duty] will be so diffused as to be in a manner insensible.'[11]

Stamp duties were thus perceived to have certain advantages over alternative forms of taxation. Diffuse incidence was regarded as a virtue as it spread the financial burden more widely across society; individual burdens would thus have been lower than targeted taxes aimed either at the wealthy alone, such as land taxes in England, or slave taxes in the American colonies. Moreover, the duty had the virtue of visibility, as payment of the tax was denoted by a clear mark or cipher, and the administrative costs would have been far lower. As Grenville said at the time, a stamp duty was the 'least exceptionable because it requires fewer officers and even collects itself.' It was, in other words, 'the perfect tax to impose upon people who were used to evading British taxes by bribery and fraud.'[12]

Oats and Sadler assert that the design of the Act was flawed from its inception. 'We argue that the logistics of implementing a highly complex form of taxation across vast geographical distances were completely underestimated by Parliament, demonstrating the failure to enact action at a distance. Even with the full cooperation of the colonists, it would have been extremely difficult to manage the efficient operation of the Act and

[10] M. Thompson, "Massachusetts and New York Stamp Acts," *William and Mary Quarterly*, **26** (1969) 253–258, p. 257.

[11] Cited in L. Oats and P. Sadler, "Accounting for the Stamp Act Crisis," *Accounting Historians Journal*, **35** (2008) 101–143, p. 109.

[12] J. Bullion, Escaping Boston: Nathaniel Ware and the Beginnings of Colonial Taxation, 1762–1763, *Huntington Library Quarterly*, **45** (1982) 36–58, p. 48. Grenville's quote is from the same source.

to reap the expected revenue.'[13] They maintain it might have succeeded had the government taken into account the social and economic conditions in individual colonies as it could have led to a different structure and by implication greater local acceptance, a doubtful argument for several reasons. First, the acceptability of stamp duties among individual American colonies derived primarily from the fact they were enacted by local legislatures, in contrast to the parliamentary measure that was imposed upon them without their consent. Had the Stamp Act been enacted, say, forty years earlier, it arguably would not have aroused serious local opposition. Also, it is doubtful, even had the Act been designed differently, that given the prevailing climate it would have made any difference. An assessment of the Act prepared by Parliament several years later indicated which colonies actually paid the tax. Only Georgia, the last of the thirteen North American colonies, remitted any revenue; the only other British colonies to have done so were Quebec, Montreal, West Florida, Jamaica, St. Kitts, and Barbados,[14] thus highlighting the extent to which the North American colonies viewed things differently from Britain's Caribbean dependencies or the French territories ceded to it by the Treaty of Paris.

And, finally, Oats and Sadler fail to consider that the Act's shortcomings did not derive from ignorance of local conditions, distance, administration, or as a by-product of the legislation but almost certainly by design: to convey, and silence opposition against, the principle of parliamentary supremacy. Parliament thus faced a serious dilemma. London merchants argued in favour of repeal on the grounds that nonimportation imposed considerable costs on the economy since colonial trade and British prosperity were closely linked. From Parliament's perspective, the more significant point of the Stamp Act was that it addressed the broader and ultimately more significant issue of supremacy. William Pitt provided Parliament with

[13] L. Oats and P. Sadler, "Accounting for the Stamp Act Crisis," *Accounting Historians Journal*, **35** (2008) 101–143, p. 138.

[14] Britain's West Indian colonies resented the interference in their internal affairs as did the North American colonies, but as the circumstances in the two regions were fundamentally different, the former did little more than register their opposition; 'Islanders faced a dilemma not shared to the same degree by North Americans: how to resist British authority without seriously jeopardizing their safety and livelihood? … geographic isolation, hostile surroundings, slave majorities, and one-crop economies clearly set limits for prudent behavior which were far more restricted than in North America.' D. Spindel, "The Stamp Act Crisis in the British West Indies," *Journal of American Studies*, **11** (1977) 203–221. In any event, the repeal of the Act applied only to Britain's North American colonies.

the answer. 'The Stamp Act must be repealed absolutely, totally and immediately. That the reason for the repeal be assigned, because it was founded on an erroneous principle. At the same time, let the sovereign authority of this country over the colonies be asserted in as strong terms as can be devised, and be made to extend to every point of legislation whatsoever. Thus we may bind their trade, confine their manufactures, and exercise every power whatsoever, except that of taking their money out of their pockets without their consent.'[15] Upon repeal of the Stamp Act, Parliament enacted the equally odious Declaratory Act, which asserted that a parliamentary majority could enact any legislation that would apply equally to British subjects and colonists.

The tax required legal and business documents of all types to be printed or issued only on paper with a royal stamp, and the paper itself had to be imported from England, substantially raising costs. Legal and business forms were to be taxed from three pence to six pounds, paperwork for indentures from two and a half to five pence, almanacs two pence and up, newspapers a halfpenny to a penny per sheet, and advertisements in newspapers two shillings. The Stamp Act was expected to raise between £60,000 and £100,000 annually, but actual receipts amounted to no more than £4000, a figure that includes revenues received from all of Britain's American colonies. The net financial impact of the Stamp Act generated a net loss of *c.* £220,000, the bulk of which is accounted for by the cancellation of stamped paper and outstanding balances due from stamp distributors in the colonies.

Traditional historiography tended to focus mainly on constitutional issues such that by violating the accepted distinction between internal and external taxes, the Stamp Act was a major factor contributing to the ensuing colonial protests.[16] Other important aspects of the legislation, by contrast, are either slighted or ignored. Priest and du Rivage, for example, point out that the stamp duty amounted to an 'institutional tax' that threatened to affect the way business was conducted in the colonies that could have had serious repercussions on the rate and pattern of regional growth. For one thing, the provisions of the Act affected commercial and

[15] E. and H. Morgan, Stamp Act Crisis,' p. 277.

[16] On the opening sentence of the preface to the third edition of the Morgan's classic study, the senior author notes that a major criticism of the book was its failure to give due weight to the important role the distinction between internal and external taxes played in colonial protests. E. and H. Morgan, *The Stamp Act Crisis*. Third Edition (Chapel Hill and London: University of North Carolina Press, 1995), p. vii.

legal transactions and, in so doing, imposed a greater financial burden on the northern than southern colonies. More than that, the Stamp Act was a deliberate attempt to use taxation to alter colonial institutions and shift the trajectory of the North American economy. 'For its supporters, the Stamp Act promised to curb the licentiousness and disorder of the colonial economy, to restrain runway land speculation, and to make the colonies more readily governed by Britain. For its opponents, the Act threatened to shred colonial property rights, while dramatically raising the cost of legal and commercial transactions. Depending on where one stood, the Stamp Act looked very different, but its importance was clear not just as a constitutional precedent for Parliament's taxation of the American colonies but as a means of changing those colonies' economy and society.'[17] The latter, undoubtedly intended, impacts were to curb land speculation by increasing the cost of buying and selling property; discourage litigation by taxing most legal papers, and minimise local dissent by taxing newspapers, pamphlets, and other publications, with the structure of taxation being the principal means of achieving these desiderata.[18]

The punitive nature of the tax is best demonstrated by its impact on the printing industry, above all, the publishers of newspapers, as it not only affected production costs but also imposed a tax on advertisements appearing therein. As the margin of difference between production cost and selling price was small, advertising revenues then as now subsidised newspaper production. Indeed, it has been argued that one of the principal reasons for the growth of colonial newspapers was the recognition by merchants and businessmen of their value as a means for advertising goods and services.[19] The onerous character of the duty is demonstrated by comparing the tax with then-current advertising rates. 'The Newport Mercury

[17] C. Priest and J. du Rivage "The Stamp Act and American Institutional and Economic History," *Southern California Law Review*, **88** (2015) 875–912.

[18] 'Colonial law at mid-century was riven with paradoxes. With Anglicisation in the law came needed sophistication and unwanted formality. Lawyers were everywhere abused for stirring up suits and everywhere employed to bring suits. The openness and fluidity of the law gave rise to litigiousness that flooded court dockets and delayed legal redress. The iniquities of private law became the iniquities of public law in what seemed to contemporaries to be a spiral of private avarice and official corruption. The law promoted greater equality for some and progressively debased others into chattel slaves.' P. Hoffer, *Law and People in Colonial America* (Baltimore, MD, and London: Johns Hopkins University Press, 1998), p. 126.

[19] C. Humphrey, *The American Revolution and the Press: The Promise of Independence*, (Northwestern University Press, 2013), p. 28.

charged 3 s. 9d. for three insertions of a notice not exceeding twelve lines and for each subsequent repetition; the Maryland Gazette asked 5 s. for an advertisement of "moderate length" and is. for each week's continuance; and the Virginia Gazette charged 3 s. for a first insertion and 2 s. for each later appearance. Probably because of less competition, advertising rates were generally higher in the South than in the North.'[20]

The deleterious impact of the tax on publisher finances was recognised early on by Benjamin Franklin in a letter to his printing partner David Hall dated February 1765: 'I think it will affect the Printers more than anybody, as a Sterling Halfpenny Stamp on every Half Sheet of a Newspaper, and Two Shillings Sterling on every Advertisement, will go near to knock up one Half of both. There is also Fourpence Sterling on every Almanack.'[21] The ultimate profitability of newspaper publishing depended upon one other source of revenue, namely, public printing. These contracts were typically awarded on a purely personal or political basis and never through competitive bidding. 'Accepting one (of these contracts) carried an explicit or implied agreement that the columns of the newspaper should carry items favourable to those in power and exclude material that was critical or hostile.'[22] As publishers of official notices, these newspapers could not so easily be replaced by others offering a less partisan perspective, thus compounding the financial impact of the stamp duties; that is, at the proposed tax rates, these marginally profitable newspapers could not possibly have survived.

The importance accorded newspapers as the principal vehicle for encouraging revolutionary fervour is widely acknowledged, notwithstanding that the number of newspapers published in the American colonies was not all that great, as well as the fact that many were loyalist. Nor should it be forgotten that publishing was also a business and where ideology coincided with profitability so much the better, as noted by David Ramsay. 'Printers, when uninfluenced by government, have generally arranged themselves on the side of liberty, nor are they less remarkable for attention to profits of their profession. A stamp duty, which openly invaded the first, and threatened a great diminution of the last, provoked their

[20] A. Schlesinger, "The Colonial Newspapers and the Stamp Act," *New England Quarterly*, **8** (1935) 63–83, p. 66, fn. 4.

[21] Cited in ibid.

[22] O. Dickerson, "British Control of American Newspapers on the Eve of the Revolution," *New England Quarterly*, **24** (1951), 453–468, p. 453.

zealous opposition.'[23] It has been estimated that there were a total twenty-four newspapers published on the eve of the Stamp Act, and at least one could be found in every colony except New Jersey, which nevertheless was served by those published in neighbouring Philadelphia and New York.[24] Some idea of the importance of newspapers in the principal port cities may be inferred from the number of master printers resident in each, with Boston having fourteen, followed by Philadelphia with nine, and New York, a distant third, with only five.[25] By 1775 the number of newspapers had risen to thirty-eight, with a conservatively estimated average circulation per newspaper, that on 'a rough calculation suggests that on the eve of the Revolution approximately one issue of a newspaper appeared weekly for every sixty-five colonists.'[26] Printing could also be quite a profitable business with margins on, say, a typical pamphlet of seventy-two pages amounting to roughly 35 per cent.[27]

Publishers appear to have been among the most innovative entrepreneurs and investors in colonial America, best epitomised by the activities of Benjamin Franklin. In addition to turning his *Pennsylvania Gazette* into one of the more influential of the colonial newspapers, Franklin also manufactured and sold materials for making ink (and even an occasional keg of the fluid itself), he collected rags and sold newsprint throughout the colonies, and he lent money to and formed partnerships with his former journeymen (as well as a couple of nephews) to set up shop in other colonies. Still other printers—Benjamin Edes and John Gill of Boston, Solomon Southwick of Newport, John Holt of New York, William Bradford of

[23] D. Ramsay, *History of the United States from Their First Settlement as English Colonies to Year 1808*. Second Edition (Philadelphia: M. Carey and Son, 1818), p. 341.

[24] Schlesinger, "Colonial Newspapers," p. 64.

[25] S. Botein, "Meer Mechanics and an Open Press: The Business and Political Strategy of Colonial American Printers," *Perspectives in American History*, 9 (1975) 127–228.

[26] R. Merritt, "Public Opinion in Colonial America: Content-Analyzing the Colonial Press," *Public Opinion Quarterly*, 27 (1963) 356–371, p. 365. Merritt goes on to note that circulation figures by themselves will underestimate readership. He goes on to note that 'In colonial America it was common practice for the owners of roadside taverns, public houses, and other places where travellers or towns people gathered to subscribe to one or more local prints, and possibly even to those from other colonies or from England.'

[27] L. Wroth, *The Colonial Printer* (New York: The Grolier Club, 1931), pp. 153–154. Wroth cautions, however, 'one may not assume that this percentage of profit was maintained everywhere and for a long period.' The capital costs associated with setting up a one-press shop in the second quarter of eighteenth-century America was of the order of £85 (*c.* £18, 400 in today's money). Ibid., p. 50.

Philadelphia, Peter Timothy of Charleston, South Carolina—were prominent patriots, 'clear-thinking and bold captains, who crystallized their discontents, formulated plans, and joined with other groups in precipitating the revolution with the movement.'[28]

The tax imposed on lawyers not only affected their income but, as recent research has argued, the potential prosperity of the American colonies. It is widely accepted that institutions play a prominent role in economic development. Where societies are free to develop their own institutions, they will tend to evolve practices that are efficient, that is, optimal in terms of the particular desideratum they are meant to promote. Du Rivage and Priest assert that the Stamp Act by targeting property and contractual arrangements that evolved against the backdrop of conditions specific to the American colonies, above all, the abundance of land and the scarcity of specie, threatened to undermine the efficient operation of both land and credit markets to the detriment of the colonies' continued economic and demographic growth. 'The Stamp Act's taxation of land conveyances and official legal documents threatened to disrupt the functioning of local colonial institutions, to suppress the recordation of land conveyances and mortgages, and to reduce litigation on the basis of credit transactions. To the extent that local institutions' central role is to publicize information about property rights and to process credit claims, those functions are impaired by excessive costs imposed on the participants.'[29]

The design of the Stamp Act, with its emphasis on the taxation of legal documents and newspapers, was not incidental but rather central to the legislation. Grenville, and his deputy Whately, admitted as much. According to the former, the Act meant 'to discourage by a high Duty the Grant of large Quantities of Land to one Person.' And the latter, the Stamp Act would serve as 'some Check to those enormous Grants and Conveyances, which are so detrimental to the Colonies.'[30] Taken at face

[28] Ibid., 360–361.

[29] J. Du Rivage and C. Priest, "The Stamp Act and the Political Origins of American Legal and Economic Institutions," *Southern California Law Review*, **88** (2015) 875–912, p. 880.

[30] 'The Law Instruments, such as Deeds Bonds, &ca. are charged nearly the same as the English except Conveyances of Land and Bonds for the Payment of money. The former of these are upon a very different footing from Ours, being proportioned to the Quantity of Land Conveyed. With Us they are all rated alike, whether the Estate they relate to be of five pounds or fifty thousand pounds value; In the Colonies it is proposed that a conveyance of 100 Acres shall pay is. 6d. of 200 acres 2 s. 8c of 320 acres 2S. 6d. which is the English duty; so that all below that Quantity is lighter taxed than here. But on the other hand all above that

value, the stamp and subsequent tax acts were meant to accomplish three things: to assert the supremacy of Parliament in all matters pertaining to the colonies; to raise additional revenues that, inter alia, would minimise the dependence on colonial governors on the local assemblies for administrative funds; and to avert the economic challenge to Great Britain resulting from steady growth and expansion of the American colonies.

> The regulations the Stamp Act placed on the colonies would reduce land speculation by raising the cost of buying and selling real property, discourage litigation by taxing most legal papers, and curb colonial civil society by raising the cost of newspapers that fanned the flames of political opposition. ... This is not surprising. Authoritarian imperial reformers in Britain had long expressed concern that colonial settlement and expansion needed to be restrained lest the colonies challenge Britain's economic supremacy within the empire. ... Keeping the colonies useful to Britain meant checking the scramble for vast tracts of the American interior, a scramble that led to conflict with Native Americans and that ultimately threatened Britain's economic control over its own empire. Using taxation to limit the acquisition of huge amounts of North American land was nominally egalitarian, but, in reality, it served to discourage territorial expansion and development while still leaving poor settlers with a significant tax burden.[31]

Du Rivage and Priest's thesis that the design of the Stamp Act was meant to undermine local institutions to the benefit of Great Britain is appealing but lacks a solid foundation. The idea that the operation of the market for land and credit was efficient is tautological in the sense it presupposes that because it evolved to meet local needs it was necessarily optimal; it confuses longevity with efficiency. As to credit, the issuance of legal tender paper currency often resulted in inflation, reflected in the depreciation of local currency against sterling, which benefitted borrowers while penalising creditors. A system that leads to an arbitrary redistribution of the benefits of transacting can hardly be described as optimal. If the

Quantity will be higher as an Additional 2 s. 6d. is proposed to be charged upon every additional 320 Acres; and this Duty being applicable equally to grants, it is hoped the effect may be some Check to those enormous grants and Conveyances which are so detrimental to the Colonies.' Whately to Temple, 9 February 1765. Nout, 'John Temple and Thomas Whately,' p. 136. It is worth noting here that the original stamp act which came into effect in 1671 was designed to minimise 'trivial and vexatious suits,' as well as to deal with land disputes which followed the Civil War and the Restoration. Hughes, 'English Stamp Duties,' p. 237.

[31] Ibid., 891–892.

measure was designed by Parliament to limit colonial expansion westwards, either because it challenged Britain's economic supremacy or incited greater Indian violence, tax policies would not have been the most effective way forward. Far more significant in this regard was the Royal Proclamation of 1763 that five years later set the western colonial boundary at the Appalachian Mountains.[32] On the other hand, George Washington, correctly, regarded the Proclamation as being 'a temporary expedient' only as he expressed in a letter to his land agent, views which may be regarded as typical of those speculating in western lands.

> I proposed in my last to join you in attempting to secure some of the most valuable lands in the King's part which I think may be accomplished after a while notwithstanding the Proclamation that restrains it at present and prohibits the Settling of them at all for I can never look upon that Proclamation in any other light (but I say between ourselves) than as a temporary expedient to quiet the Minds of the Indians and must fall of course in a few years … any person therefore who neglects the present opportunity of hunting out good lands and in some measure marking and distinguishing them for their own (in order to keep others from settling them) will never regain it. … I might be censured for the opinion I have given in respect to the King's Proclamation and then if the Scheme I am now proposing to you was known it might give the alarm to others and by putting them upon a Plan of the same nature (before we could lay a proper foundation for success ourselves) set the different Interests a clashing and probably in the end overturn the whole all which may be avoided by a Silent management and the (operation) snugly carried on by you of hunting other game.[33]

[32] 'An examination of the activities of three (major) Virginia land companies, the Ohio, Loyal, and Mississippi land companies, reveals that during the entire period the proclamation was in force, none of these enterprises was successful in carrying out collective, organized settlement in the trans-Appalachian region.' E, Del Papa," The Royal Proclamation of 1763: Its Effect upon Virginia Land Companies," Virginia Magazine of History and Biography, 83 (1975) 406–411, p. 407.

[33] Cited in T. Curtis, "Riches, Real Estate, and Resistance: How Land Speculation, Debt, and Trade Monopolies Led to the American Revolution," *American Journal of Economics and Sociology*, 73 Annual Supplement (July, 2014), pp. 474–626, p. 538. In due course, Britain closed off colonial settlement in the western regions adding yet another layer of opposition to imperial rule, as wealthy Virginians, including George Washington, Thomas Jefferson, Patrick Henry, George Mason, and Richard Henry Lee, all of whom had invested heavily in western lands and thus would have incurred huge losses on their investment in potential land sales if England retained control over its colonies. Eckenrode, long ago, rejected the 'land problem' as a factor affecting Virginians' allegiance to Britain. 'It is difficult to believe that the king's plan to form new colonies west of the Alleghanies forced the land

A second contentious feature of the Act was the way the tax was to be collected, namely, in terms of the 'sterling money of Great Britain' to be paid in 'silver ... to the proportion and value of five shillings and six pence the ounce' rather than in colonial currency, thus imposing a financial burden that would have uniformly affected all colonies. The requirement, it was claimed, would exacerbate local economic problems arising from the supposed chronic shortage of money among the American colonies, which, in turn, reflected the fact that England did not supply the colonies with sufficient coinage while prohibiting them from issuing their own. Early settlers brought coins from Europe, but these were quickly repatriated to pay for imports. Without sufficient money, the colonists were forced to resort to barter for goods or use primitive currency, including Indian wampum, nails, and tobacco[34]; in due course, the colonies began to issue their own currency, known as bills of credit, which in time were legally discouraged.

The potential consequences that would follow from the requirement to pay the duty in hard currency was widely articulated, as confirmed by

hungry Virginians ... to go into Revolutionary movement; land in the wilderness at that time was too cheap to fight about,' H. Eckenrode, *The Revolution in Virginia* (Boston, MA: Houghton Mifflin Company, 1916), p. 39. A decade later Eckenrode's conclusion was challenged by Isaac Harrell, who noted that '[l]ands were plentiful indeed, yet, as more than one colonial empire builder from Georgia to Massachusetts to his great discomfort, it was extremely difficult to secure a title to any lands west of the mountains that would stand test before a court.' I. Harrell, *Loyalism in Virginia* (Duke University Press), p. 8. Years later Curtis in a series of articles reiterated the importance of land policies in helping to forge an alliance among key elements of Colonial America against Great Britain. 'Great Britain altered her land policies after the Seven Year's War and so brought the many diffused interest groups in the colonies into a configuration of opposition. The coming together of the Southern planters, Northern merchant land speculators, backwoods farmers, the fur interest, and frontiersmen was a necessary precondition for a successful revolution.' T. Curtis, *Land Policy: Pre-Condition for the Success of the American Revolution*," *American Journal of Economics and Sociology*, **31** (1972) 209–224, p. 209 and *supra*.

[34] This problem was recognised by Adam Smith. 'A nation may import to a greater value than it exports for half a century, perhaps together; the gold and silver which comes into it during all this time, may be all immediately sent out; its circulating coin may gradually decay, different sorts of paper money being substituted in its place, and even the debts too, which it contracts in the principal nations with whom it deals may gradually be increasing; and yet its real wealth, the exchangeable value of the real produce of its lands and labour, may, during the same period, in a much greater proportion. The state of our North America colonies, and of the trade which they carried on with Great Britain, before the commencement of the current disturbances, may serve as proof that this is by no means an impossible supposition.' WN: IV. 4.

Henry McColloh, whose observations are especially relevant as he was an early supporter of the stamp duty as being 'the only Tax or Fund from which any Considerable Duty' could be raised in the colonies. At the same time, he predicted the Stamp Act as enacted by Parliament would encounter opposition in the colonies both because it neglected 'several … Matters' that 'ought to have been taken into Consideration' and because it contained several unnecessary and 'very Exceptionable' clauses.[35] Foremost among these was that it failed to take account of the fact that there was a chronic shortage of hard currency in the American colonies. 'As there is not Specie in most of the said Colonies to Enable the people Settled there to Pay in Specie the several Duties required from them So that under their present Circumstances it is impossible for many of the Colonists to pay Obedience to the said Law.'

> I have Often Considered this Matter, and have had great Opportunities of being Acquainted with the General Concerns of America; And the only Method which seems to me, practicable is, either by Issuing Exchequer Orders in the Payment of the Army, and all other contingent Charges in America, which will Obtain a Circulation by receiving the said Orders in payment of Customs, Stamp Duties, Quit Rents &ca, or also, as the Stamp Duty Act is soon to take place, to raise Money by way of Lottery, the Interest of which may be paid from the Stamp Duties in America. That when the said Money is so raised by Lottery, there should be a New Coinage for America, to be Transmitted there for the payment of the Troops, and other Contingent Charges; And as by the 6th of Queen Anne Foreign Silver is to pass in America at the rate of 6s 8d p[er]Ounce,' in the New Coinage for America there should be an Alloy of 1/4th Given to each Ounce of Silver, but I would not be Understood to pass it as Sterling, but according to the Real Value. If this Proposal is Approved of, the Stamp Duty and other Revenues arising in America will at different periods of time, be sufficient to Raise four or Five Millions Sterling, by way of Lottery; And by this means America will be supplied with Silver Specie so as to Answer all payments, both of a Public, and of a Private Nature. The only Objection that I have heard mentioned is, that if the Colonies are not at Liberty to Issue any further Bills of Currency, and their Silver is Coined upon the Credit of the above Fund, it will not remain in America. But be shipped home, which I conceive to be a Mistake, for if the Money is really Circulated, so much as is needful for the Course of Business there will remain.

[35] J. Greene and H. McColloh, "'A Dress of Horror': Henry McCulloh's Objections to the Stamp Act," *Huntington Library Quarterly*, **26** (1963), pp. 253–262, p. 258.

The arguments of McColloh and others who expressed the same concerns are specious in that the revenues to be raised under the Act were to be expended in the colonies to cover local military and administrative outlays. '[T]he expense and hazard of remitting this stamp money to England may be saved and the complaint of draining the country of money obviated by a transaction between the Paymaster-General and the Stamp Commissioners, they furnishing him with bills upon their head-distributors and he paying their value into the Exchequer.'[36] A second reason is that the Currency Act of 1764, which required that all such currency then circulating be punctually retired at the time appointed by the act of issue, 'passed at a time when most of the colonies involved still had sufficient currency circulating from wartime issues and when Americans were more alarmed by other more objectionable features of the Grenville program, the Currency Act encountered little immediate opposition, and for the first two years there were only sporadic protests.'[37]

The latter Act prohibited the American colonies from issuing legal tender paper currency that substituted for specie, except under exceptional circumstances, as during the French and Indian Wars.[38] The motivation for several acts that restricted or prohibited the issuance of paper currency was directly influenced by British merchants who feared that colonial legislators would attempt to force payment of sterling debts in depreciated paper, a perspective formally stated in the preamble to the Act: 'Whereas such bills of credit have greatly depreciated in their value, by means whereof debts have been discharged with a much less value than was contracted for, to the great discouragement and prejudice of the trade and commerce of his Majesty's subjects, by occasioning confusion in dealings, and lessening credit in the said colonies or plantations.'[39]

[36] Cited in Hughes, 'English Stam Duties,' p. 259.

[37] J. Greene and R. Jellison, "The Currency Act of 1764 in Imperial-Colonial Relations, 1764–1776," *William and Mary Quarterly*, **18** (1961) 485–518, pp. 486–487.

[38] In 1751, under pressure from these trading interest, Parliament intervened in colonial note issue, passing an act aimed at the New England colonies, restricting the maturity of new issues in Rhode Island, Connecticut, and Massachusetts to two years and prohibiting their designation as legal tender in private transactions. This was followed in 1764 by a second act applying to the remaining colonies and prohibiting legal tender provisions both for private debts and for public obligations. A number of colonies, including New York and Pennsylvania, defied these prohibitions, however, and continued to issue new notes.

[39] Yale law School, *Avalon Project*, Great Britain: The Currency Act; April 19, 1764.

Various expedients adopted by the American colonies to attract or increase the supply of specie likewise failed owing mainly to parliamentary opposition. For example, in 1652, the Massachusetts government began re-minting coins issued by other nations for purposes of producing so-called pine tree shillings, which were minted from anything made of silver (silver bars, dishes, candlesticks, and jewellery), with individuals induced to do so by the profits to be obtained from selling these items to the mint at an above-market price for silver. 'The General Court established a standard of 72 grains of 0.925 fine sterling silver to the shilling, which represented a 22.5 per cent reduction of the English standard of 92.9 grains per shilling. By minting coins of lesser weight, it was hoped they would not be exported out of the Commonwealth. In England, the Boston shilling (as it was called) would be slightly over 22 per cent lighter than the English counterpart and therefore would be valued at about 22 per cent less than the English shilling. Thus, one was more likely to spend the coin in Massachusetts where it would be worth a shilling (12d) rather than to pay a shilling for it in Massachusetts and take it back to England where it would be worth only about 10d.'[40]

Imperial authorities were unsympathetic to colonial issuance of paper money and sought to curb the practice as early as 1720, when Parliament first instructed colonial governors to forbid state legislatures from enacting laws permitting their production without a suspending clause. These prohibitions appear especially harsh given the colonies perennial shortage of specie, exacerbated by various Parliamentary measures meant to encourage the flow of specie from the colonies to Great Britain. Among the more important were direct prohibitions on specie exports from Britain, colonial production of coins made of silver, duties that biased the terms of trade in favour of the home country, prohibitions on competing trade and manufacturing within the colonies, and restrictions on colonial trade with foreign powers. 'Colonial bills were restricted in supply by prohibitions and limitations originating in Britain, as well as by local government prohibitions of private paper issues and local limits on emissions of legal-tender currency. Parliament enacted its prohibitions at the behest of British and colonial creditors who saw in paper money a means to reduce the value of hard-currency debt. Some colonials complained that government

[40] L. Jordan, "Massachusetts Silver, 1652–1682: An Introduction," (accessed at: https://coins.nd.edu/ColCoin/ColCoinContents/Contents01.html).

regulations and government unwillingness to supply sufficient paper bills caused unnecessary monetary scarcity.'[41]

The situation appears to have reached a crisis point when Virginia in 1755 issued paper currency, the last of the colonies to do so, to cover military expenditures incurred in connection with the French and Indian Wars. In subsequent years Virginia issued a further £440,000 in legal tender bills. 'Beginning in 1757 the issuing statutes all provided that the General Court should take depreciation into account when awarding judgments for sterling debts. Nevertheless, British merchants trading to Virginia procured an additional instruction to Lieutenant Governor Francis Fauquier in January 1759 requiring him to induce the Burgesses to amend the statutes so that sterling debts contracted before the acts became law would be payable only in sterling money and so that the bills would be legal tender only if the creditor were willing to accept them. But the Burgesses flatly refused to comply, and during the next three years they provided for four additional issues without the required limitations.'[42]

Against this backdrop Parliament passed the Currency Act, which among other things defined Pounds Sterling to be legal tender in the colonies as in Britain, hence the widespread concern aroused by the requirement that stamp duties could only be paid in hard currency. On the other hand, the terms of the original Act and subsequent modifications to it did not actually outlaw the issuance of paper currency, but rather imposed conditions on its issuance. 'This was not as great a hardship as might have been expected, for, as the experience of Maryland demonstrated, currency did not have to be legal tender to circulate as a medium of exchange. After 1750, the Maryland legislature had been able to build up a reserve fund by buying capital stock with the interest from its land-bank loans. By 1766, it had a reserve of £35,000, of which £26,000 was invested in stock of the Bank of England. When the old money issued by the colony had expired, the legislature was still able to issue new bills, but not as legal tender. Yet, these circulated freely, for the land-bank commissioners were able to draw on the reserve in London when the paper currency was presented for redemption.'[43]

[41] C. Calomiris, "Institutional Failure, Monetary Scarcity, and the Depreciation of the Continental," *Journal of Economic History*, **48** (1988) 47–68, pp. 47–48.

[42] J. Greene and R. Jellison, "The Currency Act of 1764 in Imperial-Colonial Relations, 1764–1776," *William and Mary Quarterly*, **18** (1961) 485–518, pp. 486–487.

[43] J. Sosin, "Imperial Regulation of Colonial Paper Money, 1764–1773," *Pennsylvania Magazine of History and Biography*, **88** (1964) 174–198, p. 188.

The impact of the Seven Years War and subsequent years on colonial monetary developments is shown in Chart 9.1. Owing to the shortage of specie, most colonies issued large amounts of bills of credit with the result that their currencies depreciated against sterling. In Virginia, the exchange rate vis-à-vis sterling depreciated by about one-fifth and even more if measured against the 'official' parity of 125:1. After the enactment of the Currency Act in 1764, most colonial currencies appreciated against sterling; on the eve of the Revolution, the exchange rate for Virginia's currency actually surpassed its notional parity. These trends suggest a degree of monetary stringency, and possible risks to commercial activity implied by the Stamp Act's hard currency requirement. The data indicate the risks

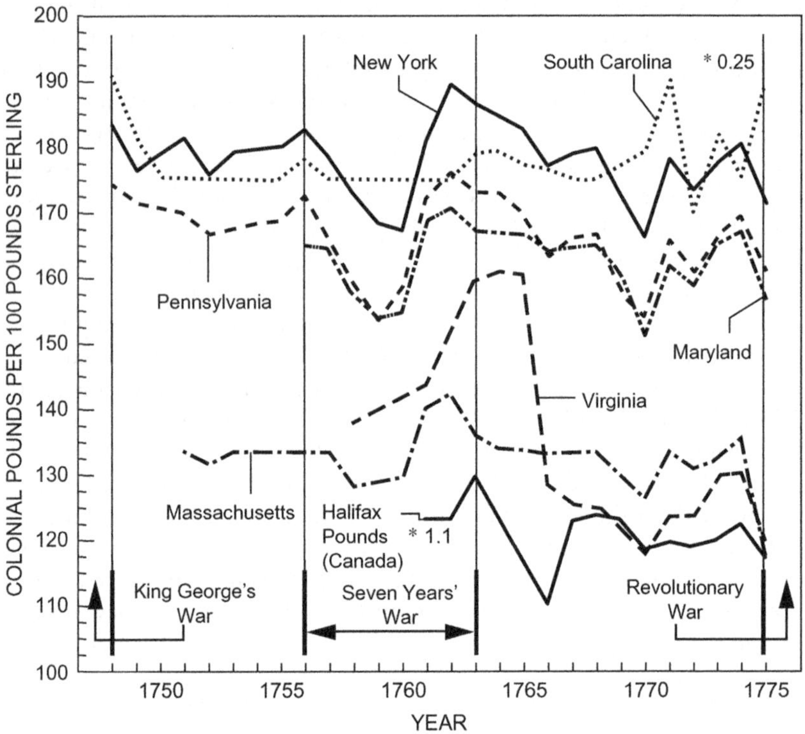

Chart 9.1 Colonial currency exchange rates vis-à-vis sterling. (Source: F. Grubb, "Theory, Evidence, and Belief—The Colonial Money Puzzle Revisited: Reply to Michener and Wright," *Econ Journal Watch*, **3** (2006) 45–72, p, 56, Fig. 1)

were greatest for Virginia, given the magnitude of its currency's appreciation, but none of the other colonial currencies appreciated that sharply; in most instances, exchange rates vis-a-vis sterling (silver) reverted more or less to pre-war levels, a period for which there is little evidence of monetary insufficiency.

There are three interrelated aspects of the debate that have yet to be settled. The first has to do with how much revenue the tax was expected to raise, the second with the scarcity of hard currency, and, closely related, whether the loss of silver and gold would necessarily ruin the colonial economy. As to the first issue, Edmund and Helen Morgan, among others, conceded that the amounts to be paid under the Stamp Act were unlikely to cause any great hardship. To underline the point, the tax was expected to raise £60,000–100,000 annually from about 2 million British colonists in North America and the Caribbean region; at the higher estimate, that would have been equivalent to *c.* about one shilling per person annually, or less than 0.5 per cent of colonial per-capita income.[44]

Others argued the revenues generated by the Act could be even higher, but attended with greater risks. In a letter (dated 10 September 1764) addressed to Thomas Whately, John Temple estimated that were the Act to be put 'on the same footing that it is in England, I suppose it might produce upwards of Forty thousand a year in my District (the Eight Northern Colonies).' But Temple thought the Act would ultimately prove counterproductive as the amount remitted would be offset by an equivalent reduction in American imports. 'But then for a Moment consider Great Britain & her Colonies on the large Scale, and think whether it would be either Expedient or prudent to lay such a Duty here:—For it is an undoubted Fact, *that the Produce of all these Colonies in the Course of Trade goes NOW to Great Britain in return for her Manufactures*, and if they produced three times as much as they do, it would all go for the same purpose; Our People are Extravagantly fond of Shew and Dress, and have no bounds to their Importation of English Manufactures but their want of Money: Suppose then that a Stamp Act should take place, and yield Sixty thousand a year, to be Collected in the Colonies and sent home, there certainly would be Sixty thousand pounds worth of English goods less Imported, besides the Inconvenience of such a Sum of Money laying still

[44] A. Edwards, "Grenville's Silver Hammer: The Problem of Money in the Stamp Act," *Journal of American History*, **104** (2017) 337–362, p. 339.

in Coffers for the Crown, instead of Circulating in the Colonies already very much drained of Cash.'[45]

The shortage of specie is another matter and has generated an ongoing debate that continues more or less unbated. The issue long ago was stated by Curtis Nettles: 'the provinces south of Pennsylvania afforded commodities that England herself did not produce-and in much greater abundance than needed by English consumers. The surplus was re-exported to Europe, where it had the effect either of paying for British imports and thereby stopping the outflow of coin, or of creating a favourable balance of trade that caused the importation of specie. ... the trade between England and her colonies was so balanced that they bought more than they sold; in consequence, they shipped to their British creditors such of the precious metals as they obtained in Spanish America, in the West Indies, and in southern Europe. It was estimated by one observer that coin did not circulate in the colonies more than six months until it was gathered up and remitted to England.'[46] David Hume attributed the scarcity of specie to the introduction of paper currency.[47] More recent research

[45] Stout, "Temple-Whately Papers," p. 132. Temple, a Loyalist, was born in Boston and served as surveyor general of customs for the northern district of America, a commissioner of the Board of Customs for North America, and lieutenant governor of New Hampshire. Contrary to the Act's intent, that the receipts would be used to defray local defence and administrative costs, Temple assumed instead they would be remitted, which explains the pound for pound loss in exports. Otherwise, the result would be a redistribution of expenditure from the household to the government sector.

[46] C. Nettles, "British Policy and Colonial Money Supply," *Economic History Review*, 3, (1931) 219–245, p. 220. According to Nettles, British attitudes towards colonial monetary arrangements were dictated by concerns that the increasing monetisation of the colonial economy would not only lessen their dependence on England, but ultimately become formidable competitors. Nettles focused primarily on trade, ignoring other components of the balance of payments. G. Walton and H. Rockoff, *History of the American Economy*. Thirteenth Edition (Cengage, 2018), pp. 68–70, provides estimates of the overall colonial balance and reach the conclusion that invisibles, mercantile credits, and military and administrative outlays by the British government offset the visible deficit.

[47] D, Hume, "Of the Balance of Payments," *Hume: Political Essays*, K. Haakonssen (Ed.) (Cambridge University Press, 1994), p. 143. Several economists have pointed out the flaw in Hume's argument, arguing that the composition of the money supply as between specie and notes is irrelevant. 'While specie can be driven out by currency substitution, money per se is not made scarce by this mechanism. Being held in a fixed exchange rate with specie, paper money is a perfect substitute for specie. Domestic transactions do not resort to barter, and so chronic specie scarcity does not impact the real economy. *As such, the colonists were misguided and their complaints of chronic specie scarcity should not be taken seriously. Either chronic specie scarcity did not exist or it did not matter*' (emphasis added). F. Grubb, "Chronic Specie

is divided on the issue, with several economists claiming the amount specie relative to the total money supply was small,[48] while others argue the opposite.[49] Scholars acknowledge that the failure to reach any consensus is complicated by the lack of reliable data on the magnitude and composition of the colonial money supply.[50]

McColloh wasn't the only observer who considered the silver provision was unwise, would ruin local commerce, and, accordingly, would be widely opposed throughout the colonies. Massachusetts' former agent in London claimed the demand for payment in silver was the 'most extraordinary' aspect of the Stamp Act; John Adams likewise wrote that 'we have Reason to think that the Execution of that Act for a short Space of time, considering the present Scarcity of Money, would dreign (*sic*) the Country of its Cash'; and the governor of North Carolina, William Tryon acknowledged 'the parliamentary Right of Taxation' but also 'took Notice of the Impossibility of the Stamp-Act operating in all its Parts in this Province, where the whole Cash of the Country would scarcely pay a single Year of the Tax.'[51]

Nor was this perspective unique to America; even senior members of the British government, including George Grenville, knew that demanding 'Sterling Money,' as one 1763 British Treasury document urged, could make paying taxes and fees a 'Matter of real Terror & Punishment' for American colonists.[52] The implication that contracting the colonial money supply would necessarily undermine trade to the detriment of British exporters may not have been lost on the government, but neither does it figure prominently in Parliamentary debates. Both of these points, however, were stated explicitly in the Stamp Act Congress resolves. Article IX specifically states: That the duties imposed by several late Acts of

Scarcity and Efficient Barter: The Problem of Maintaining an Outside Money Supply in British Colonial America," NBER Working Paper 18,099, May 2012; Revised 2018), p. 3.

[48] B. Smith, "The Relationship Between Money and Prices: Some Historical Evidence Reconsidered," *Quarterly Review*, **12** (1988): 18–32.

[49] R. Michener, "Backing Theories and the Currencies of Eighteenth-Century America: A Comment." *Journal of Economic History*," **48** (1988): 682–692.

[50] E. Wicker, "Colonial Monetary Standards Contrasted: Evidence from the Seven Years' War," *Journal of Economic History*, **45** (1985), 869–884, p. 871; B. McCallum, "Money and Prices in Colonial America: A New Test of Competing Theories," *Journal of Political Economy*, *100* (1992), 143–161, p. 144.

[51] Cited in A. Edwards, "Grenville's Silver Hammer: The Problem of Money in the Stamp Act Crisis," *Journal of American History*, **104** (2017) 337–362, pp. 341–343.

[52] Ibid., p. 343.

Parliament, from the peculiar circumstances of these colonies, will be extremely burthensome and grievous; and *from the scarcity of specie, the payment of them absolutely impracticable*. Article XI claims: 'That the restrictions imposed by several late Acts of Parliament, on the trade of these colonies, will render them *unable to purchase the manufactures of Great-Britain*.'[53]

The bulk of transactions carried in the colonial period depended largely upon paper money ('bills of credit') and book (mercantile) credit owing to the local shortage of precious metals.[54] Thomas Paine (*The Crisis*, IX) famously declared that 'there are two distinct things which make the payment of taxes difficult; the one is the large and real value of the sum to be paid, and the other is the scarcity of the thing in which the payment is to be made.' Americans, in their own estimation, had the latter problem in 1765.[55] Paine's observation made sense mainly within the context of the Currency Act of 1764 that affected all colonies, with the exception of 'Maryland, where the legislature had worked out in 1766 an acceptable scheme to issue a non-legal tender currency secured by specie invested in the Bank of England, and New York, where the legislature had established a land bank after it had obtained a special favour from Parliament in 1770, achieved more permanent solutions and surmounted the problems presented by the Currency Act.'[56] Unlike the Stamp Act, Parliament refused to repeal immediately the Currency Act; it was subsequently amended in 1773 to resume the issuance of paper currencies.

[53] *Resolutions of the Continental Congress October 19, 1765*. The Avalon Project. (Lillian Goldman Law Library. Yale law School), emphasis added.

[54] 'Colonial coinage is interesting numismatically, but economically it was too slight to be of consequence. Most circulating specie was minted abroad. The gold and silver coins circulating in the colonies were generally of Spanish or Portuguese origin.' R. Michener, Money in the American Economy, EH.net (https://eh.net/encyclopedia/money-in-the-american-colonies/).

[55] T. Paine, "The Crisis, IX." *The Writings of Thomas Paine*, Vol. 1 Collected and Edited by M. Conway, 1774–1779 (New York: G. P. Putnam's Sons, 1894).

[56] J. Greene and R. Jellison, "The Currency Act of 1764 in Imperial-Colonial Relations, 1764–1776," *William and Mary Quarterly*, **18** (1961), 485–518, p. 517.

CHAPTER 10

The Townshend Duties

The Townshend Duties were the last major revenue act passed by Parliament before the American colonies declared their independence from Great Britain.[1] Parliament no doubt had learnt to its cost that the Stamp Act was the wrong way to go about taxing the colonies. Even so, any new tax package would have to reflect certain broad principles if it were to prove acceptable. The first issue to be addressed was the question of parliamentary supremacy. Following the repeal of the Stamp Act, this issue was dealt with via the Declaratory Act (1766), designed to better secure 'the dependency of his majesty's dominions in America upon the crown and parliament of Great Britain.'[2] The second issue was what type of tax was likely to be acceptable to the Americans. This issue was of sufficient concern that the government sought the advice of colonial officials on the best way forward. Thomas Whately, Townshend's Treasury secretary, writing to John Temple, Surveyor General of Customs, Boston, in August 1764 admitted as much. 'It will be a principal object of attention here to make this Tax as little burthensome as possible, but for this

[1] While these and other acts were meant to generate revenues, other measures adopted by Parliament involved what amount to taxes in kind, such as the Quartering Act of 1764 that required colonists to British military units with housing, provisions, and transportation. In many respects these 'taxes' may have been more objectional than those paid in cash. The two together, however, provided compelling reasons for Americans to reconsider their loyalty to the British Crown.

[2] Avalon Project: Great Britain: Parliament—The Declaratory Act; March 18, 1766.

G. Pollio, *The Rise and Fall of Britain's North American Empire*,
https://doi.org/10.1007/978-3-031-07484-4_10

purpose it will be necessary to know whether ye same Duties as are imposed in England on Obligations, Instruments of Conveyance & Indentures of Apprenticeship would be too heavy on the Colonies? Which of ye English Duties will be burthensome? which should be omitted? & which lightened & why?'[3] In any event, drawing on the distinction between internal and external taxes, Townshend seems to have believed Americans were not averse to being taxed, so long as it was not an excise tax.

Townshend's cousin, a member of the Treasury Board, provides a concise description of Parliament's state of mind as it enacted the new measures.

> It was not the opinion of one man, but of numbers. It was absolutely necessary to do something. It was the opinion of (Charles Townshend). He exerted all that ability which made him the delight of this House and all who knew him. He desired taxes agreeable to the American themselves. He flattered himself too far. In those hopes he was misled by the Americans themselves, who told him take the tax, let it but bear the appearance of port duties, it will not be objected to. A Chancellor of the Exchequer at that time who had not attempted something of that kind would have been looked upon as blameable.[4]

These measures were not, as noted, enacted solely for the purpose of regulating trade between England and her colonies. Rather, they were explicitly designed as revenue-raising measures to ensure that the colonists made a financial contribution, inter alia, towards covering the salaries of royal governors and other executive and judicial officials in the colonies so that 'these men would become more dependent on the crown than on the legislative assemblies in the colonies that had previously paid their salaries. Pitt may have ignored the political purposes of these customs duties, but the American colonists did not.'[5] Chaffin's[6] assessment that the Townshend

[3] "Letter from Thomas Whately, Esq. to John Temple, 14 August 1764," Massachusetts Historical Society.

[4] Cited in N. Koehn, *The Power of Commerce: Economy and Governance in the First British Empire* (Ithaca, NY and London: Cornell University Press, 1994), pp. 139–140.

[5] H. Dickinson, "The Failure of Conciliation: Britain and the American Colonies 1763–1783," *Kyoto Economic Review*, 79 (2010) 2–20, p. 4.

[6] R. Chaffin, "The Townshend Acts of 1767," *William and Mary Quarterly*, 27 (1970) 90–121, pp. 120–121. The necessity for, and disposition of, the revenues raised were clearly stated in the Act's preamble: 'a revenue should be raised in your Majesty's dominions in America, for making a more certain and adequate provision for defraying the charge of the

Acts were 'moderate' and 'in the main mild compared to other plans offered' is seconded by Dickson,[7] who adds that the Act's main objectionable feature was that it reiterated the principle of parliamentary superiority in all matters relating to England's colonies.

It was not the rates that were objectionable per se. Even if they were in fact moderate, the more relevant issue was the greater efficiency with which the new duties were collected. As noted, the Townshend Acts were in fact structured in ways designed to maximise tax efficiency by, among other things, authorising the use of writs of assistance (general warrants), creating a board of customs commissioners whose compensation was beyond local control, the transfer of authority to Admiralty Courts of functions formerly were discharged by colonial courts subject to the oversight of provincial legislatures. As their legal establishment derives from Roman rather than Common Law, Admiralty Courts could dispense with juries drawn from the local population. Taken together, these measures succeeded in raising customs revenues from an annual rate of £2000 to £30,000, while total administrative costs rose by only 40 per cent, converting an annual net revenue loss of £7000 to net gain of £17,000.[8]

One way to measure American reaction to the enactment of the various acts passed by Parliament is to observe the frequency with which certain words appear in American publications from before passage of the Stamp Act to the Declaration of Independence. The words chosen for analysis are 'Taxation,' 'Representation,' and 'Tyranny,' words that recur frequently throughout the period studied. While it is true that the sample of texts analysed is small, the results broadly conform with the thrust of traditional American historiography. Charts 10.1a and b present the lexical data on an annual and smoothed basis, the former on the annual count and the latter on a three-year moving average. The first panel highlights the immediacy with which American colonists responded to the announcement of each

administration of justice, and the support of civil government, in such provinces where it shall be found necessary; and towards further defraying the expenses of defending, protecting, and securing, the said dominions.' Avalon Project, Great Britain: Parliament—The Townshend Act, November 20, 1767.

[7] 'These duties were clearly not burdensome and were not constitutional innovations like the Stamp Act. ... they were resented primarily because they served the political purposes of Britain and supported the British claim that Parliament was the sovereign authority across the British empire.' Dickson, 'Conciliation,' p. 16,

[8] D. Van Rijsbergen, "Townshend Acts" (accessed at: http://www.let.rug.nl/usa/essays/before-1800/townshend-duties-dylan-van-rijsbergen.php).

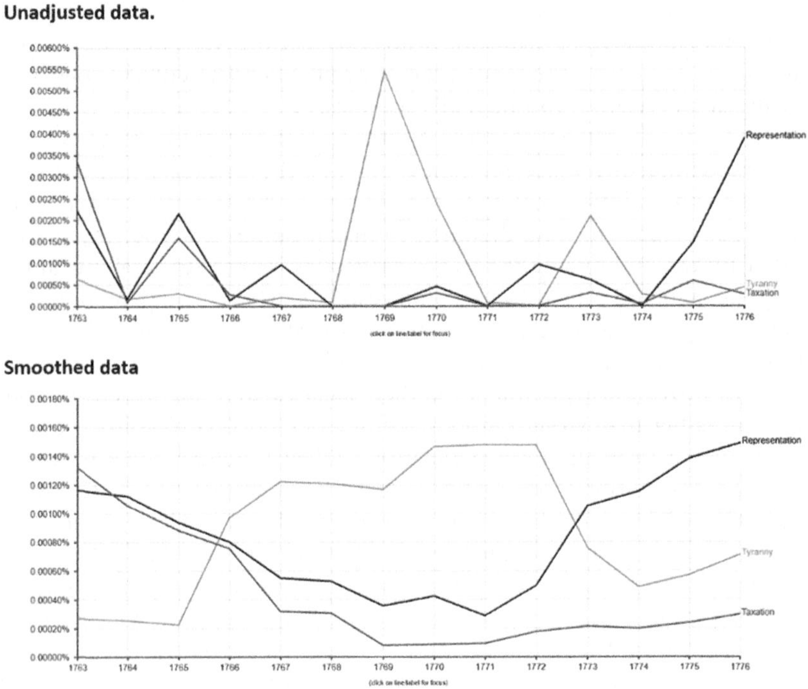

Chart 10.1 Lexical analysis, 1763–1776 ('Taxation,' 'Representation,' 'Tyranny': American English) (**a**) Unadjusted data. (**b**) Smoothed data. (Source: Google Ngram)

new Parliamentary measure, while the second panel identifies underlying trends in colonial reactions. Popular reaction to both the Stamp Act and the Townshend Acts reflected a greater concern with issues related to Representation than either Taxation or Tyranny; in fact, taxation appears to have been of virtually no importance in writings concerning the latter measures. The spike in the use of 'Tyranny' that occurred in 1769 is connected with a number of concurrent political developments such as the Virginia Resolves, dissolution of the House of Burgesses, and the adoption by a number of colonial legislatures or merchant and traders encouraging the boycott of British imports. The use of the noun reappeared in 1773, but thereafter 'Representation' dominates written usage.[9] The

[9] Parliament's intent was clearly demonstrated by the fact that on the same day it repealed the Stamp Act, the government passed the Declaratory Act, which stated the British govern-

smoothed data identify two further important lexical characteristics. Between 1763 and 1769/1770, after the Stamp Act peak, there is a steady decline in concerns over taxation, interrupted only briefly by the enactment of the Townshend duties. From 1765 to 1772, 'Tyranny' tends to dominate public writings, but begins a steep decline thereafter, the mirror image of which is an increase in the frequency and relative importance of 'Representation.'

The 'moderate' nature of the Townshend legislation belies its complexity. The taxed articles included paints, glass, red and white lead, and painters' colours as well as sixty-three grades of paper and paper products (e.g., wallpaper). With regard to the latter, the Act also distinguished between paper manufactured in England and the Continent, the duties applying to the latter being two to three times higher than those applying to English paper. Domestic paper, by contrast, was not taxed, notwithstanding the risk the higher duties might stimulate domestic paper production and thus circumvent one of the key provisions of the Acts. However, 'because equipment, rags, and skilled workmen were scarce in the colonies. At best, domestic manufacture could meet local needs for the paper used for newspapers and some job work. But in quality, quantity, and price the domestic "white paper" used for writing paper and in book printing could not compete with its imported counterpart.'[10] This is to be contrasted with the duty imposed by the Stamp Act, which applied to the *uses* of domestic and imported paper. On the other hand, the Act reduced duties applying to

ment had the full power and authority to make laws governing the colonies 'in all cases whatsoever,' including taxation. The colonists clearly did not want the taxes imposed them by Parliament. 'To escape them, they implored Parliament to recant with arguments both economic (that such taxes and duties would retard commerce) and constitutional (that the enactment and manner of enforcement of these acts were illegal). Parliament, as is well known, was impressed by the economic argument: it repealed the Stamp Act, but expressly rejected the constitutional claims. Soon thereafter it imposed the Townshend duties. Subsequent American protest emphasized constitutional claims. ... On both sides of the Atlantic, it seems that rhetoric was employed to move popular sentiment, loyalty, and acquiescence, rather than to state ultimate and unanimously held ends. Yet, the opportuneness of pronouncements does not imply that the statements made were insincere then, or that the statements did not reflect the later sentiment of the masses, and perhaps even the sentiment of the leaders. ... But the fact that reactions on both sides of the Atlantic moved with trade suggests that constitutional arguments had economic motivations throughout.' Reid, 'Economic Burden,' pp. 91–92.

[10] R. Harland, "David Hall and the Townshend Acts," *Papers of the Bibliographical Society of America*, 68 (1974), pp. 19–38, pp. 225–26.

tea, partly as a way of discouraging smuggling. It would thus appear that it was not the duties per se that enraged colonists, but rather the Act's ancillary measures, above all, the very real prospect of future tax increases as a way of achieving the British government's colonial policy objectives.

American merchants, in New York and in other American colonies, initially welcomed Townshend's ascendency owing largely to his part in repealing the Stamp Act. Behind such support was the conviction the British government would be sympathetic to the types of reforms merchants in New York and elsewhere favoured. Among the more important of these were rejection of the creation of a freeport in the West Indies, which in no way would have been of benefit to them; greater protection from foreign competition; and the modification of certain features of the Navigation Acts.

In the traditional historiography, once Parliament demonstrated its unwillingness to adopt the sorts of policies favoured by American merchants, nor reconsider the principle of its supremacy in all matters pertaining to England's colonies, the business sector's response was rapid and predictable: merchants and traders in Boston followed by those in New York and, somewhat later, Philadelphia adopted nonimportation agreements.[11] The hostility of some sectors was clearly motivated by the fact that the new duties would have raised input costs. It is unsurprising, therefore, that publishers, printers, bookseller, and stationers, for example, opposed the Townshend duties as they would have been among the most affected by its enactment.[12]

Harlan provides an estimate of the impact the tax would have had on the publisher of the *Pennsylvania Gazette*, founded by Benjamin Franklin, which range from a minimum of £21 16 s 10½ d to a maximum of £39, with a mean of £30 8 s 5¼ d. On Hall's order paper amounting to about

[11] See, for example, L. Gipson, *The Coming of the Revolution, 1763–1775* (New York: Harper and Brothers, 1954) pp. 187–188.

[12] Years ago Andrews argued that 'which aroused apprehension in the colonies and created unrest was, in the beginning at least, the effect of the laws on the cost of living.' C. Andrews, *The Colonial Background of the American Revolution* (New Haven: Yale University Press, 1961), p. 135. Elsewhere, Andrews extends the argument noting that 'Northern merchants agreed to non-importation when local business conditions made such an end to competition most desirous; merchants abandoned non-importation when their own inventories were well depleted, and efforts to coordinate the start or end of non-importation agreements among the merchants of different ports with appeals to loyalty and such intangibles as "the Rights of Man" floundered.' "The Boston Merchants and the Non-Importation Movement," *Transactions of the Colonial Society of Massachusetts*, **19** (1916–17), 159–259.

£350, the approximate duties would add to this figure 'at the rate of from 6.3 to 11.2 per cent, with a mean of 8.75 per cent.'[13] Notwithstanding the implied increase in printing costs the *Pennsylvania Gazette*, the paper initially provided a list of the new duties but without commenting upon them. Harlan explains the publisher David Hall's, and other American publishers', reticence as reflecting the hope that Parliament 'would realise its mistake before another crisis developed—that it would have learned something from the Stamp Act fiasco.' But another consideration may lie behind his initial restraint, namely, that notwithstanding his preference for printing the *Gazette* on imported English stock, he managed to substitute domestically produced paper, thus averting any rise in printing costs. Hall, however, ended his silence once the legislation was enacted. Apart from the expected indignation, and partly as a result of the paper's own experience, the *Gazette* began to trumpet the virtues of local manufacturing.

Like most other newspaper publishers, Hall was unwilling to let a crisis to go waste. But these were not the only opponents of British 'tyranny,' with lawyers joining the ranks of newspaper publishers. 'Lawyers had long taken the lead in public affairs; the art of special pleading, refined in the courtroom, proved equally successful in the political arena. They nearly always dominated the legislatures … had drunk deep of English constitutional theory as well as of the natural rights philosophy. "Nothing is too wicked of them to attempt which serves their purposes—the press is to them what the pulpit was in times of Popery," asserted New York's Lieutenant Governor Cadwallader Colden. The Stamp Act, levying taxes on important legal documents and imposing a £10 fee for admission to the Bar (much higher than in England), aroused their initial ire against Britain. … Each successive crisis repeated the story. Advocates of the calibre of (John) Adams, John Dickinson, James Iredell and Thomas Jefferson analysed the issues with legal and philosophical acumen, and their prestige in the community further aided the cause. It is not surprising the profession furnished over half the members of the first Continental Congress and as well as a like proportion of the signers of the Declaration of Independence.'[14]

[13] R. Harlan, "David Hall and the Townshend Acts," *Papers of the Bibliographical Society of America*, **68** (1974), 19–38, pp. 27–28.

[14] Cited in A. Schlesinger, *Prelude to Independence: The Newspaper War on Britain, 1764–1776* (New York: Alfred A. Knopf, 1958), pp. 10–11. Schlesinger identifies clergymen as equally articulate spokesmen for independence, but like the two other professions, they too had their own agenda. As Schofield points out: 'Many historians have commented on this

Hall's initial hesitation was repeated elsewhere in the American colonies notwithstanding the risks faced by those who opted not to do so. An excellent example of both effects is provided by a Boston broadside published by merchants and traders in January 1770,[15] the gist of which is that after local merchants agreed to submit their businesses to public scrutiny, four of their members opted out of the arrangement. Those supporting the practice put the matter to a second vote in which it was agreed that: 'in refusing and delaying to comply with so reasonable and just a Demand, have abused the Lenity and Patience of their Fellow Citizens ... We do (therefore) fervently wish all who with us are exercising themselves to maintain and secure the invaluable Rights of our country, may refuse to sell to, buy of, or have any Intercourse (with the named offenders), not only during the present Struggle for Liberty, but *for ever* thereafter.' Other more stringent forms of intimidation were applied against recalcitrant.

Act in terms of British acceptance of French Catholicism. The real effect for the Colonies was, however, noticed by Thomas Paine. "Should affairs be patched up with Britain, and she to remain the governing and sovereign power of America ... we shall deprive ourselves of the very means of sinking the debt we have, or may contract. The value of the backlands which some of the provinces are clandestinely deprived of, by the unjust extension of the limits of Canada, valued only at five pounds sterling per hundred acres, amount to upwards of twenty-five millions, Pennsylvania currency; and the quit-rents ... to two millions yearly." Marc Egnal has also argued that "the revolutionary movement was led by an upper-class faction whose passionate commitment to the rise of the New World was evident well before 1763. The changes in property rights implied by the Quebec Act means expectations of many of the colonial elite (including Washington) of wealth from land speculation were dashed."' N. Schofield, "Evolution of the Constitution," *British Journal of Political Science*, **32**, (2002) 1–20, pp. 10–11.

[15] The broadside is reproduced in Breen, 'Marketplace of the Revolution,' p. 258.

CHAPTER 11

Nonimportation

Reactions to the Townshend Acts were stronger than those that followed enactment of the Stamp Act, suggesting the former were more broadly supported than the latter. In the traditional view, by pauperising Americans, Parliament made it impossible to maintain normal commercial or financial relations with Great Britain. The crisis, in other words, was the direct result of obnoxious trade and tax policies enacted by Parliament to discipline the recalcitrant American colonies regardless of the dire consequences for Great Britain that would follow from their implementation. Consider in this connection the Boston Non-importation Agreement of August 1768, where again scarcity of hard currency and the reasons for the shortage are reiterated.

> The merchants and traders in the town of Boston, having taken into consideration the deplorable situation of the trade and the many difficulties it at present labours under on account of the scarcity of money, which is daily decreasing for want of the other remittances to discharge our debts in Great Britain, and the large sums collected by the officers of the customs for duties on goods imported; the heavy taxes levied to discharge the debts contracted by the government in the late war; the embarrassments and restrictions laid on the trade by the several late Acts of Parliament; together with the bad success of our cod fishery this season, and the discouraging prospect of the whale fishery, by which our principal sources of remittances are like to be

G. Pollio, *The Rise and Fall of Britain's North American Empire*,
https://doi.org/10.1007/978-3-031-07484-4_11

> greatly diminished, and we thereby rendered unable to pay the debts we owe the merchants in Great Britain, and to continue the importation of goods from thence.[1]

Whether liquidity pressures were as acute is questionable for the reasons given above. But the fact is the 1764 Currency Act did lead to the appreciation of most colonial currencies against sterling, as British money lenders had hoped, being keen to protect the real value of their loans. Boycotts and nonimportation agreements, although second best, provided Americans with the means 'of giving coercive effect, comparable to that of law' in dealing with parliamentary intransigence.[2] The logic of collective action suggests that large groups with heterogenous interests would be less successful creating collective goods than would smaller, more cohesive groups with narrowly defined objectives. These considerations indicate that the efficacy of nonimportation agreements had less to do with the shared political values of consumers than with their manipulation by highly motivated cliques, who achieved their desiderata by being able to mobilise mass support to coerce opponents into supporting their agenda. They may have been popularly led, but the driving force behind nonimportation were economic and political interests, often one and the same, abetted by others, who while not necessarily supportive of the elites' private agenda were willing nevertheless to back their public aspirations. These would include publishers of newspapers, whose commercial interests supported their liberal orientation, and mainly non-conformist clergymen who were convinced enactment of Quebec Act of 1774, which, inter alia, formally recognised the Catholic Church, would eventually lead to the establishment of an Anglican episcopate in the American colonies.

There are, of course, alternative explanations that correspond more closely with normative American social values, what Breen has described as 'public awareness of private actions.'[3] On the face of it, the Boston nonimportation agreement noted above provides a compelling example of the normative model of social behaviour. According to the Agreement's

[1] *Avalon Project*, Boston Non-Importation Agreement, August 1, 1768.

[2] A. Peck, "Revisiting the Original 'Tea Party': The Historical Roots of Regulating Food Consumption in America," *UMKC Law Review*, **80** (2011) 1–43, p. 5.

[3] 'Private enjoyments (has) a social price. Each purchase—no matter how justified in terms of the finances of a given household—spoke not simply of self-fulfilment but also of responsibilities to communities of local purchasers who happened to be experiencing straitened times.' Breen, 'Marketplace of Revolution,' p. 206.

preamble, the actions to be taken were motivated by the impoverishment of Americans by the various revenue measures enacted by Parliament that necessitates the forbearance being demanded by the Agreement.

> *We, the subscribers, in order to relieve the trade under those discouragements, to promote industry, frugality, and economy, and to discourage luxury and every kind of extravagance, do promise and engage to and with each other as follows:*
>
> *That we will not send or import from Great Britain this fall, either on our own account, or on commission, any other goods than what are already ordered for the fall supply.*
>
> *That we will not send for or import any kind of goods or merchandise from Great Britain, either on our own account, or on commissions, or any otherwise, from January 1, 1769, to January 1, 1770, except salt, coals, fish-hooks and lines, hemp, duck, bar lead and shot, wool-cards, and card-wire.*
>
> *That we will not purchase of any factors, or others, any kind of goods imported from Great Britain from January 1, 1769, to January 1, 1770. That we will not import on our own account, or on commission, or Purchase from any Who shall import from any other colony in America, from January 1, 1769, to January 1, 1770, any tea, glass, paper, or other goods commonly imported from Great Britain.*
>
> *That we will not, from and after January 1, 1769, import into the province any tea, paper, glass, or painters' colours, until the Acts imposing duties on these articles have been repealed.*

The major difficulty with the public awareness of private actions hypothesis is that, if correct, voluntarism would have ensured compliance; economic pressures alone would have produced the desired result. That the truth is otherwise was recognised a long time ago. 'It is perfectly evident that behind these mob captains there was some guiding force. Though all the facts concerning the power behind the crowd leaders in each city are not available, we know enough to outline the general situation. All the evidence points to the general conclusion that behind every mob leader there was a small group of men, keeping their identity secret, who had gotten together before the actual outbreak against the stamp distributors, made their plans for this step, and thereafter charted the course of popular opposition.'[4] This was even more true of the reaction to the Townshend duties than to the Stamp Act.

[4] P. Davidson, "Sons of Liberty and Stamp Men," *North Carolina Historical Review*, 9 (1932) 38–56, p. 39, See also E. and M. Morgan, 'Stamp Act Crisis, Chapter 11.

The economic impact of nonimportation varied considerably across time and space. The simplest, but not necessarily the most accurate, measure of the impact of such agreements would be the behaviour of British imports following their implementation. On this basis, American imports from Britain fell 14 per cent and 7 per cent in 1765 and 1766, respectively. This pattern has been explained as reflecting the fact that while colonial merchants seized the opportunity to reduce large inventories that had been built up during the recession that followed the initial boom at the end of the French and Indian War. The falloff in North American orders occurred at a time when Britain likewise was experiencing an economic downturn. British merchants responded to the twin economic burdens by flooding Parliament with petitions describing the additional financial hardship and loss of employment arising from the cancellation of American orders for their goods; such intense lobbying appears to have been the catalyst leading to repeal.

Subsequent nonimportation agreements were implemented more slowly while local opinion was divided as between merchants whose support for the movement was lukewarm at best and local artisans and craftsmen who enthusiastically embraced the proposed boycotts. The ambivalence of the former derived from the fact their livelihoods depended on being able to import English goods, while the fervour of the latter reflected the fact the goods they produced often competed with those made in Britain and thus boycotting English manufactures would encourage local production.

It is possible the Townshend Act may have encouraged the development of colonial manufacturing industry, notwithstanding the specific goods taxed were selected precisely because they were thought to offer minimal scope for domestic substitution. 'By creating a protective tariff by taxing imported glass, paints and paper products,' and reinforced by nonimportation, Parliament unintentionally promoted the expansion of local industry.[5] This may have been true in certain instances; it was noted above, for example, that the publisher of the *Philadelphia Gazette* somehow managed to replace imported stock with locally manufactured newsprint, even though it was widely assumed that such substitution was infeasible. There may have been other similar instances, but in the absence of evidence as to how widespread the practice was, the claim amounts to little more than

[5] L. Peskin, *Manufacturing Revolution: The Intellectual Origins of Early American Industry* (Baltimore, MD: Johns Hopkins University Press, 2004), p. 42.

speculation. For one thing, there is no indication where the capital needed to develop these new industries would come from, and for another, the contention presupposes investors assumed the duties were likely to be permanent. Merchants in the main, but with exception, showed little inclination, then or subsequently, to invest their funds in industrial ventures, while the purpose of nonimportation was to get Parliament to repeal the Townshend duties, the prospects for which must have seemed favourable against the backdrop of the success of past boycotts.

Chart 11.1 illustrates the behaviour of colonial exports and imports during the nonimportation period. The decline in British imports associated with the reaction to the Stamp Act was modest in comparison with what followed the Townshend duties. Far more interesting is the weak rebound following repeal. This can be explained by the fact the Stamp Act was enacted at a time when colonial demand was already depressed suggesting that the contribution of nonimportation was correspondingly

Chart 11.1 Colonial trade with Great Britain, 1760–1770 (pounds sterling). (Source: *Historical Statistics of the United States*, "Colonial and Pre-Federal Statistics," Series Z 213–226, p. 1176)

moderate; the anaemic post-repeal recovery indicates that colonial demand remained weak. However, business conditions towards the end of the decade appear to have improved. The reduced frequency with which merchants referred to poor trading conditions points in that direction. So, too, does data on Philadelphia merchants' margins: between 1763 and 1765, retail mark-ups amounted to 13 per cent compared with an average 35 per cent over the balance of the decade.[6] Even so, Jensen notes that throughout this period business failures continued, culminating in the failure in 1767 of Baynton, Wharton, and Morgan, 'general merchants, Indian traders, and land speculators,' the largest failure in the colonial history of Pennsylvania.[7] Of course, we should not automatically extrapolate developments in Pennsylvania to the rest of the American colonies, but there are reasons to believe the colony-wide inventory correction had not fully run its course. By the end of the decade, the colonial economy appears to have improved, which would account for the steep rise in British imports. While the Townshend Act provoked a larger negative response, colonial demand for British exports post-repeal soared. It is reasonable to suppose the stronger rebound reflected the larger depressing impact nonimportation had on the economy, but the magnitude of the increase must have reflected the expectation of continued strong demand growth.

Who benefitted the most from nonimportation policies? Among the strongest supporters of coercive economic measures were, first, those directly affected by the Townshend taxes, second, those who opposed them on principle, and, finally, those that had been adversely affected not by current but rather by the provisions of the prior Trade and Navigation Acts. Thus, each group albeit for different reasons found common ground for participating in consumer boycotts and nonimportation agreements. The overarching objective was to eliminate any measures that favoured British over American interests, that is, to demonstrate to Parliament the folly of such measures because ultimately they were inimical to British commercial and financial interests; for others, local merchants, in particular, support was motivated by self-interest, and many correctly concluded that public outrage used to cover their narrower agenda.

[6] M. Egnal and J. Ernst, "An Economic Interpretation of the American Revolution," *William and Mary Quarterly*, **29** (1972) 3–32, p. 14.

[7] A. Jensen, *The Maritime History of Colonial Philadelphia*, (Madison, WI: State Historical Society of Wisconsin, 1963), p. 122.

To understand the latter's interests, we have to return to some of the key features of the Trade and Navigation Acts and the structural changes they encouraged. True, these Acts shielded American merchants from direct foreign competition, but at the cost of intensified competition vis-à-vis their British counterparts, notwithstanding that vigorous competition from British merchants actually enhanced consumer welfare in the colonies. From around the mid-eighteenth century, English and Scottish merchants had seized control of British manufactured goods imports into the colonies by exploiting the opportunities created by the Trade and Navigation Acts. These merchants arrived in the colonies with a large consignment of goods which were sold in one of two ways: either by bypassing American intermediaries and selling their goods on generous credit terms directly to American shopkeepers or by disposing of them via auction sales, often with very low mark-ups. To underline the extent of the threat, Scottish merchants in the Chesapeake region in due course established stores in the backcountry displacing local merchants by selling British goods directly to farmers. Thus, matters of principle and self-interest coalesced to help repeal the Townshend duties.

The first nonimportation agreement was adopted in Boston; the agreement, however, was limited to one year, and there was no indication it would automatically have been extended if Parliament refused to rescind the measure. It was either assumed the intended result would be achieved within one year or, more likely, the time limit represented a compromise designed to keep local merchants on side. In March 1770, all Townshend duties, with the exception of those applying to tea, were cancelled. Fortunately, we have eyewitness accounts of merchants grappling with whether they should support, oppose, or adopt a neutral position with regard to nonimportation. The correspondence between Henry Drinker, a Philadelphia merchant, and his partner Abel James, who was in London at the time, provides a clear picture of the state of mind of individual merchants.[8] Drinker's correspondence begins in 1769, when the Townshend Act was still in effect, but its demise appeared imminent.

[8] Henry Drinker, "Effects of the "Non-Importation Agreement" in Philadelphia, 1769–1770, *Pennsylvania Magazine of History and Biography*, 14 (1890) 41–45. Drinker was one of the exceptions in that he had investments in both an ironworks and sawmill, the former one of the industries in which Quakers were actively involved in. 'A scrutiny of the iron trade during the eighteenth century soon reveals that the Quakers were a very prominent element in the structure of the industry, and were contributing heavily, not only by the provision of capital, but by technical improvements, to the trade's advancement.' A. Raistrick,

In a letter dated 12 February 1770, Drinker was not convinced that there would be widespread compliance with nonimportation, and in consequence withdrew from the committee created to oversee compliance. 'The accounts from England after the Parliament has proceeded to business will be expected here with great earnestness by many; their disposition as to the Colonies is indeed of great importance at this critical juncture. Should they determine to pass by us unnoticed, or what amounts to the same thing, grant us no relief in the burthens we complain of, then shall we see how far our publick spirit and patriotism will hold out. I rather apprehend it is but skin deep with a great many and principally with the fierce and violent, as they appeared to be at first setting out. Already do we see those making breaches in the Agreement who were the first in promoting it. I expect ere long to write thee of some important changes in our measures here, not that I by any means wish or shall promote them, but so I believe it will be. I mentioned to thee sometime past that I had withdrawn myself from the Committee, which step upon due deliberation I am not dissatisfied with.'

In a long letter written two months later (29 April 1770), Drinker acknowledged the cruel dilemma he faced. On the one hand, he expressed sympathy for those who were no longer willing or able to comply with the agreement. On the other, he was reluctant to abandon 'a measure we had deliberately gone into for the securing and supporting our Liberties and valuable Rights, drawing on ourselves at once the contempt and indignation of the other Colonies, not to say the exultation and derision of the Mother Country.' The anguish caused by the thought of deserting the cause was compounded by an awareness that the merchants at that time might have been on the verge of having succeeded in convincing Parliament to repeal the Act: 'and this at a time when we were hourly expecting such accounts from England as would either save our Credit or lastingly determine what we ought to depend on from Parliament.'

Having gotten much of what they wanted, Drinker reported in May 1770 the local merchants continued to bemoan retention of the tax on tea, and, notwithstanding the appalling behaviour of Rhode Island, those in Philadelphia and New York were determined to carry on with the agreement until the last vestige of the Act was cancelled. 'Since my last respecting the state of our Non-importation Agreement, the face of things has

Quakers in Science and Industry: Being an Account of the Quaker Contributions to Science and Industry during the 17th and 18th Centuries, York: Sessions Book Trust, 1993, p. 89.

altered much, notwithstanding the little dirty Colony of Rhode Island has shamefully broken faith with the others, and has imported a ship load of goods as usual, put their Committee to defiance, and are proceeding in the Sales without regard to their suffering neighbors; yet this flagrant violation and breach of their plighted honour has not staggered the merchants of New York or this place, but rather left them more determined than ever to persevere untill (*sic*) the Revenue on Tea is removed. ... A few days past in consequence of printed notices, were convened together a very great number of our respectable Tradesmen, Artificers and Mechanics, when it was unanimously resolved to strengthen the hands of all Merchants who were for supporting and continuing the Agreement as it now stands; and not to purchase of, but by all lawful and prudent means to discourage and discountenance any that may depart from said Agreement.'

Four years later, Drinker switched sides, when his firm accepted appointment as one of the four Philadelphia consignees for the tea that East India Company planned to sell in the American market, and to which the Townshend duties still applied. After hesitating for two months, they finally decided to resign the commission, less out of principle, than at the insistence of the Committee for Tarring and Feathering. It is unclear whether such threats reflected opposition to continuation of the tax on tea or to the fact that the law limited the number of consignees who could sell the now lower priced tea thus cutting into the income of merchants who were excluded from selection. Doerflinger provides a concise summary of the sources of merchant ambivalence to the pressures put upon them by those having a stronger interest in nonimportation.

> The behaviour of Henry Drinker encapsulates an essential paradox in the political motivations of Philadelphia merchants before the Revolution. They genuinely feared British encroachments on American rights and were willing to make real financial sacrifices to oppose them. Yet their opposition was qualified and inconsistent, their attitudes complex and conflicted; the merchants never offered sustained, united support for the resistance and Revolutionary movements. They neither strenuously lobbied against the Sugar Act, nor led the opposition to the Stamp Act, nor initiated the boycott of I 769-I770, nor supported strongly the convening of the Continental Congress. If it had been left to the city's merchants, the Revolutionary movement would have been more circumspect and cautious, more judicious and temperate, less eager to make the final break with Britain. In short, it would not have been a revolutionary movement at all. One reason for this ambivalence was that Philadelphia's economy was not especially disordered

> or depressed between 1760 and 1775, as some neo-Progressive historians have suggested; indeed, the period offered notable entrepreneurial opportunities. The merchants thus had no compelling financial reason to break with England. Quite to the contrary, they were restrained by a variety of countervailing factors. They had close commercial and personal ties with England; they wished to avoid disruption of their trade by boycotts and protests; and the Quakers among them not only discountenanced tumultuous extra-legal protests but also feared that the Revolutionary movement would sweep Pennsylvania's turbulent Presbyterian faction into power.[9]

The reaction in Boston was no different as confirmed by the Statement of Theophilus Lillie, published in the *Boston News-Letter*, 11 January 1770, in response to his continued refusal to join in the nonimportation movement and the malevolence to which he was exposed. True, Lillie eventually agreed to comply with nonimportation, on the understanding that it would expire on 1 January 1770 as stipulated in the original Agreement. However, on 17 October 1769, the Agreement was revised making its operation now contingent upon repeal of the Townshend duties. 'Late in December, the Merchant's Committee of inspection made an examination of the goods which had been stored by various merchants in their won shops in rooms for which the committee held keys. They found a considerable quantity wanting in the instance of John Taylor and Theophilus Lillie, and they heard several other merchants declare their intention to sell stored goods after January 1, 1770. A meeting of the Boston merchants on December 28 voted a boycott against Taylor and Lillie and all those who should trade with them.'[10]

Lillie's statement describes the pressures applied to comply with the terms of the Agreement. However, with the shift from a one year to an open-ended commitment, he concluded the pledges that he had made, having been extracted by intimidation, were no longer binding. According to his account, merchants were initially 'invited' to participate in nonimportation. 'When the Subscriptions for non-importation were carrying about, they were repeatedly brought to me, and as often as they were brought, I refused signing. I knew many worthy Gentlemen had refused, and I was told there was no compulsion. I therefore went on sending for

[9] T. Doerflinger, "Philadelphia Merchants and the Logic of Moderation, 1760–1775," *William and Mary Quarterly*, **40** (1983) 197–226, pp. 197–198. Henry Drinker, as noted, was a Quaker.

[10] Schlesinger, 'Colonial Merchants,' pp. 174–175.

my goods as usual [from Britain], for the support of my family depended upon it.' Those that refused were intimidated, by being publicly named and shamed, or physically threatened. 'The Merchants met and voted that my name, with others, should be published in the newspapers and in handbills as Enemies to our Country, &c., which was done accordingly, and ... (handbills were spread) immediately throughout many of the Country towns; and the greatest pains were taken to stop my customers from coming to my shop, my signboard was defaced, and my name brushed out, and I suffered many other indignities.' Lillie as noted eventually pledged to support the agreement, but recorded that not all Boston merchants were treated equally, some who continued to sell British goods were unmolested. After 'finding that where there was one person who had imported and was called to account for it, there were ten who had no notice taken of them, and were selling freely—the partiality was so gross that I openly declared I would sell my goods, too. And for this I am a third time (December 1769) exposed in the newspapers and charged with breach of faith.'[11]

[11] 'Statement of Theophilus Lillie,' published in the *Boston News-Letter*, 11 January 1770 (accessed at: https://americainclass.org/sources/makingrevolution/crisis/text4/townshendactsresponse1767.pdf).

PART IV

Rebellion: Revolution and Its Aftermath

War tore the country apart; refugees and soldiers wandered the countryside; armies stole cattle and crops; people starved. Trade atrophied; money lost its value; jobs disappeared ... The war ended but the misery continued ... This depression seared the memories of all who lived through it.[1]

Could the American Revolution have been avoided? Several contemporaries proposed ways in which the rupture could be averted. Adam Smith, among others, thought the forfeiture of the colonies a great loss to Britain and to head off that prospect proposed a compromise he felt was fair and would end the matter. In contrast to David Hume, who argued that colonial independence must come in the ordinary course of nature so that the matter lacked the importance commonly attached to it,[2] Smith maintained, first, it was nonsensical to imagine 'Great Britain should voluntarily give up all authority over her colonies ... would be to propose such a measure as never was and never will be adopted by any nation in the world,' while arguing that a colony could only be beneficial to the empire

[1] A. Kulikoff, "'Such Things Ought Not to Be:' The American Revolution and the First National Depression, in A. Shankman (Ed.) *The World of the American Revolution and Republic: Land, Labour and the Conflict for a Continent* (New York: NY: Routledge, 2014), p. 134.

[2] "I am an American in my Principles, and wish we woud (sic) let them alone to govern or misgovern themselves as they think proper," *The Letters of David Hume* (Ed.) J. Greig 2. Vols. (Oxford: Clarendon Press, 1969), 2:303. See also E. Benians, "Adam Smith's Project of an Empire," *Cambridge Historical Journal*, **1** (1925) 249–283, p. 255 and D. Livingston, "Hume and America," *The Kentucky Review*, **4** (1983) 15–38.

of which it belongs, not only to defray the expenses of its own defence but equally to contribute its fair share to the support of the general government.

> The Parliament of Great Britain insists upon taxing the colonies; and they refuse to be taxed by a Parliament in which they are not represented. If to each colony which should detach itself from the general confederacy Great Britain should allow such a number of representatives as suited the proportion of what it contributed to the public revenue of the empire, in consequence of its being subjected to the same taxes and in compensation admitted to the same freedom of trade with its fellow subjects at home; the number of its representatives to be augmented as the proportion of its contribution might afterwards augment; a new method of acquiring importance, a new and more dazzling object of ambition would be presented to the leading men of each colony. (WN: IV:5)

While the British made a last-ditch attempt at conciliation, the focus remained on taxes and not on the broader issue of the proper relationship between taxation and representation. The views of Smith and others like him who proposed the only rational solution was a compromise that addressed both issues concurrently. In his *Conciliatory Resolution* of January 1775, the British government's final attempt to avoid war, Lord North eschewed such advice.

> That it is the opinion of this Committee, that when the Governor, Council, and Assembly, or General Court, of any of his Majesty's Provinces or Colonies in America, shall propose to make provision, according to the condition, circumstances, and situation of such Province or Colony, for contributing their proportion to the common defence, (such proportion to be raised under the authority of the General Court, or General Assembly, of such Province or Colony, and disposable by Parliament,) and shall engage to make provision also for the support of the Civil Government, and the Administration of Justice, in such Province or Colony, it will be proper, if such proposal shall be approved by his Majesty and the two Houses of Parliament and for so long as such provision shall be made accordingly, to forbear, in respect of such Province or Colony, to levy any Duty, Tax, or Assessment, or to impose any farther Duty, Tax, or Assessment, except only such Duties as it may be expedient to continue to levy or to impose for the

regulation of commerce; the nett produce of the Duties last mentioned to be carried to the account of such Province or Colony respectively.[3]

The colonists rejected the proposal, as should have been expected given that it addressed the issue of taxation in isolation.

Upon the whole, this proposition seems to have been held up to the world, to deceive it into a belief that there was nothing in dispute between us but the **mode** of levying taxes; and that the Parliament having now been so good as to give up this, the Colonies are unreasonable if not perfectly satisfied: Whereas in truth, our adversaries still claim a right of demanding ***ad libitum***, and of taxing us themselves to the full amount of their demand, if we do not comply with it. This leaves us without any thing we can call property. But, what is of more importance, and what in this proposal they keep out of sight, as if no such point was now in contest between us, they claim a right to alter our Charters and established laws, and leave us without any security for our Lives or Liberties. The proposition seems also to have been calculated more particularly to lull into fatal security our well-affected fellow subjects on the other side the water, till time should be given for the operation of those arms, which a British Minister pronounced would instantaneously reduce the "cowardly" sons of America to unreserved submission. But when the world reflects, how inadequate to justice are these vaunted terms; when it attends to the rapid and bold succession of injuries, which, during a course of eleven years, have been aimed at these Colonies; when it reviews the pacific and respectful expostulations, which, during that whole time, were the sole arms we opposed to them; when it observes that our complaints were either not heard at all, or were answered with new and accumulated injury; when it recollects that the Minister himself on an early occasion declared, "that he would never treat with America, till he had brought her to his feet," and that an avowed partisan of Ministry has more lately denounced against us the dreadful sentence ***"delenda est Carthago,"*** that this was done in presence of a British Senate, and being unreproved by them, must be taken to be their own sentiment, (especially as the purpose has already in part been carried into execution by their treatment of Boston, and burning of Charlestown) when it considers the great armaments with which they have invaded us, and the circumstances of cruelty with which these have commenced and prosecuted hostilities; when these things, we say, are laid together, and attentively considered, can the world be deceived into an opinion that we are unreasonable, or can it hesi-

[3] 394 "Conciliatory Resolution," P. Force (Ed.). *American Archives*. (Washington, D.C.: Clarke and Force, 1837–1853).

tate to believe with us, that nothing but our own exertions may defeat the ministerial sentence of death or abject submission.[4]

The American colonists were well aware the British government would refuse to consider the issue of representation. As John Adams noted in a letter written one year before the Resolution was drafted, parliamentary representation, all the more so if it was based on population rather than fiscal capacity, was 'impracticable.' Parliament would never consider such a proposal based on population alone as Americans would have demanded 'at once 250 representatives and in time 1000, so that in due course the Crown and legislature would have to migrate to America.'[5]

Adams' exaggeration was meant to make a point. The white population of the colonies just about equalled that of Scotland which, following the Acts of Union, was granted representation greater than would be expected on the basis of financial, economic, and demographic factors alone. In principle, there was no reason why a comparable agreement could not have been reached with the Americans. There was, however, one crucial difference that militated against such an outcome. Whereas in the Acts of Union, agreement was mutually beneficial, with England's northern border secured against French invasion and the Hanoverian settlement formally acknowledged, in exchange for economic and political concessions,[6] the latter inter alia in the form of disproportionate parliamentary representation as a further demonstration of the English government's commitment to supporting the terms of the Act. As to the American colonies there was no comparable congruence of interests, no similar commitment

[4] Avalon Project, *Resolutions of Congress on Lord North's Conciliatory Proposal*; THE SEVERAL Assemblies of NEW JERSEY, PENNSYLVANIA and VIRGINIA, having referred to the Congress a resolution of the House of Commons of GREAT BRITAIN, which resolution is in these words (20 February 1775).

[5] E. Benians, "Adam Smith's Project of an Empire," Adam Smith Critical Assessments. Volume 4 in J. Wood (Ed.) (New York and London: Routledge, 1984) p. 28.

[6] The Scots' interests were succinctly summarised by Lord Roxburgh as 'Trade with most, Hanover with some, ease and security with others, together with a generall aversion to civill discords, intolerable poverty and … constant oppression.' Not all scholars agree with Roxburgh as to the importance accorded economics, although in whatever alternative order they might prefer, trade undoubtedly was an important input. On the current state of scholarly debate see A, Whatley, "Economic Causes and Consequences of the Union of 1707: A Survey," *Scottish Historical Review*, 68 (1989) 150–181. For the English perspective see J. Pocock, "The Union in British History," *Transactions of the Royal Historical Society*, 10 (2000), 181–196.

mechanism, that would have led to British acceptance on the same or similar basis.

Game theoretic models of the American Revolution have shown that with one exception, and a minor one at that, there was no real possibility of agreement given the vast differences between what each side wanted or expected.[7] Galliani and Torrens demonstrate that adding to the dissonance was the fears of the incumbent government, then controlled by members of the landed gentry, granting political concessions to the colonies would undermine their dominant position by strengthening the incipient democratic movement, to which American parliamentarians would almost certainly have supported thus intensifying social pressures for the reform of a political system based on land ownership.[8] In short, what was possible for Scotland, was not feasible for Britain's North American colonies. Revolution may not have been a dead certainty, but the odds favouring military conflict were very high.

Rebellion and dysfunctional government during the Confederation era imposed huge costs on the new Republic. Prior to the Revolution, per capita and household incomes were actually higher in Colonial America than in England and were more equitably distributed[9]; by 1800 these advantages had been squandered. 'The causes seem clear: war damage, mortality and morbidity among young adult males, the destruction of loyalist social networks, a collapse of foreign markets for American commodity exports, a dysfunctional financial system, and much more. The per capita income loss up to 1790 may have been as large as 30 percent.'[10] Estimates of the out-of-pocket costs of the War vary from $130–170 million, while Bullock's estimates suggest a figure of $101–104 million in specie value. Together with the $60 million expended by France on behalf

[7] C. Kromkowski, *Recreating the American Republic* (Cambridge University Press, 2002).

[8] S. Galliani and G. Torrens, "Why Not Taxation and Representation? A Note on the American Revolution?" NBER Working Paper No. 22724 (October 2016, Revised January 2018).

[9] The Gini coefficient for the thirteen American colonies is 0.44 (1774; free only), and 0.35 (New England) and 0.42 (Middle Atlantic), and 0.38 (South; whites only). The comparable figures for England and Wales (1759) and Holland (1732) are 0.52 and 0.61, respectively. P. Lindert and J. Williamson, *Unequal Gains: American Growth and Inequality Since 1700* (Princeton, NJ and Oxford: Princeton University Press, 2016).

[10] Ibid., p. 10.

of the American cause, the total amount was considerably less than the war costs incurred by Great Britain, officially estimated at £119 million.[11]

These figures do not include the indirect costs of the War, which imposed an even heavier burden on the national economy. The resulting depression, deeper than that of the 1930s, impoverished Americans, forcing a reconsideration of existing institutions and practices. Economic decisions taken during the war, while ill-conceived, reflected in many instances existing institutional and political constraints. For example, it was difficult or impossible for governments to borrow from their own citizens. 'Private capital was tied up in lands or commodities, and no banks or business corporations had been formed. When war or other contingencies required large outlays, colonial governments discovered no alternative to paper money.'[12] Printed in ever-increasing amounts, it resulted in a steady depreciation of its value. By December 1780, after the British had invaded the South and the French departed to fight in the West Indies, the value of the continental traded at 100:1 *vis-à-vis* the pound sterling. As monetary creation increased inflation accelerated causing a breakdown in trade and credit; payments could now only be made either in specie or goods. International trade likewise ground to a halt, reflecting the combined impact of military demands, production disruptions, blockades, embargoes, and privateering. Severe as these financial and economic pressures were during the war years, once peace was established these issues were in due course addressed and corrected laying the foundation for the Republic's future growth and its subsequent economic and political ascendency.

Once war was declared, the Republic's most pressing need was to find ways to cover the associated large increase in military expenditure. Table 1 indicates the costs connected with the Revolutionary War and how they were financed. The favoured option, as noted, was printing money, an expedient forced upon the new Republic owing mainly to Congress' inability to tax or impose tariffs, leaving it without an independent source of revenue[13]; of course, if Congress lacked the power to tax, it virtually

[11] C. Bullock, *The Finances of the United States from 1775–1789 with Special Reference to the Budget, Bulletin of the University of Wisconsin*, **1** (1895) 117–273, pp. 180–181.

[12] E. Ferguson, *The Power of the Purse: A History of American Public Finance, 1776–1790* (Omohundro Institute and University of North Carolina Press (1968), pp. 8–9.

[13] Robert Morris, Superintendent of Finance, sought to expand governmental powers beyond the limits set by the Articles of Confederation. He released a *Report on Public Credit*, calling for the Confederation government to assume the entire national debt, issue new interest-bearing debt certificates, and impose tariffs and internal taxes to pay the interest costs. This plan essentially prefigured Alexander Hamilton's later fiscal program.

ruled out the option of being able to raise finance in the bond market. 'Without revenues,' Alexander Hamilton warned, 'a government can have no power.' One obvious source of revenue was confiscation of the estates of loyalists or others deemed to have provided support to, or fought on behalf of, Great Britain.[14]

Table 1 Funding Sources for the American Revolution

	Sterling (£)	Percentages
Fiat currency		
Congressional monies	46	28
States' monies	64	39
Total fiat currency	110	67
Borrowed funds		
Congress: domestic bonds	6	3
Congress: debt certificates	16	10
Congress: foreign loans	10	6
States' indebtedness	23	14
Total debts	54	33
Total cost of war	165	100

Source: E. Perkins, *American Public Finance and Financial Services, 1700–1815* (Columbus, OH: Ohio State University Press, 1994), p. 103, Table 5.4

Note: a. The actual sum in circulation may never be known. Congress officially voided $41.5 million and offered a swap programme because of problems related to counterfeiting. As a result of escalating depreciation, the sums issued in 1779 and 1780 had only one-third of the purchasing power of the initial emissions in 1775 and 1776. By January 1780 it took more than $40 in paper to exchange for $1 in coin; a year later the exchange ratio had fallen to 100:1 or worse. Grubb presents the annual breakdown of Congressional expenditure for the period 1975–1979, but excludes state indebtedness. F. Grubb, "The Distribution of Congressional Spending during the American Revolution, 1775–1780: The Problem of Geographic Balance," NBER Working Paper 14,267 (August 2008), p. 27, Table 5. With exception of New England, data on state indebtedness are unreliable. Ratchford, 'State Debt' p. 45 reports Massachusetts' debt (1785) at $5 million, New Hampshire (1784) at $0.5 million, Rhode Island (1783) at $0.48, and Connecticut (1783) at $3.783 million. The dollar/sterling for Massachusetts averaged exchange rate c. £1.35 prior to the War, implying the state's debt amounted to c. £3.8 million

[14] 'The number of Loyalists in each colony varied. Recent estimates suggest that half the population of New York was Loyalist; it had an aristocratic culture and was occupied throughout the Revolution by the British. In the Carolinas, back-country farmers were Loyalist, whereas the Tidewater planters tended to support the Revolution. During the Revolution, most Loyalists suffered little from their views. However, a minority, about 19,000 Loyalists, armed and supplied by the British, fought in the conflict.' American History, "Loyalists During the American Revolution," (accessed at: http://www.let.rug.nl/usa/outlines/history-1994/the-road-to-independence/loyalists-during-the-american-revolution.php

CHAPTER 12

Confiscation

The issue of confiscation was first raised by the Continental Congress which, however, left the final decision to the discretion of the rebelling states. 'Resolved, that it be earnestly recommended to the several states, as soon as may be, to confiscate and make sale of all the real and personal estate therein, of such of their inhabitants and other persons who have forfeited the same, and the right to the protection of their respective states, and to invest the money arising from the sales in continental loan office certificates, to be appropriated in such manner as the respective states shall hereafter direct.'[1] One of the more brazen legal justifications, the 'absentee crimes' doctrine, was articulated in the preamble to Massachusetts' 1779 sequestration act. 'Whereas every government hath a right to command the personal services of all its members whenever the exigencies of the state shall require it, especially in times of an impending or actual invasion, no member thereof can then withdraw himself from the jurisdiction of the government, and thereby deprive it of the benefit of his personal services, without justly incurring the forfeiture of all his property, rights and liberties, holden under and derived from that constitution of government.'[2] All thirteen states passed confiscation legislation, although

[1] Library of Congress, *Journals of the Continental Congress, 1774–1789*, Vol. IX (Washington, D.C.: Government Printing Office, 1904), p. 971.

[2] Cited in R. Brown, "The Confiscation and Disposition of Loyalists' Estates in Suffolk County, Massachusetts," *William and Mary Quarterly*, **21** (1964) 534–550, p. 539.

G. Pollio, *The Rise and Fall of Britain's North American Empire*,
https://doi.org/10.1007/978-3-031-07484-4_12

the amount of land and chattels sequestered and sold varied widely. Confiscations in Maryland, a relatively small state, resulted in the seizure and sale of more than 200,000 acres, raising £450,000, in contrast to, say, Pennsylvania, a considerably larger state, in which sequestrations totalled only 40,000 acres.[3]

The question naturally arises as to the potential number of loyalists (or Royalists, as Benjamin Franklin preferred to call them)[4] then living in the United States, which would provide an indication of the fiscal potential of sequestration. For present purposes it appears useful to differentiate active from passive loyalists. The former provided either direct support to the British, including serving in the military,[5] or opted to emigrate to England or elsewhere in the British world; the latter, by contrast, were unwilling to abandon the goal of reconciliation and/or fight a war for independence and thus stayed put. The total number of British sympathisers is estimated at up to 500,000,[6] while a further 60,000–100,000 chose to depart the colonies.[7] Smith's estimate implies that one-fifth of Americans were

[3] The state also assumed control over more than 20 million acres of the Penn family's proprietary lands, for which it granted £130,000 in compensation (perhaps one-tenth of its true value). Maryland confiscated more land than Pennsylvania. M. Gallo, "Property Rights, Citizenship, Corruption, and Inequality: Confiscating Loyalist Estates during the American Revolution," *Pennsylvania History: A Journal of Mid-Atlantic Studies*, **86** (2019) 474–510, p. 474. An early study on state sequestration that covers the laws of all the states is R. Allen, *The Legislation for the Confiscation of British and Loyalist Property During the Revolutionary War* (doctoral dissertation, University of Maryland, 1937).

[4] Letter from Benjamin Franklin to Baron Francis Maseres, June 26, 1785, *The Works of Benjamin Franklin*, Vol. XI Letters and Misc. Writings 1784–1788 (NY: G.P. Putnam's Sons, 1904). A useful summary of past and recent research on American Loyalists see J. Bannister and L. Riordan, "Loyalism and the British Atlantic, 1660–1840," in J. Bannister and L. Riordan (Eds.) *The Loyal Atlantic: Remaking the British Atlantic in in the Revolutionary Era* (Buffalo, NY: University of Toronto Press, 2012). 'Loyalists had diverse backgrounds and commitments as well as different memories and notions about what loyalty meant that included unpredictably mixed assessments of multivalent English and British cultural, legal, commercial, and political ways of understanding themselves and their world' p. 24.

[5] On Loyalist regiments in the American Revolution see S. Salmon, "The Loyalist Regiments of the American Revolutionary War, 1775–1783" (doctoral dissertation, University of Stirling, 2009).

[6] P. Smith, "The American Loyalists: Notes on Their Organization and Numerical Strength," *William and Mary Quarterly*, **25** (1968) 259–277, p. 269. The author frankly admits that because these 'calculations rest upon some rather tentative figures, several subjective decisions, and a bastard methodology, one can make no claim to such precision.'

[7] The higher figure us attributed to a Canadian historian, of whom some 60,000 emigrated to Canada. G. Wrong, *Canada and the American Revolution: The Disruption of the First*

loyalist, which compares with John Adams' widely cited one-third figure.[8] Most scholars now favour the lower estimate as well as accepting that the majority of loyalists stayed behind.

Various factors have been adduced to explain loyalist motivations. For some, including William Franklin, Governor of New Jersey, and the Tory son of Benjamin Franklin, it was a matter of principle. '"Every breach of the [English] Constitution, whether it proceeds from the Crown or the People, is, in its Effects, equally destructive to the Rights of both." It is the Duty, therefore, of those who are entrusted with Government to be equally careful in guarding against Encroachments from the one as the other. But It is (says one of the wisest of Men), a most infallible Symptom of the dangerous State of Liberty, when the chief Men of a free Country show a greater Regard to Popularity than to their own Judgment."[9] It is generally conceded that opposition to British rule was broadly based, and that their patriotic opponent's characterisation of their behaviour—'self-interested men, greedy parasites who profited from the imperial connection or weak and cowardly individuals who feared anarchy more than appreciated liberty'—was short of the truth. Apart from Crown officials, 'there was not a common determinant for ending up on the Loyalist side. The Loyalists came from every social class in colonial society, every occupation, and every region on the continent.'[10]

William Franklin, along with many others, elected to emigrate after concluding that the possibility of any sort of meaningful reconciliation was possible. As tensions increased the states found it necessary to identify those that opposed revolutionary aspirations, the favoured method was to enact laws requiring the male population to take oaths of allegiance to the new states, applying in effect, albeit in reverse, the earlier British practice requiring signed oaths confirming loyalty to the Crown. Individuals who refused to sign such oaths typically forfeited their property and were often imprisoned or made to work for the new local revolutionary order. The

British Empire (NY: Cooper Square Publishers, 1968 [original: 1935]), pp. 376, 468–9. Reviewers of his study dismissed the estimates as unrealistic as even Wrong admitted that he could only identify 6000 Tory family names could be discovered in Canada.

[8] Cited in M. Tyler, "The Party of the Loyalists in the American Revolution," in *American Historical Review*, 1 (1895) 24–45.

[9] L. Gerlach (Ed.), *New Jersey in the American Revolution, 1763–1783: A Documentary History*, (Trenton, NJ: New Jersey Historical Commission, 1975), pp. 110–111.

[10] "Loyalists," Washington Library, Centre for Digital History, Digital Encyclopaedia, "Loyalists."

mere fact of signing the oath did not necessarily imply support for independence, but rather ensured the safety of one's family while protecting its wealth.

Estimates of the loyalist element in the American colonies amount, in most instances, to little more than guesses, although contemporary evidence indicates their number varied widely across individual states. In Connecticut, for example, just under one in ten males aged 15–60 identified themselves as loyalist[11]; in Philadelphia alone, an estimated '15 to 20 percent of white colonial men actively aided the British in their attempts to suppress the Revolution.'[12] The numbers of those that departed are in principle more susceptible to quantification; although data exist that would support such an endeavour, the fact is they, too, are incomplete and subject to various limitations. A recent widely cited study by Maya Jasanoff estimates the number of emigrees at 75,000, comprising 60,000 white loyalists—Flick estimated (erroneously) that New York alone accounted for three-fifths of that total[13]—and 15,000 slaves. 'Seven thousand or so went to Britain, often to find themselves strangers in a strange land. By far the largest group, more than half the total, fled to Canada and settled in the present-day provinces of the Maritimes, Ontario, and Quebec. Notably, about three thousand black loyalists moved to Canada, some of the thousands of former slaves who had gained freedom by fighting for the

[11] G. Gilbert, "The Connecticut Loyalists," *American Historical Review*, **4** (1899) 273–291, p. 278. Newtown was likewise located in Fairfield County. A more recent study of loyalism in Connecticut is S. McGrath, "Connecticut's Contrarians: The Loyalists of Fairfield County," *Connecticut History Review*, 54 (2015) 243–255.

Connecticut Quarterly, 1.21895: 'During the first few years of the revolutionary war, this state was literally full of Tories. They filled our jails to overflowing; many of them were confined within the court-house at Hartford, and others were confined under guard or within certain limits on parole in various parts of the state where they would be out of contrast with the British, while many others of fighting age and burning zeal for their King left their families, property and homes and took up arms against the American cause.'

[12] S. Duffy, 'Loyalists,' *Encyclopaedia of Greater Philadelphia* (accessed at: https://philadelphiaencyclopedia.org/archive/loyalists/).

[13] A. Flick, *Loyalism in New York During the American Revolution, New York* (NY: Columbia University Press, 1901, p. 277.

British.'[14] Her estimates indicate that, overall, more than one in forty residents of what became the United States opted to emigrate.[15]

Philip Ranlet, in a detailed review of Jasanoff's data, concludes that her 60,000 estimate of loyalist refugees is 'inflated and unreliable.'[16] An important consideration in Ranlet's analysis, and one that can be quantified independently, is that Jasanoff's estimates include children, who for obvious reasons were in no position to dispute, reject, or develop political views that differed from those of their parents and thus should be excluded from the totals. To provide an indication of their importance, Ranlet relies on two returns covering the number of New York residents intending to depart for Nova Scotia and New Brunswick, the ultimate destination of the bulk of the State's emigrees. According to the first return, dated 12 October 1783, which lists a total of 29,278 emigrees who had signed up (or been signed up) to embark for Canada, the number of dependent children, at 9140, account for *c.* one-third of the total number defecting.[17] It would be too facile to apply the same percentage to Jasanoff's estimate, but if nothing else it underlines the extent to which her figures are artificially inflated. Moreover, these data refer to those intending to emigrate not those that actually did thus adding to the overstatement.

The discrepancy between the aggregate and city- or state-wide estimates noted above demonstrates that a much large number of colonials supported Britain, but were unwilling to act upon their convictions by emigrating, while those that did nevertheless constituted a significant percentage of the local population. To underline the point, consider the 1783 data for New York discussed above, which after deducting children from the total indicates a loyalist percentage of 10 per cent, more or less in line with the estimates cited above for Connecticut and Philadelphia; this compares with Jasanoff's 2.5 per cent ('one in forty') estimate. We now know

[14] M. Jasanoff, "The Other Side of Revolution: Loyalists in the British Empire," *William and Mary Quarterly,* Third Series, 65 (2008) 205–232, p. 208. She notes that the 1 in 40 estimate compares with 1 in 100 that emigrated from revolutionary France. The two figures are unlikely to be comparable. Jasanoff includes children in her estimate, who quite obviously were in no position to sympathise with either the Loyalist (or Republican) cause.

[15] M. Jasanoff, "The Other Side of Revolution: Loyalists in the British Empire," *William and Mary Quarterly,* Third Series, **65** (2008) 205–232.

[16] P. Ranlet, "How Many Loyalists Left the United States?" *The Historian*, **76** (2014) 278–307, p. 306.

[17] Ranlet 'Loyalists,', p. 296. The second return, dated 24 November 1783, mentions a figure 32,224.

that the latter's loyalist estimates are overstated, which would widen the discrepancy even further.

Finally, such comparisons may be misleading given the extent to which Americans remained loyal to Britain had a strong regional bias. John Adams, for example, believed that New York and Pennsylvania would have joined the British if strongly patriotic Virginia and New England had not kept them in line. As for Connecticut, it has long been recognised that loyalist support was concentrated in the southwestern part of the state, Fairfield County in particular, which, both 'religiously and politically, (was) the most conservative county in Connecticut,'[18] largely explained by the fact it was the centre of Anglicanism in the state. 'Nowhere in the colony ... was the (Anglican) church so strong as in Fairfield County where it embraced about one-third of the people ... while at Newtown—the hot-bed of Toryism—there was found an equal division.'[19] The extent to which the views of Anglicans were at odds with the rest of the state is indicated by an article appearing in the *Connecticut Courant*, of 20 May 1776. 'A gang of Tories has been discovered in the neighbourhood of Fairfield, taken and imprisoned ... If these internal enemies are suffered to proceed in their hellish schemes, our ruin is certain; but if they are destroyed, the power of Hell and Britain will never prevail against us. Rouse then, my countrymen, search out the nest of these vultures, and bring them to the punishment they merit.'[20]

Philadelphia's support for the British Crown may also have been motivated by religious considerations. Anglicans, who formed a minority among the city's population, remained loyal because they needed the protection of the King,[21] while Quakers and other pacifistic sects, opposed to or unenthusiastic about the war, added further support.[22] Yet another

[18] McGrath, Loyalists, p. 243.

[19] G. Gilbert, "The Connecticut Loyalists," *American Historical Review*, **4** (1899) 273–291, p. 278. Newtown was likewise located in Fairfield County.

[20] Cited in ibid., p. 283, fn. 2.

[21] W. Nelson, *The American Tory* (Oxford University Press, 1971). A more recent review of the relationship between religion and the American Revolution is D. Davis, "Religion and the American Revolution," *Journal of Church and State*, **36** (1994) 709–724.

[22] 'The reluctance of the (Quakers) ... to support of the war against England in 1775 and the early part of 1776 gave the radicals, who desired the overthrow of the hegemony of the Quakers and the wealthy, their opportunity and their excuse. Since the Tory Party, which was dominant in the Assembly, was slow to support the war and had instructed their delegates to the Second Continental Congress to vote against independence, the majority in congress who were determined on independence turned to the Whigs in Pennsylvania. On May I,

perspective that emphasised the importance of religious differences dates back to the late eighteenth century, when Joseph Galloway, a member of the Pennsylvania Assembly and close friend of Benjamin Franklin, opposed the Revolution and fled to England in 1778. Like many Tories he believed that the Revolution was, to a considerable extent, a religious quarrel caused by Presbyterians and Congregationalists whose 'principles of religion and polity [were] equally averse to those of the established Church and Government.'[23] Of course, an event as complicated as the American Revolution cannot be reduced to a single cause, but it is undoubtedly true that religion figured more prominently in some sections of the country than others.

How much of the revenue raised from confiscations was committed to the purchase of continental loan certificates is unclear, but it is doubtful the yield in any way approximated to the amounts anticipated. In many instances the oft-cited figures represent the nominal, not the actual, amount raised; in many instances the purchases were made on credit, were never completed, or paid for in the depreciated currency of the state in which the auctions were held.[24] Indeed, the suspension of sales in Suffolk County, Massachusetts, in 1780 'appears related to the General Court's dissatisfaction with the amount of revenue the sales were producing.'[25] There is also evidence of venality on the part of the Commissioners

1776, Congress passed a resolution calling on the various colonies to change their forms of government to conform to the changed political situation.' H. Seyler, "Pennsylvania's First Loyalty Oath." *History of Education Journal*, **3** (1952) 114–126, p. 115.

[23] J. Galloway, *Historical and Political Reflections on the Rise and Progress of the American Rebellion* (London: G. Wilkie, 1780), p. 54.

[24] 'Although efforts were made after 1781 to have all business in the state (of New York) transacted on a specie basis, it was not until the Act of May 12, 1784, was passed that the relative value of the various kinds of money was determined. Gold and silver were to be accepted at their "legal and current values." The bills of credit of New York and the continental paper money were to be taken at the rate of one silver dollar for $120 in currency. Other special certificates and warrants were to be received on more favourable terms.' A. Flick, *Loyalism in New York During the American Revolution* (London: P.S. King & Son, 1901), Chapter 7. In the same chapter there is a discussion of monetary values and rates of exchange vis-à-vis specie and Spanish dollars.

[25] Brown, 'Confiscations in Suffolk County,' p. 542. He goes on to note that a 'suspicion prevailed among members of the Court that bidders at the Suffolk auctions had conspired to hold down prices, to the damage of the state and the creditors. In fact, the low prices may equally have been caused by a general scarcity of cash and a consequent dearth of investors. But for whatever reason, there was no doubt that the estates had been purchased "on very advantageous terms."'

conducting the auctions.[26] Many of these issues are explicit in the experience of the State of Georgia.

> Certainly the confiscation of Loyalist estates did not prove to be the fiscal panacea that many had hoped for. The recorded transactions of the commissioners from 1782 to 1786 reached a total for gross sales of £410,118. Of this sum the state had received bonds from purchasers of confiscated property in the amount of £281,716. The difference between these figures is largely accounted for by the fact that property which had sold for £84,744 reverted to the state for non-payment under the terms of the Releasing Act of July 1783, and that £29,448 in claims by Whigs had been drawn against the confiscated property. But nearly five years after the program was begun only about one-third, or £93,783, had actually been received by the treasury, and much of that amount had not been paid in specie.[27]

Many of the properties confiscated were large estates, and it was thought that apart from the revenues generated from their sale, a potential ancillary benefit was the possibility of creating a more equitable distribution of land ownership throughout the United States. Thomas Jefferson, in particular, argued that widespread landownership was vital for a healthy republic, insisting that 'dependance (sic) begets subservience and venality, suffocates the germ of virtue, and prepares fit tools for the designs of ambition.'[28] The alternative perspective that favoured limiting enfranchisement was articulated by William Blackstone, the well-known British jurist. 'The true reason' he wrote, 'of requiring any qualification with regard to property, in voters, is to exclude such persons as are in so mean a situation that they are esteemed to have no will of their own. If these persons had votes, they would be tempted to dispose of them under some undue influence or other. This would give a great, an artful, or a wealthy man, a larger share in elections than is consistent with general liberty.'[29]

[26] 'In February 1780, Thomas Hale, Agent for Forfeited Estates in Philadelphia County, was accused of using public money for speculation. When a review of his books revealed a shortage of £50,000, he was relieved of his duties and his case turned over to the attorney general for prosecution.' A. Ousterhout, "Pennsylvania Land Confiscations During the Revolution," *Pennsylvania Magazine of History and Biography*, **102** (1978) 328–343, p. 337.

[27] Georgia, R. Lambert, "The Confiscation of Loyalist Property in Georgia, 1782–1786," *William and Mary Quarterly*, **20** (1963) 80–94, p. 91.

[28] *Notes on Virginia* (Philadelphia: Prichard and Hall, 1788), p. 175.

[29] W. Blackstone, *Commentaries on the Laws of England: A Facsimile of the First Edition of 1765–1769.* (Chicago. IL: University of Chicago Press, 1979, Volume 2, Article 1, Section 2, Clause 1, Document 3).

In most of the former colonies, suffrage was contingent upon the ownership of property (not necessarily restricted to owning a freehold) and varied considerably across individual states. In Delaware, for example, voters were required to own 50 acres of land or property worth £40; Rhode Island set the limit at land valued at £40 or worth an annual rent of £2; Connecticut required land worth an annual rent of £2 or livestock worth £40; in New Jersey, the property requirement was set at £50[30]; and in Maryland, the right to vote was restricted to those who possessed £20 or fifty acres of land. Property qualifications were even more stringent for those aspiring to hold office. In Maryland, to run for 'governor required £5000; members of the Senate needed £1000; members of the House required £500. To put these numbers in some perspective, Jackson Turner Main suggested that a typical 289-acre farm on the Eastern Shore in the late colonial period could only yield £170 per year. This meant that only substantial planters owning about 1000 acres could qualify for office under Maryland's revolutionary constitution.'[31]

While attitudes towards suffrage evolved in the decades following independence,[32] these shifts had little or nothing to do with loyalist land

[30] E. Crews, "Voting in Early America," *Colonial Williamsburg Journal* (Spring 2007).

[31] M. Gallo, "Property Rights, Citizenship, Corruption, and Inequality: Confiscating Loyalist Estates during the American Revolution," *Pennsylvania History: A Journal of Mid-Atlantic Studies*, **86**(2019) 474–510, p. 493. Gallo goes on to note that as 'Maryland's elites controlled its government, so it should not surprise us that confiscations tended to put large properties in the hands of those elites. Corruption in this case was not overt, but it was systemic: the wealthy were the men best positioned to benefit from any opportunity for investment or speculation and most likely to comprise the state's leadership. Having gained control, Maryland's leaders did not conduct the revolution to level social differences: they sought to protect private property whenever possible and had little interest in democratizing wealth beyond the necessity of avoiding popular revolt.'

[32] In due course, suffrage was extended even to those who did not own property. There are two dimensions to this evolution. The first had to do with the fact that an increasing number of Americans had become taxpayers, and who by right should be enfranchised. The other was philosophical: 'On the one hand, Americans continued to adhere to the classical republican notion that only property ownership conferred independence on a man. On the other hand, they had also come to believe that "all men were by nature equally free and independent and had certain inherent and unalienable rights." 'One view pointed toward a world in which all men, whether or not they owned property, were assumed by nature to be free and independent, and capable of political discretion. The other assumed that the polity was divided at bottom into two groups, those who owned property and those who did not. According to this view, the propertyless should never exercise political authority precisely because they were not free and independent agents.' R. Steinfeld, "Property and Suffrage in the Early American Republic," *Stanford Law Review*, **41** (1989), 335–376, p. 338

sales; on the contrary, such sales would have helped to consolidate the political dominance of incumbents. Given the urgent need to raise funds, it is unsurprising the primary beneficiaries of the sale of confiscated loyalist land were wealthy individuals, many of whom were merchants. But a disproportionately large number of Maryland's political and military officers, many of whom were large landholders, were among the principal recipients of the land sales ensuring the state's politics would continue to protect their interests. Things were much the same in other former colonies, with the scale of corruption, as in the neighbouring state of Pennsylvania, being the principal difference.

> Many Pennsylvanians sought to cheat the state through the process of acquiring confiscated lands. Pennsylvanians' dishonest dealings resembled those in Maryland but took place on a grander scale. For example, in 1780 the state re-confiscated lands sold to purchasers in Northampton County. Taking advantage of the rapid depreciation of the currency, purchasers there sought to delay payment for their lands to gain the lands at a lower real price. In Bucks County accusations of intimidation at auctions emerged, indicating that prices could be kept low to benefit buyers at the expense of the state. Throughout the state, officials made little effort to meticulously record property sales, and much of the land appears to have fallen into the hands of a small number of well-connected men. In 1780 the government prosecuted Thomas Hale, the agent overseeing land confiscations in Philadelphia County, for fraud. His books showed a shortfall of £50,000.[33]

The presumption that the right to vote was limited to only to a small number of Americans ignores the fact that the abundance of land meant that there were many smallholders who could in fact vote. This was

[33] Ibid., p. 478. According to Ousterhouse, 'since the purpose of the confiscations was to raise money for the state, the property of the richest defectors was taken and sold under conditions that would discourage its purchase by anyone who was not moderately affluent. Thus, it is not surprising that among the 196 persons who bought estates, either singly or with others, were many prominent citizens. Fifty-two have been identified as army officers; John Bull, William Coates, and Charles Willson Peale served in the Assembly; James Smith represented Pennsylvania in Congress; and Thomas McKean was Chief Justice of the state. While the largest number were merchants, there were at least seven Congress; and Thomas McKean was Chief Justice of the state. While the largest number were merchants, there were at least seven doctors, three ministers and two lawyers.' A. Ousterhouse, "Pennsylvania Land Confiscations during the Revolution," *Pennsylvania Magazine of History and Biography*, **102** (1978) 328–343, p. 340.

especially true where the requirement was expressed in terms of acreage rather than value, as was customarily the case in the southern colonies, it being much easier to acquire (and to measure) 50 acres than land worth, say, £50. Even so, voting in the early Republic remained highly circumscribed: in most instances, the enfranchised appointed electors who in turn cast votes that resulted in the appointment of state or federal officials; the electoral college, which elects the US president, is a remnant of this process. Six colonies allowed alternative qualifications to freehold ownership in the form of personal property or payment of taxes, opening the suffrage to owners of urban property, and even to prosperous farmers who rented their land or held it on some form of leasehold.

Throughout the early post-war era there was a tendency to liberalise voter qualifications.[34] Contemporary observers correctly predicted that each concession would be followed by further adjustments. Alexis de Tocqueville was a leading proponent of this view. In his classic *Democracy in America* (1835), he wrote: 'The further the limit of voting rights is extended, the stronger is the need felt to spread them still wider; for after each new concession the forces of democracy are strengthened, and its demands increase with its augmented power. The ambition of those left below the qualifying limit increases in proportion to the number of those above it. Finally, the exception becomes the rule; concessions follow one another without interruption, and there is no halting place until universal suffrage has been attained.'

Estimates of those permitted to vote range from 50–75 per cent of eligible (freehold) voters across individual states, the national figure estimated at 60 per cent. This compares with a figure of less than 20 per cent of enfranchised adult males in Great Britain.[35] Over time, both the

[34] D. Bateman, "Democratization in the USA? The Impact of Antebellum Suffrage Qualifications on Politics and Policy," Cornell University, Government Department Working Paper July 2020.

[35] D. Ratcliff, "The Right to Vote and the Rise of Democracy, 1787–1828" *Journal of the Early Republic*, **33** (2013) 29–254, p. 221. In Virginia, the largest American colony, the percentage was a high as 70 per cent, comprised of *c*. 50 per cent of adult white male Virginians qualified by outright ownership and another 20 per cent entered the electorate as life tenants, *Encyclopaedia Virginia*, "Elections in Colonial Virginia" (accessed at: https://encyclopediavirginia.org/entries/elections-in-colonial-virginia/). For the United States, the figure was closer to 30 per cent of the total white population of 2.2 million on the eve of the Revolution. For reasons given in the text, this figure somewhat understates the true percentage.

number of eligible voters and the range of officials they could elect increased transforming the Republic from an indirect to a direct democracy, as there was a more or less progressive easing of restrictive qualifications that inhibited the rate of enfranchisement that began even before the end of the Revolutionary War as each of the former colonies introduced new or amended their existing constitutions.[36]

Electoral reforms, however, had less to do with matters of principle than with strategic partisan calculation—expanding the number of supporters eligible to vote[37] to promote the policies of incumbents or, alternatively, to frustrate them—the elimination of inconsistencies inherent in

[36] New Jersey emerged as the most progressive of the former colonies. The 1776 New Jersey constitution conferred the vote on 'all inhabitants' (women and free blacks) who met specified property and residence requirements. ('50 pounds clear estate'). In 1790 the state's constitution was reworded substituting 'he or she' for 'all inhabitants.' In 1807, the state legislature restricted voting rights to tax-paying, white male citizens, likewise disenfranchising African Americans. I Gertzog, "Female Suffrage in New Jersey, 1790–1807," *Women and Politics*, **10** (1990) 47–58. See also J. Klinghoffer and L. Elkins, "'The Petticoat Electors': Women's Suffrage in New Jersey, 1776–1807," *Journal of the Early Republic*, **12** (1992) 159–193, L. Garbaye, "Opacity and Transparency in eighteenth Century New Jersey Electoral Reforms: The Case of Women's Voting Rights," *XVII-XVIII Revue de la Société d'études anglo-américaines des XVIIe et XVIIIe siècles,* (2012) 231–246 and C. Curry-Ledbetter, "Women's Suffrage in New Jersey, 1776–1807: A Political Weapon," *Georgetown Journal of Gender and the Law*, **21** (2020) 705–723. On the social and political impact of enfranchising women see J. Lott and L. Kenny, "Did Women's Suffrage Change the Size and Scope of Government?" *Journal of Political Economy*, **107** (1999) 1163–1198. Free blacks, so long as they could meet the property requirement, were likewise eligible to vote in New York and Pennsylvania (rescinded in 1838). New York's second constitution (1821) abolished property qualifications for white male voters, but introduced for 'persons of colour' the requirement they must own $250 worth of property, 'over and above all debts,' in order to vote. White male voters were instead required to pay a tax, but this rule was abolished in an 1826 amendment. *The Second Constitution of New York, 1821* (accessed at: https://www.nycourts.gov/history/legal-history-new-york/documents/Publications_1821-NY-Constitution.pdf).

[37] The elimination of property qualifications appears to have had the largest impact on enfranchisement rates. Data for New York indicate that the removal of property qualifications resulted in a huge increase in the number of eligible voters, rising from 33 per cent to 85 per cent in gubernatorial contests and 67 per cent to 85 per cent in Assembly elections. The elimination of the tax qualification, by contrast, appears to have had no impact at all on either rate. D. Bateman, "Democratization in the USA? The Impact of Antebellum Suffrage Qualifications on Politics and Policy," Cornell University, Government Department Working Paper July 2020 (accessed at: https://csap.yale.edu/sites/default/files/files/apppw-bateman-10-7-20.pdf).

the existing voter qualifications, and as a response to economic developments, above all, the shift from farming to manufacturing (as in New England and the Middle Atlantic states), the growing importance of heavy investments in transportation (roads, canals, later railroads) and communications (a more effective post office system, the magnetic telegraph, the expansion of print media) that led to national integration of formerly local markets.[38] To cite a single example of pressures for change, with more than '60 percent of the adult white men in Virginia entered the Revolutionary War period as experienced electors in local contests. As independence progressed, they hoped to continue and expand these opportunities while their less-fortunate white cousins with little or no land began to demand the same privileges as their landowning relatives. Neither would be completely satisfied for many decades to come.'[39] Could these and others like them in other states—property owners, tenant farmers, self-employed artisans, and so forth—still be regarded, as Blackstone's expressed it, men with 'no will of their own'?

In contrast to its failure to achieve the objectives of Jeffersonian Republicans, confiscation did address other, more pressing needs. While Howard Pashman's analysis of these 'broader purposes' relates to New York, his findings would appear to apply equally to other states. 'Confiscation,' he writes 'had a major transformative effect, because it offered material relief and revenge against enemies to a society that demanded both. During the War, New Yorkers suffered internal displacement, shortages of basic goods, and inflation. For people struggling in such conditions, property redistribution provided them with a desperately needed subsistence. Moreover, it created a constituency with a stake in the revolutionary regime, people whose material security, sometimes even their survival, depended upon the regime's stability. War also stoked a desire for revenge against Britain and its supporters. New Yorkers wanted

[38] 'When one considers a pre-industrial or early industrialized society comprised of different social groups, one can imagine preferences over the character of economic growth to differ across (and potentially within) each group. As such, the enfranchisement or disenfranchisement of these groups is a means for political parties to pursue economic policies benefitting their constituencies,' H. Llavador, and R. Oxoby, "Partisan Competition, Growth, and the Franchise." *Quarterly Journal of Economics*, **120** (2005) 1155–1189, p. 1156. See also J. Huston, "Economic Change and Political Realignment in Antebellum Pennsylvania," *Pennsylvania Magazine of History and Biography*, **113** (1989): 347–95.

[39] Ibid.

to strike back at the occupying army, and expropriation resonated with that desire for vengeance.'[40]

The variability in the scale of seizures would seem to vindicate Franklin Jameson's view that what mattered most in the design of such legislation among financially hard-pressed states was the number of potential loyalists or 'absentees' which, in turn, determined the scale of potential revenue extraction.[41] This was undoubtedly true, but other factors too entered into consideration, given the different objective circumstances facing individual states. To underline the point, consider the contrasting experiences of Vermont and New York. 'It was natural that the small, community of Vermont, with its highly informal government, and its few loyalists, should find confiscation by the simplest and most direct methods entirely adequate.'[42] 'Since the primary concern of (Vermont's) ruling faction was to maintain and nurture an independent state on an exposed frontier ... Those who lost most land were ... land speculators who opposed the independent Vermont movement.'[43] At the opposite extreme, was New York, 'with its large area and population, its numerous body of loyalists, its British garrison in New York City, and its very complicated system of state and local government, was destined from the first to require an elaborate body of statutes for the purpose.'[44]

> The issue of allegiance was particularly complicated in New York, where the heterogeneity of the population in terms of ethnicity, religion, and wealth resulted in a similar heterogeneity in political beliefs. ... Those of questionable allegiance were particularly vulnerable in New York because the state was wedged between the British forces occupying New York City and the threat of invasion from the north. Both the British and the Americans believed that silent Tories would be encouraged to declare their true allegiance and threaten the state from within if the British forces were able to advance into the interior. It was therefore incumbent upon the authorities in New York to find a method to deal with the Loyalist threat, whether real or phantom. The government imprisoned suspected Tories, often in extremely

[40] H. Pashman, "The People's Property Law: A Step Toward Building a New Legal Order in Revolutionary New York," *Law and History Review*, **31** (2013), pp. 587–626, p. 589.

[41] J. Jameson, *The American Revolution Considered as a Social Movement* (Princeton: Princeton University Press, 1926).

[42] Ibid., p. 271.

[43] S. Kalinoski, "Sequestration, Confiscation, and the 'Tory' in the Vermont Revolution," *Vermont History*, **45** (236–246), p. 245.

[44] Allen, 'Confiscation of British and Loyalist Property,' p. 270.

substandard facilities and without due process of law. Particularly feared Tories were exiled, others were put to hard labor (although many authorities denounced such punishment). The property of some Loyalists was confiscated; Patriot vigilantes occasionally tarred and feathered their opponents.[45]

Among other factors affecting the design and implementation of confiscation policies, the most important, other than the proximity of British forces, were existing land tenure arrangements and the process by which sequestrations were carried out. As to the importance of land tenure, Allen writes 'as typified by Virginia, with its active acceptance of the full implications of the theory of eminent domain, with its attendant prerogatives of tenure subject to continuing compliance with the terms of some contractual relationship with the original proprietor, identified with the sovereign, leading to the working out of a regular, and frequently applied law of escheatment and reversion, gave the revolutionary governments of that group of states a tremendous functional and psychological advantage over the state governments of the northern divisions. In the New England area particularly, the land system of tenure in fee simple, reinforced to a great extent by the religious and social convictions of the bulk of the inhabitants, led to a firm belief in the almost sacrosanct character of private property, and caused the responsible citizens to turn instinctively from any suggestion embodying the negation of this principle.'

As to the way by which the confiscations actually were carried out, Allen identifies two principal approaches: in the first group, 'the legislature simply conferred the supervision of confiscation, as an added duty, upon men already acting as public officers. Among the states in this class may be included New Hampshire, where the selectmen of the towns were given the task, and Pennsylvania, where the occupants of the other extreme of the political hierarchy, the president and council acted as supervisors of confiscation. The second group of states created special commissions or committees to handle the processes of seizure. New York and Maryland are typical of this category.' States falling into the first group, 'in spite of, or perhaps because of, their rather cavalier treatment of the problem, had, as a general rule, far less difficulty in converting the property of their enemies into money or credit than those of the second,' attributing the

[45] K. Shefsiek, "A Suspected Loyalist in the Rural Hudson Valley: The Revolutionary War Experience of Roeloff Josiah Eltinge," *Hudson River Valley Review*, **20** (2003) 27–52, pp. 27–30.

differences to the fact that 'states employing the commission type of administration were obliged to pass a much larger body of remedial legislation, on the average, than the states of the other group.'[46]

The confiscation laws enacted in New York were among the most extreme, even vindictive,[47] of any that were approved by the other twelve American states. The justification for their harshness, according to the preamble of the resolution empowering Commissioners to sequester land, was that 'diverse ill- disposed persons ... have joined our cruel and inveterate foes and the effects of such persons ... are liable to waste or maybe employed for wicked purposes within this State ... or consist of goods & merchandise useful to the well affected inhabitants of the same.'[48] The fact that throughout the War New York City was occupied by British troops almost certainly added to the severity of the measures adopted. All in all, the state confiscated 1 million acres of land. To carry out the 1779 law, three 'Commissioners of Forfeiture' were appointed in each of New York's four districts—the southern district encompassed New York, Kings, Queens, Richmond, Suffolk, and Westchester counties; the middle district included Dutchess, Orange, and Ulster counties; the western district was made up of Albany and Tryon (renamed Montgomery, in 1784) counties; and the eastern district, which covered Charlotte (renamed Washington) County, as well as Gloucester and Cumberland counties, though the latter

[46] Ibid., pp. 272–273.

[47] 'Thomas Jones, a lawyer and representative of the loyalist cause, attested to this description, finding that the most prevalent loyalist complaint focused on the idea that the government, under military control, was confiscating loyalist property for their own "ease, pleasure, diversion, and emolument." Furthermore, there were no courts that would hear their cases except for those "arbitrary, illegal, despotic, and unconstitutional Courts, called "Courts of Police."'' D. Hulsebosch, *Constituting Empire: New York and the Transformation of Constitutionalism in the Atlantic World, 1664–1830* (Chapel Hill: University of North Carolina Press, 2005), 160–163.

[48] Ibid., p. 598. 'The commissioners seized more than just land; they claimed the entire contents of confiscated estate. These included, bushels of wheat, com, rye, and barley; mill stones; wheat still growing in the ground; blankets; joiners' tools; an anvil; a pair of tongs; sleighs; tackling for the sleighs; a yoke of oxen; ten sheep; a sow; a sow with pigs; five looms; a piece of polished tin; a pair of stockings; axes; three sloops; windows and doors stripped out of houses; a single stick of ash wood. The Commissioners also offered more elegant items: table linens, feather beds, costume jewellery, mahogany desks, silver plate, mirrors, bolts of finished cloth, even a jacket for £20, which was more than the going rate for an ox.'

two were part of Vermont, which had seceded from New York in 1777.[49] The final verdict on the policies pursued by New York was that they were not only the most aggressive but in consequence of which suffered from 'inefficiency, clashes of a jurisdictional character, and confusion as inescapable concomitants.'[50]

The peace treaty that ended the War was first published in New York on 26 March 1783. Only two articles in the Treaty addressed Loyalist interests. Article Five provided for the restitution of the confiscated property of British subjects, 'and therein to remain twelve months unmolested in their endeavours to obtain the restitution of such of their estates, rights, and properties as may have been confiscated; and that Congress shall also earnestly recommend to the several states a reconsideration and revision of all acts or laws regarding the premises, so as to render the said laws or acts perfectly consistent not only with justice and equity but with that spirit of conciliation which on the return of the blessings of peace should universally prevail. And that Congress shall also earnestly recommend to the several states that the estates, rights, and properties, of such last mentioned persons shall be restored to them, they refunding to any persons who may be now in possession the bona fide price (where any has been given) which such persons may have paid on purchasing any of the said lands, rights, or properties since the confiscation.'

The Sixth article was intended to guard the Loyalists against any future persecutions or confiscations, as well as to allow for their release from confinement after the treaty was ratified: 'there shall be no future confiscations made nor any prosecutions commenced against any person or persons for, or by reason of, the part which he or they may have taken in the present war, and that no person shall on that account suffer any future loss or damage, either in his person, liberty, or property; and that those who

[49] M. Boonshoft, "Dispossessing Loyalists and Redistributing Property in Revolutionary New York," New York Public Library (September 19, 2016). '[It has been estimated that] "Two-thirds of the property of New York was supposed to belong to the Tories."' If this statement be intended to include the crown lands, as well as the forfeited estates, it is undoubtedly true. Approximating the total sales from the partial sales which are left, it seems fair to conclude that the state received one million two hundred and sixty thousand pounds in standard money, or three million one hundred and fifty thousand dollars in Spanish coin, from the sale of forfeited real estate. The total loss for personal and real estate would be nearly three million six hundred thousand dollars.' Flick, 'Loyalism in New York,' Chapter 7.

[50] Allen, 'Confiscations,' p. 270.

may be in confinement on such charges at the time of the ratification of the treaty in America shall be immediately set at liberty, and the prosecutions so commenced be discontinued.' In practice, things worked out rather differently: congressional restrictions meant the States were free to ignore all such recommendations, to harass any Loyalists that remained within their borders, and bar them from entering their state. Understandably, Loyalists regarded the peace treaty as a betrayal of their cause.[51]

[51] Library of Congress, *Treaty of Paris: Primary Documents in American History* (accessed at: https://www.loc.gov/law/help/us-treaties/bevans/b-gb-ust000012-0008.pdf). 'Their support helped Britain's war effort considerably. But Britain never trusted or fully used its Loyalist allies, and after the war, Britain offered Loyalists only limited financial support. The majority reintegrated into the new United States, promising to be good citizens and to support the national project they had opposed,' R, Brannon, "Loyalists and the American Revolution," *Oxford Research Encyclopaedia, American History* (2021). On the reintegration of Loyalists post-Treaty of Paris see A. Coleman, "Loyalists in War, Americans in Peace: The Reintegration of the Loyalists, 1775–1800" (doctoral dissertation, University of Kentucky, 2008). Benjamin Franklin expressed a different and more popular view: 'The enormities committed by [the Loyalists], under the direction of British generals, but of those committed by the British troops themselves, will form a record that must render the British name odious in America to the latest generations. In that authentic record will be found, the burning of the fine towns of Charlestown, near Boston, of Falmouth just before winter, when the sick, the aged, the women, and children, were driven to seek shelter where they could hardly find it; of Norfolk, in the midst of winter; of New London, of Fairfield, of Esopus, &c &c besides near a hundred and fifty miles of well settled country laid waste, every house and barn burnt, and many hundred of farmers, with their wives and children, butchered and scalped.' Franklin to Richard Oswald, Esq., (November 26, 1782). Franklin then proposed that the claims on both sides be submitted to commissioners for their determination of the total losses and that the side with lesser losses compensate the other. *The Papers of Benjamin Franklin,* Vol. 38, *August 16, 1782, through January 20, 1783,* (Ed.) Ellen R. Cohn (New Haven and London: Yale University Press, 2006), p. 350.

CHAPTER 13

Repudiation

Loyalists were not the only ones to have suffered during the Revolutionary War; British merchants, who had extended vast amounts of credit, mainly for the purchase of British manufacturers, were similarly affected. The disposition of debts incurred by Americans to British creditors prior to the American Revolution long remained a contentious issue between the two countries. Americans railed against the repayment of British debts, as a series of resolutions proposed in June 1783 in Halifax County, Virginia, attest. 'The payment of debts contracted before the Revolution (as unprecedented and ruinous) to the suffering citizens of this state, who, we think, are unable to comply with comply with the demands, without producing great injury to the state itself. The debts of the British merchants are equally forfeited with their rights of property among us, and we can never consent that the good citizens of this state shall lay at the mercy of British creditors on account of such debts; neither do we think that there is any authority in the laws to compel the payment of such debts to British subjects.'[1]

British creditors, by contrast, demanded repayment of outstanding debts either in sterling or in specie, and not in the depreciated local currency. They likewise baulked at the actions taken by some state authorities,

[1] I. Harrell, *Loyalism in Virginia* (Duke University Press, 1926), p. 129. The resolutions were in response to the Treaty of Paris' requirements concerning the repayment of debts owed to British creditors.

G. Pollio, *The Rise and Fall of Britain's North American Empire*,
https://doi.org/10.1007/978-3-031-07484-4_13

most notably in Virginia, that in practice amounted to de facto repudiation. The most conspicuous example was the confiscation of Loyalist property that adversely affected the security interests of British creditors; other measures included debt sequestration, that is, paying the amounts owed into respective state treasuries,[2] or barring or restricting the ability of creditors and their representatives to collect debts. The sums involved (including accrued interest) were considerable, amounting in total to £4.9 million pounds (with a current value of *c.* £1 billion or $1.4 billion). Southern states collectively owed four-fifths of the total amount outstanding, with Virginia alone accounting for more than half that total.[3] Among the Middle Atlantic and New England states, only Pennsylvania and Massachusetts owed substantial sums to British creditors. One other significant feature of the table is that virtually the entire amount outstanding was owed by Virginia's most prominent citizens and leading revolutionaries whose debts, according to Virginia law, could be discharged in local currency as opposed to specie or pounds sterling, which had been and remained in short supply.

The demand for repayment in sterling or specie derived from the high rates of inflation that affected Virginia and most of the other former colonies. The resulting inflation, higher in Virginia and other states with large outstanding debts to British creditors, quite obviously eased the real burden of repayment. Virginia's currency depreciated by 10.7 per cent per month during the war years, and in the last few months of the inflation, the rate of increase came close to meeting the current definition of hyperinflation (50 per cent or more per month). Many prominent

[2] Virginia's Bill for Sequestering British Property (13 January 1778) states with respect to debts incurred prior to the Revolution that 'it shall and may be lawful for any Citizen of this Commonwealth owing money to a subject of Great Britain, to pay the same, or any part thereof, from time to time, as he shall think fit, into the said continental loan-Office taking thereout a certificate for the same in the name of the Creditor, with an endorsement under the hand of the Commissioner of the said Office, expressing the name of the payer, and shall deliver such certificate to the Governor and Council, whose receipt shall discharge him from so much of the debt.' *Papers of Thomas Jefferson*, Vol. 2, *1777–1718 June 1779*, J. Boyd (Ed.). (Princeton, NJ: Princeton University Press, 1950), pp. 168–171. *Ware v. Hylton* 3 U.S. 199 (1796) invalidated a Virginia law allowing Virginia residents Revolutionary War debts to British creditors to be paid off in depreciated currency or confiscated property and affirmed the terms of the federally negotiated Treaty of Paris (1783), establishing the principle that federal treaties always take precedence over conflicting state laws.

[3] S. Bemis, *Jay's Treaty: A Study in Commerce and Diplomacy* (New York, NY: Macmillan and Co.mpany, 1926), p. 103 fn. 18.

Virginians—including Thomas Jefferson, who owed British and Scottish creditors an estimated ten thousand pounds—availed themselves of this option; an additional five hundred less prominent debtors did likewise.[4] Some of these debts involved mortgages financed by British firms; the bulk, however, were incurred in connection with the purchase of merchandise,[5] further evidence of the planters' extravagant lifestyle and the willingness, even eagerness, with which British merchants were willing to allow Virginia planters to finance luxury purchases with credit. On the other hand, it reduced the amount of debt owed to Virginians, while lowering the value of their leases. The fact that George Washington lamented that 'it is much to be wished that remedy could be applied to the depreciation of our currency' provides an indication of his net financial position, in contrast to those like, say, Alexander Hamilton or Tom Paine, who regarded inflation as both a necessity and reasonable substitute for taxation.[6]

On the other hand, Harrell's claim that the sizeable debts owed to British creditors was a major source of local discontent and revolutionary support merely recapitulated Beard's earlier argument to the same effect,[7] a perspective challenged long ago and discarded by later research.[8] Evans

[4] Recent research indicates that initially there was little enthusiasm for Virginia's loan sequestration law. Unless moved by patriotism, debtors had little incentive to pay since British creditors could not recover from them during the war. The measure was initially intended as fiscal measure, not unlike a public loan, to help restore the parlous condition of the state's finances. 'The great depreciation of the paper money, however, soon made it possible for Virginians to pay off their debts at a fraction of their real value. Not surprisingly most of the payments occurred during the last two months of the act, when the depreciation was sixty to one.' But the more important point is that 'even at the height of the depreciation, the number of debtors taking advantage of the sequestration law was strikingly small. Of those who did, some undoubtedly saw an easy opportunity to escape their indebtedness. Others simply tried to protect themselves by depositing in the loan office the depreciated paper which they as creditors were required by law to accept from their own debtors.' C. Hobson, "The Recovery of British Debts in the Federal Circuit Court of Virginia, 1790 to 1797," *Virginia Magazine of History and Biography*, **92** (1984) 176–200, p. 178.

[5] Ibid., p. 28.

[6] D. Stabile, *The Origins of American Public Finance* (Westport, CT: Westwood Press, 1998), p. 24.

[7] (It) 'is generally known, the debts due to British merchants and other private citizens constituted one of the powerful causes leading to the Revolution,' C. Beard, *Economic Origins of Jeffersonian Democracy* (New York, NY: Macmillan, 1915) p. 270.

[8] 'If indebtedness had any relationship to the coming of the Revolution other than as a political weapon to secure a change in British policy, it was certainly as no more than an

argues that non-repayment was more a matter of pressuring the British Parliament to reconsider its policies towards the colonies, in effect, the financial analogue to the nonimportation and boycotts of English goods. Even as late as April 1775, Richard Randolph, a prominent Virginia planter, wrote his British creditors in March 1775, that 'we are endeavoring as much as ever for a Crop of Tobacco in hopes of a favourable measure being adopted by your Rulers respecting the Colonys (sic) as we sincerely wish to continue in the Old Chanel having the greatest aversion to the new mode lately prescribed by them.'[9]

There was always some question as to whether such measures were lawful or valid. Thomas Jefferson thought they were; Alexander Hamilton, by contrast, took the opposite view. Although written many years after Virginia's debt sequestration legislation was enacted, there is little doubt that these views were consistent with Hamilton's underlying principles long before Jay's Treaty was drafted and debated.

> [T]hose 'who represent the confiscation or sequestration of debts as our best means of retaliation and coercion, as our most powerful and sometimes our means of defence. So degrading an idea will be rejected with disdain by every man who feels a true and well informed national pride; by every man who recollects and glories, that in a state of still greater immaturity we achieved independence without the aid of this expedient. The federal Government had no power on the subject; but the reverse of this is truly the case. The Federal government alone had power. The State governments had none, though some of them undertook to exercise it. This position is founded on the solid ground that the confiscation or sequestration of the debts of an enemy is a high act of reprisal and war, necessarily an exclusively and incident to the power of making war, which was always with the Federal Government.'[10]

It is generally accepted that Hamilton, not Jay, was the author of the 1794 Treaty—he was as Secretary of the Treasury responsible for the

unconscious and unarticulated conditioning element that helped to make Virginians more receptive to rebellion and independence.' E. Evans, "Planter Indebtedness and the Coming of the Revolution in Virginia," *William and Mary Quarterly*, **19** (1962) 511–533, p. 533.

[9] E. Evans, "Planter Indebtedness and the Coming of the Revolution in Virginia," *William and Mary Quarterly*, **19** (1962) 511–533, p. 532.

[10] A. Hamilton, *A Defence of the Treaty of Amity, Commerce, and Navigation, entered into between the United States of America & Great Britain, as it has appeared in the papers under the signature of Camillus, Hamilton. Alexander,1757–1804, King, Rufus, 1755–1827., Jay, John, 1745–1829* (New York: Francis Childs and Co., 1795), p. 106.

preliminary negotiations on its behalf, for Jay's negotiating instructions, and most significantly, the substantial effort to elicit support for what became the most controversial foreign relations effort of Washington's presidency[11]—since the views expressed therein are imbued with pro-British Federalist sentiment and that as a banker, lawyer, and resident of New York there is little reason to suppose he would side on such matters with southern planters.[12] Indeed, his principal opponents were Jefferson and Madison, both of Virginia, while the former was unable to impose upon the latter to write a critique of Hamilton's views; Madison refused to do so because Hamilton's 'impassioned defence, (was) so intimidatingly comprehensive,' that the effort was pointless.[13]

The Treaty of Paris officially ended the war between Britain and its former American colonies. Britain's primary interest in these negotiations was to ensure the new Republic's neutrality, which goes a long way towards explaining Britain's lax position vis-à-vis both the confiscated property of Loyalists and the impairment of debts. The government counted on international norms and opinion to persuade America to make a just debt settlement, and therefore gave its negotiators ample leeway on the issue. For their part, the Americans were unwilling to make debts part of any settlement. Indeed, the initial draft of the treaty made no mention of debts. The British cabinet rejected that draft insisting the American negotiators address debt collection, to include in addition to the principal amount outstanding, interest accumulated during the course of the War, and other economic issues. In due course, the American negotiators came around to accepting the principle as acknowledged in the Treaty's Article Four: 'It is agreed that Creditors on either Side shall meet with no lawful Impediment

[11] 'Hamilton understood that the Jay Treaty was the best a new nation could expect from a world power, which was not obligated in the least to even consider its trading rights let alone treat with it like an equal. Hamilton's defense did not work its usual immediate magic: Washington thought on it for several weeks before signing the document and putting into effect what was essentially Hamilton's treaty,' L. de Carolis, *A Biography of Alexander Hamilton, 1755–1804* (accessed at: http://www.let.rug.nl/usa/biographies/alexander-hamilton/).

[12] 'For Hamilton, the Jay Treaty victory represented the culmination of his work with Washington. By settling all outstanding issues left over from the Revolution, the treaty removed the last impediments to improved relations with England and promised sustained prosperity,' R. Chernow, *Alexander Hamilton* (Penguin Books, (2004), p. 500.

[13] J. Alvarez, "Alexander Hamilton's Defense of Foreign Capital," New York University, Institute for International Law and Justice, 2017 (accessed at: https://www.iilj.org/working-papers/alexander-hamiltons-defense-foreign-capital/).

to the Recovery of the full Value in Sterling Money of all bona fide Debts heretofore contracted.'

Owing to an increase in tensions between the United States and Great Britain, arising from the presence of military posts located in America's north-western territory, the encouragement of Indian attacks against settlers, its refusal to move forward with a trade treaty, the seizure of American merchant vessels,[14] and so forth, all of which, the British insisted, were justified by America's failure to comply with the terms of the Treaty of Paris. Nor was there constructive engagement over the issue of debt. In fact, individual States resumed their former harassment of creditors by, inter alia, closing their courts to debt cases, denying admission to creditors and their agents, disallowing the accumulation of interest during the war, and terminating debts, nor were they willing as noted *supra* to restore the confiscated property of Loyalists, as prescribed by the Treaty's Article Five. However, once the US constitution established a Supreme Court and declared treaties to be the law of the land, federal courts began to adjudicate debt cases in accordance with the Treaty of Paris. Even so, the deterioration of relations was especially acute from 1792 to 1793, which prompted the negotiation of a second treaty designed to avoid war, improve commercial relations between the two nations, and repay debts contracted prior to the War.

The resulting agreement—officially titled 'Treaty of Amity Commerce and Navigation, between His Britannic Majesty; and The United States of America' and less formally as Jay's Treaty—was signed on 19 November 1794. Jay was only partially successful in getting Britain to meet America's demands and opposition to the treaty in the United States remained intense. The Treaty was opposed by, among others, Thomas Jefferson, John Adams, and James Madison, all three subsequent presidents of the United States, on the grounds that it made too many concessions to the

[14] Seizure of American vessels occurred against the backdrop of the war between France and England. Initially, the Order in Council (8 June 1793) permitted British commanders to stop and detain all vessels loaded wholly or in part with corn, flour, or meal, bound to any port in France, where the provisioning cargoes could be purchased by the British, and the vessels released. This Order was followed five months later by a more drastic measures directing British commanders to detain all ships carrying supplies for the use of any French colony and to bring them in as prizes for adjudication in the British court, which was subsequently superseded (8 January 1794) by a new order substantially restoring the original order of June 1793. All these orders gave rise to seizures of American ships and cargoes, notwithstanding its neutrality in the war. J. Newcomb, "New Light on Jay's Treaty," *American Journal of International Law*, **28** (1934) 685–692.

British that in practice weakened America's trade rights—including limiting trade with the British West Indies to vessels of a maximum burden of 70 tons, setting limitations on the types of goods that could be sold there, and conceding most favoured nation status to British imports without obtaining a reciprocal commitment for American exports to Britain—and committing the US government to paying off British creditors. Support for and opposition to the treaty followed along geographic lines. Merchants in large cities, such as Boston, New York, and Philadelphia, believing that ratification would benefit international trade, were among the treaty's most important supporters. They were, moreover, less affected by the treaty's mandate requiring repayment of debts owed to British creditors than were, say, southern planters, who largely opposed the measure. Although the American President, George Washington, was similarly disappointed with the treaty's provisions, he felt it offered the best hope to avert war with Great Britain and submitted it to the Senate for approval. The Treaty passed the Senate on 24 June 1795, by a vote of 20 to 10, precisely the two-thirds required for approval.[15]

Jay's Treaty lengthy Article 6 goes well beyond the terse commitment made in the Treaty of Paris, in effect, setting out the terms upon which the US government would compensate British creditors for pre-War debts. The first section committed the United States to compensate British creditors resulting from Americans who through 'various lawful impediments ... not only the full recovery of the said debts has been delayed but also the value and security thereof have been, in several instances, impaired and lessened, so that by the ordinary course of judicial proceedings, the British creditors cannot now obtain, and actually have and receive full and adequate compensation for the losses and damages which they have thereby sustained.' The amount of any such losses or damages are to be

[15] 'By taking an early public role in the campaign, providing direction and encouragement to others, and using the powers of his office to shape public opinion and withhold the treaty from Congress until the effects of the pro-treaty campaign had run their course, Washington guided and shaped the ultimate result. At every turn, the president provided strong, forceful leadership—both in public and behind the scenes—calling on the vast reserves of goodwill most Americans had for him and deploying with great skill and impeccable timing the discretionary powers he had regarding submission of the treaty. On this matter, Washington stood tall, and the case of the treaty debate offers not only convincing evidence of his leadership in this matter but also forces a reconsideration of the larger questions of the first president and the effectiveness of his presidential leadership.' T. Estes, "The Art of Presidential Leadership: George Washington and the Jay Treaty," *Virginia Magazine of History and Biography*, **109** (2001) 127–158, p. 158.

determined by a commission comprised of five members, 'two of whom are to be appointed by his Majesty, two by the President of the United States with the advice and consent of the Senate, and the fifth by the unanimous vote of the other four. The award of the Commission, or of any three of them, shall in all cases be final and conclusive, both as to the justice of the claim and to the amount of the sum to the sum to be paid to the creditor or claimant ... the sum so awarded to be paid in specie.'[16]

The five-member commission sat at Philadelphia from May 1797 to July 1799, when the Americans walked out during a particularly bitter debate. The commissioners were unable to agree on such matters as the commission's jurisdiction, the nature of legal impediments, the question of the solvency of debtors, and wartime interest on the debts. A settlement was finally negotiated by Rufus Kingand Henry Addington, the-then British Prime minister. In January 1802, King convinced the British government to accept a payment of £600,000 from the United States for the full satisfaction of all claims recoverable at the end of the Revolutionary War that could not be recouped through ordinary legal procedures. US courts in the future would, furthermore, be open to British creditors. A British commission sat until 1811 adjusting the claims and found that only *c.* 20–25 per cent of the claims were valid. Even so, it was able to pay with the £600,000, only about 45 per cent of the approved claims.[17]

Although considerably less than the amounts claimed by the merchants, far more important was that it reaffirmed the fourth article of the earlier Paris peace treaty, which in its future operation was 'to be binding and obligatory.' American courts, moreover, remained open to British creditors for the recovery of their old debts, and the reaffirmation of the fourth article promised to place them on a more secure footing than they had been during the preceding two decades. In keeping with this new understanding, the Supreme Court soon disallowed the statute of limitations as a defence against recovery. This ultimate resolution of the British debts issue by means of a public diplomatic settlement and continued private litigation 'reflected the dual political and legal dimensions of the controversy that had been present since the beginning.'[18]

[16] Library of Congress, *A Century of Lawmaking for a New Nation: U.S. Congressional Documents and Debate, 1774–1875*, pp. 119–120. (accessed at: https://memory.loc.gov/cgi-bin/ampage?collId=llsl&fileName=008/llsl008.db&recNum=133).

[17] W. Williams, "British Debts," in W. Powell (Ed.) *Encyclopaedia of North Carolina* (University of North Carolina Press, 2006).

[18] Hobson, 'Recovery of British Debts,' p. 200.

CHAPTER 14

Foreign Loans

The second potential source of support, namely, foreign financial and material support, which in due course were to become increasingly important (Table 14.1). In the war's early stages, foreign involvement was minimal and would remain so as long as the outcome of the conflict was in doubt. Only as the odds favouring an eventual American victory improved was there an increased willingness on the part of European creditors—mainly the Netherlands,[1] and France, with a token contribution from Spain—to provide significant amounts of debt, mainly in the form of loans

[1] Dutch-American relations stemmed from two sources: trade and finance. 'Already before 1775 Dutch smugglers were providing (Americans) with arms and ammunition. The free-trade island of St. Eustatius played an enormous role in the support of the colonies. History books often mention only the French supply, but it should be noted that long before the much-advertised house of Hortalez & Cie was even founded, the Dutch were sending the American rebels all they needed. Moreover, the Americans were of course very much interested in Dutch money. Amsterdam bankers were still the moneylenders of the world, and there was nothing the revolutionaries needed so much as money. That was finally the chief motive for John Adams' visit to Holland in the summer of 1780.' J. Schulte Nordholt, "The Recognition of the United States by the Dutch Republic," *Proceedings of the Massachusetts Historical Society*, 94 (1982) 37–48, p. 38.

On the background to the foreign loans see A. Bolles, *Financial History of the United States from 1774–1789*. Third Edition (New York, NY: D. Appleton and Company, 1892), Chapter 17.

G. Pollio, *The Rise and Fall of Britain's North American Empire*,
https://doi.org/10.1007/978-3-031-07484-4_14

Table 14.1 Foreign debt and arrears, 1 January 1790

Loans from Farmers-General of France		153,688
French loan of 18,000,000 livres		3,267,000
Loan from Spain in 1781		174,017
French loan of 10,000,000 livres		1,815,000
Holland loan of 1782		2,000,000
French loan of 6 million livres		1,089,000
Holland loan of 1784		800,000
Holland loan of 1787		400,000
Holland loan of 1788		400,000
Total principle of foreign loans		10,098,705
Due France for military supplies		24,332
Arrears of interest, 1 January 1790		1,640,069
Of which:		
Five-year interest on 6 million livres @5%	$277,777	
Six-year interest on 18 million livres @5%	99,999	
Four-year interest on 10 million livres @4%	296,296	
Spanish loan, seven-year interest on $174,000 @5% arrears thru 1782	65,997	
Total Principal and Arrears		11,763,106

Source: P. M. Garber, "Alexander Hamilton's Market-based Debt Reduction Plan," *Carnegie-Rochester Conference Series on Public Policy* **35** (1991) 79–104, Table 2, p. 85

and subsidies and, in France's case, direct military aid. France and Holland each accounted for *c.* one-half of the face value of outstanding debt; including other claims and interest arrears, France accounted for three-fifths of the Republic's total $11.8 million total outstanding debt.[2]

One of the ostensible benefits of foreign credits was that their cost was lower than the interest rate applicable to loans raised in the domestic market. In a 1783 report to Congress, Robert Morris, Superintendent of Finance during the Confederation period, noted that the 'foreign debt

[2] An alternative estimate of financial support based upon French diplomatic sources amounted to 34 million livres ($7 million) in loans as well as 12 million livres ($2 million) in gifts and interest arrears, representing *c.* 20 per cent the total receipts of the French state in 1787, a difference of 15 per cent compared with Graber's estimate. If gifts are excluded the difference amounts are virtually identical, A. Potofsky, "The Political Economy of the French-American Debt Debate: The Ideological Uses of Atlantic Commerce, 1787 to 1800," *William and Mary Quarterly*, **63** (2006) 489–516, p. 493.

drew four and five percent and the domestic debt one percent more.'[3] Interest charges, however, constitute only one element of borrowing costs, the other being commission charges. While fees on early Dutch loans actually exceeded interest costs, they declined sharply but, with one exception, never amounted to less than 4 per cent. It is understandable why foreign financial markets imposed higher overall charges on American loans. For one thing, until the adoption of the Constitution in 1789, the American government lacked the authority to impose taxes. Instead, it had to rely upon revenue quotas assigned to individual states (but lacked the power to compel a state to meet its quota) and land sales. And even after Congress was authorised to raise taxes, things remained as before with most borrowed funds being used to cover current deficits, pay interest charges, and amortise outstanding debts. 'From 1789 through 1795 American spending for current operations and interest payments alone regularly equalled or exceeded tax revenues. Through 1794 those two areas surpassed the cumulative total of tax revenues by $20.8 to $18.2 million, and all spending exceeded tax revenues by $33.2 to $18.2 million.'[4]

France was not only the main source of foreign loans but even willing to provide funds on novel terms that were vital for averting disruptions to the war effort. In this regard, France proposed, in 1781, to underwrite and to guarantee unconditionally an offering of roughly $1.8 million of US securities in the Amsterdam market. As underwriters, the French government advanced the entire proceeds of the proposed Dutch issue to US agents a few months before plans were finalised to offer the securities on the Amsterdam market, thus permitting the immediate purchase of military supplies for shipment across the Atlantic. 'The Amsterdam offering subsequently hit a snag when private investors showed disdain for the French guarantee, and the Dutch government had to be called in to act as a second, joint guarantor.'[5]

French motives for supporting the American cause were more complex than redressing the country's military defeat and territorial losses in the Seven Years (French and Indian) War. Being traditional enemies, whatever weakened England militarily, of course, benefitted France. Years ago, the

[3] A. Bolles, *The Financial History of the United States, from 1774–1789*, Volume One, (New York, NY: D. Appleton & Co., 1879), p. 317.

[4] Riley, 'Foreign Credit,' p. 666.

[5] E. Perkins, *American Public Finance and Financial Services, 1700–1815* (Columbus, OH: Ohio State University Press, 1994) p.105

American historian Edward Corwin provided a succinct summary of the regime's motives:

> France's intervention in the American Revolution is often described as an act of revenge. The description is less erroneous than incomplete, for while it calls to mind the fact that France had humiliations to be redressed, it fails to indicate the even more important fact that she had also a role to be retrieved. Furthermore, it leaves entirely out of account the logic by which, in an Age of Reason, the purpose of either revenge or restoration was brought into relation with a concrete situation. The line of reasoning by which France was brought into the American Revolution comprised for the most part the following ideas: that France was entitled by her wealth, power, and history, to the preponderating influence in Continental affairs; that she had lost this position of influence largely on account of Great Britain's inter-meddling; that Great Britain had been enabled to mingle in Continental concerns by virtue of her great naval strength, her commercial prosperity, and her preparedness to maintain Continental subsidiaries; that these in turn were due in great part to her American colonial empire and especially to the policies controlling her trade therewith; that America, become independent, would be an almost total loss from the point of view of British interests; that this loss would mean a corresponding- diminution of British power; that since the two were rivals, whatever abased the power of Great Britain would elevate the power of France. This, from the point of view of France's chief objective in intervening in the Revolution.'[6]

One unintended (but not unanticipated) consequence of French support for American independence was that it contributed to undermining the monarchy, unleashing the second major popular revolution of the eighteenth century. It was not so much the commitments per se that mattered, but rather the fact they were undertaken against the backdrop of previous large military expenditure connected with the Seven Years War. In short, French finances were already parlous, with the large sums paid out to support the American Revolution adding to the county's underlying financial distress. The importance of these pre-existing debts is often ignored in traditional historiography, as illustrated by the following quote.

[6] E, Corwin, "The French Objective in the American Revolution," *American Historical Review*, **21** (1915) 33–61, pp. 59–60.

'If it was financial difficulty which forced the king to convene the States-General of 1789, then the American war must bear a heavy responsibility for the French Revolution. Some French historians have therefore bitterly regretted the intervention of France in the American Revolution.' Marcel Marion wrote in 1914, "Due to the wretched condition of French finances, a long war led France to the abyss." An American historian (Samuel Bemis) has likewise written that "if Louis XVI had followed Turgot's advice in 1776 he might not have lost his head in 1793."[7] Settlement of debts owed to France was approved by the Secretary of the Treasury in 1795, and made in the form of domestic US bonds, $1.8 million in certificates bearing interest from 1 January 1796, at the rate of 5.5 per cent, in lieu of an equal sum due at 5 per cent; $176,000 in certificates bearing interest at 4.5 per cent also from the same period in lieu of the portion at 4 per cent, and a cash payment of $64.04. These certificates were promptly liquidated, the proceeds used for gathering and forwarding supplies to France.

It is well known that Turgot, the-then controller-general of finances, had strongly advised the King to refrain from intervention in American affairs because he anticipated the catastrophic consequences it would have on royal finances.[8] Adding further to French financial pressures was that

[7] Debt management practices in France were inferior those of Great Britain in consequence of which the cost of debt was far higher for in France thus adding further to its financial difficulties. 'The market expected default, was paid in advance for it, and received it in every crisis until 1788. Louis XVI rejected the practice. Without it, the old system could not last. A satisfying historical explanation of why he opted for calling up the Estates General instead of renouncing some of his more expensive debts would go far toward explaining the true causes of the French Revolution,' F. Velde and D. Weir, "The Financial Market and Government Debt Policy in France, 1746–1793," *Journal of Economic History*, **52** (1992) 1–39, p. 39.

[8] R. Harris, 'French Finances and the American War,' *Journal of Modern History*, **48** (1976) 233–258, p. 233. See also the earlier study by J. Perkins, "France and the American Revolution," *Proceedings of the New York State Historical Association*, 4 (1904) 74–78. 'Would the French Revolution have come in 1789 had it not been for the impression produced on French thought by the successful revolution in America, and the increasing embarrassment of the French treasury resulting from the cost of that war? Certainly the old regime could not have lasted much longer, but its overthrow might have been delayed' (p. 74). Settlement of debts owed to France was approved by the Secretary of the Treasury in 1795, was made in the form of domestic bonds of the United States, $1,848,900 in certificates bearing interest from January 1, 1796, at the rate of 5.5 per cent, in lieu of an equal sum due at 5 per cent; also $176,000 in certificates bearing interest at 4.5 per cent also from the same

the financially hard-pressed US government had difficulty servicing its foreign loans. It ceased making interest payments on the French debt in 1785 and defaulted on further instalments that were due in 1787. Americans were more punctilious in respect of their financial obligations to the Dutch since Amsterdam was then, after London, a major centre of European finance and thus might be required to provide additional loans in the future should they be needed by the new Republic, as indeed occurred in during Alexander Hamilton's tenure as Secretary of the Treasury.

As a result of Hamilton's financial reforms, there was a steady flow of foreign capital directed towards the United States, manifest most clearly in the substantial amount of Federal debt held by Europeans. Samuel Blodget, relying on Treasury and other data, estimated that by 1803 more than half of the debt of $81 million (which included $11.25 million in US securities paid to France that year for the Louisiana Purchase) was held in Europe, mostly by English and Dutch investors. Blodget also found that more than three-fifths of the stock of the Bank of the United States (another Hamiltonian innovation) was held by European investors.[9]

Unlike Albert Gallatin, his successor—who believed that debt should be paid off in full and avoided in the future—Hamilton felt that by relying upon financial markets, not only would the government be able to raise funds on favourable terms but it would also attract the large capital inflows essential for national economic development.[10] His views on financial matters were shaped largely by the experience of the British government during the Seven Years War. Because British bonds, issued through the Bank of England, traded freely in the market, the government was able to borrow at lower rates than its larger rival France. 'The French by contrast,

period in lieu of the portion at 4 percent, and a cash payment of $64.04. These certificates were promptly disposed of for cash, for gathering and forwarding supplies to France.' Newcomb, 'New Light on Jay's Treaty,' pp. 391–392.

[9] S. Blodget, *Economoica: A Statistical Manuel for the United States of America* (City of Washington:1806). Sylla concludes that one of the main reasons behind large-scale foreign capital inflows was 'the ready markets they commanded in U.S. cities,' R. Sylla, "U.S. Securities Markets and the Banking System, 1790–1840," Federal Reserve Bank of St. Louis *Review* (May–June 1998) 83–98, p. 88.

[10] 'It is ... an advantage peculiar to domestic loans that they give stability to Government by combining the interests of moneyed men for its support and consequently in this Country a domestic debt would greatly contribute to that Union, which seems not to have been sufficiently attended to, or provided for in the forming the national compact.' C. Day, 'Hamilton's Law and Finance—Borrowing from the Brits (And the Dutch),' 2019.' (Accessed at: file:///C:/Users/rosin/Downloads/SSRN-id3428606%20(1).pdf).

were reduced to begging or stealing. As Bishop Berkeley put it, credit was "the principal advantage which England hath over France." The French economist Isaac de Pinto agreed: "It was the failure of credit in time of need that did mischief, and probably was the chief cause of the late disasters." Behind every British naval victory stood the National Debt; its growth from £74 million to £133 million during the Seven Years War—was the measure of Britain's financial might.'[11]

Hamilton's financial programme is best understood as an attempt to ameliorate or eliminate the limitations imposed upon Congress by the Articles of Confederation. During the 1780s, merchant groups organised three banks—the first ones in the United States—in Philadelphia, New York, and Boston. Two received corporate charters from their state legislatures, but New York's bank waited until 1791 for this privilege. These were isolated, local banks; there was no banking system. States serviced the debts they had incurred in the War of Independence, sometimes by raising taxes and sometimes by printing bills of credit, fiat paper money that had long colonial-era precedents. The domestic US debts incurred by Congress during the war were essentially un-serviced 'junk' bonds, with interest payments due settled by issuing more IOUs because the Confederation Congress lacked the power to raise revenue through taxation. Foreign debts were serviced by means of new loans from European investors, who had an interest in rolling over their previous American loans and probably hoped for a favourable turn in the new nation's finances.[12]

Largely as a result of Hamilton's initiatives, the United States was able to develop well-functioning financial markets, which, in turn, attracted a significant volume of foreign capital. What was the principal attraction of the American market to foreign investors? Three broad criteria have long been recognised as essential for smoothly functioning financial markets, all of which were addressed in Hamilton's financial programme: (1) the credibility in the debtor's commitment to honour its promises; (2) the role of national banks in facilitating the development of a national debt; and (3) the extent and depth of financial and monetary innovations.[13] Hamilton's

[11] Cited in ibid., p. 17.

[12] Sylla, 'US Securities Markets and Banking,' p. 85.

[13] M. Fartianni and F. Spinelli, "Did Genoa and Venice Kick a Financial Revolution in the Quatrocentro?" Working Paper Oesterreichische Nationalbank, Economic Studies Division

first priority was to establish a viable system of taxation to fund the government. 'Reliable and fair taxation was required for any nation. Hamilton concluded that there must be non-discrimination regarding creditors, that is, all creditors would have the debt securities honoured at face value.'[14] The federal government would assume all the state debt at par value, making investors dependent upon the federal government for payment and strengthening the union. A national or central bank was created along the lines of the Bank of England. The Bank of the United States would monetise the debt, giving rise to strong capital markets and increasing the money supply, spurring the growth of manufacturing and commerce. Monetising the debt would enable investors to use the government bonds as collateral for new commercial purposes. First, Federal authority was exercised in 1789–1790 to raise revenue from customs duties and domestic excise taxes, the income resulting therefrom was pledged to pay interest in hard money on national and assumed state debts.

In 1790 the public debt was consolidated into three new issues of Treasury securities—6 per cent and 3 per cent issues that paid interest immediately, and a deferred 6 per cent issue that would pay interest commencing after ten years. These issues funded some $65 million of domestic debt; the $12 million of additional debts owed to foreigners, chiefly the French government and Dutch investors, was provided for separately. Second, Congress enacted Hamilton's proposal for a Bank of the United States to aid federal financial operations and exercise leadership in developing a US banking system. The last major Hamiltonian reform was enacted in 1791 to establish a mint for coining gold and silver into a dollar denominated monetary base.

One final point concerning the way the Revolutionary War was financed is worth noting. As a result of Hamilton's fiscal reforms, in that it was not until the twentieth century that the pattern of financing the War for Independence was revived. In the three subsequent nineteenth century wars—the War of 1812, the Mexican War, and the Civil War (North)—the bulk of military expenditure was covered by domestic borrowing. This is not to say that printing money was of no importance, only in the case of

(2006.). The authors that features could be found in fifteenth-century Venice and Genoa thus anticipating developments in Holland, England, and the United States centuries later.

[14] Day, 'Hamilton's Law and Finance,' p. 36. See also M. Edling and M. Kaplamoff, "Alexander Hamilton's Fiscal Reform: Transforming the Structure of Taxation in the Early Republic," *William and Mary Quarterly*, **61**, (2004) 713–744.

Mexican War (1846–1848) was it not resorted to, but rather was demoted to secondary (War of 1812) or tertiary (Civil War) importance. In three of the twentieth-century wars, the Spanish-American War (1898–1902), World War Two (1941–1945), and the Korean War (1950–1953), taxes were the main source of war finance; the remaining three twentieth-century wars were financed principally by borrowing. And while printing money remained a source of some importance in all of America's wars, Hamilton's reforms meant that it would never again be the nation's principal financial option, but rather part of a mix of policy options to be determined in keeping with the prevailing economic conditions.[15]

[15]'The one partial exception is the Vietnam War. The war … did contribute to the excessive monetary growth that characterized the late 1960s and early 1970s. But there were other factors besides the war,' H. Rockoff, "War and Inflation in the United States from the Revolution to the Forts Iraq War," Rockoff, 'War and Inflation,' p. 3, fn. 1.

CHAPTER 15

Fiat Money?

The contribution of foreign loans to the successful outcome of the Revolutionary War while important should not be overstated, as they covered less than 10 per cent of its total cost. The printing press was the principal means by which the £165 million (£30.4 billion in 2021 prices) cost of the War was financed with continental dollars from 1775 to 1779; no new emissions occurred after November 1779.[1] The first two emissions (1775) consisted of bills with denominations that ranged from $1–30; in later emissions, while large denominations continued to dominate subsequent emissions, a large tranche (45 per cent, but only 5 per cent in value terms) consisted of bills denominated as fractions of the dollar. Considering that $1 would be worth *c.* $20 in today's money, it is clear that the Revolutionary War Continentals were not initially meant to circulate as 'pocket money as, *inter alia*,' no change could be provided for transactions that would have required it. George Mason argued that without recourse to issuing currency it 'is arguable whether the War could have been won.'[2]

[1] F. Grubb, "The Continental Dollar: Initial Design, Ideal Performance, and the Credibility of Congressional Commitment," *National Bureau of Economic Research, Working Paper 17,276* (August 2011), p. 1.

[2] George Mason of Virginia, the state's delegate to the Constitutional Convention, is reported to have said referring to the Revolutionary War that it 'could not have been carried on, had such a prohibition (on the issuance of paper money) existed,' cited in F. Grubb, "State Redemption of the Continental Dollar, 1779–1790," *William and Mary Quarterly*, **69** (2012) 147–180, p. 148. In fact, the three main sources of financing for the war were

G. Pollio, *The Rise and Fall of Britain's North American Empire*,
https://doi.org/10.1007/978-3-031-07484-4_15

Before considering the volume of currency issued by the Continental Congress, three matters arise that must be addressed. The first is conceptual, how should the emissions of bills of credit be regarded, as fiat money or something else; second, unlike bills of credit issued by individual colonies, which were backed by a pledge of future tax receipts, as the Continental Congress lacked the right to levy taxes, so that those it issued could not be regarded as equivalent instruments; and third, the importance of British counterfeiting of American currency, the volume of which has yet to be determined but which nevertheless must have been considerable if the objective of the policy was to be achieved.

As to the first point, Grubb has argued that the Continental dollar was ultimately a zero-interest bearer bond, not a fiat currency. 'The public could redeem it at face value in specie at fixed future dates. Being a zero-interest bearer bond, discounting must be separated from depreciation. Before 1779 there was no depreciation, only discounting. In 1779 and again in 1780 Congress passed ex post facto laws which altered the redemption dates of past Continental dollars in ways that were not fiscally credible. These laws were the turning point. Depreciation and collapse followed.'[3]

For reasons noted above, Grubb may well be correct, but the discount rate would have to reflect both prevailing interest rates (forgone income)—at the time 6 per cent was the government's borrowing rate—and the uncertainty that either the terms of redemption would be changed or that they would never be redeemed, meaning that the discount would vary directly with the likelihood of a military victory, in which case, Continentals

direct and indirect taxes which previously had been collected by the colonial administration, printing and issuance of paper money, and (mainly shirt term) loans raised from the public. Higgins claims that the combined value of the three sources of support was sufficient to meet all expenses of the Revolutionary government (of South Carolina) prior to the siege and capitulation of Charleston to Admiral Marriot Arbuthnot and General Sir Henry Clinton on May 12, 1780; total borrowings over the same period amounted to £15.3 million. He further demonstrates the breadth of subscribers ranging from 'the extremely wealthy and powerful Gabriel Manigault to a free Negro, identified simply as Joe, who lent £1510 to the state on March 27, 1779. Large numbers of people who were not citizens of the state also provided funds to the Revolutionary government.' W. Higgins, "The South Carolina Revolutionary Debt and Its Holders, 1776–1780," *South Carolina Historical Magazine*, 72 (1971) 15–29, p. 21.

[3] F. Grubb, "The Continental Dollar: Initial Design, Ideal Performance, and the Credibility of Congressional Commitment," (accessed at: https://eh.net/eha/wp-content/uploads/2013/11/Grubb.pdf), p.1.

as bonds payable upon the successful conclusion of the War. Of course, there was no guarantee Americans would win the War, so that the greater the probability of success the smaller would be the default premium and vice versa; changes in redemption dates would likewise affect valuations. If a secondary market for such bills had existed, the magnitude of the discount could be directly determined; alternatively, fluctuations in the specie value of the Continental should provide an alternative indication of their perceived worth.

With exception, there was a more or less steady decline in the value of the continental between 1776 and 1780 when the redemption rules were changed. The exception, between April and November 1778 when the specie value of total dollar emissions rose, highlights the importance of military events, in the case to hand the American victory at Saratoga, as affecting asset valuations. They also had wider ramifications, being instrumental in encouraging the French to help finance the war and enter into a formal alliance with the Americans.[4]

Any discussion of monetary creation in Revolutionary War period must differentiate amounts authorised from the amounts outstanding. Several factors account for this difference. Some issues were intended to replace previous emissions; several issues were withdrawn; and, as noted, as a matter of policy Britain sought to further debase the American currency via counterfeiting. The actual policy was implemented in three stages: preparation and distribution of actual counterfeits of the American paper money; encouragement of Loyalists to counterfeit and pass counterfeits independently; and the production of propaganda as to the excellent quality and enormous quantity of counterfeits in circulation.[5] Josiah Bartlett, statesman and former Governor of New Hampshire, described British policy as a 'most diabolical scheme to ruin the paper currency by counterfeiting it,' noting that the fakes were 'so neatly done that it is extremely difficult to discover the difference.'[6]

[4] B. Baack, "America's First Monetary Policy: Inflation and Seigniorage during the Revolutionary War," *Financial History Review*, **15** (2008) 107–121, p. 116.

[5] E. Newman, "The Successful British Counterfeiting of American Paper Money During the American Revolution," *British Numismatic Journal*, **29** (1958) 174–187, p. 174.

[6] Josiah Bartlett to William Whipple 21 April 1777, Gilder Lehrman Collection, No. GLC00193, Gilder Lehrman Institute of American History. Towards the end of letter, Bartlett, notes 'Since so much money has been found to be counterfeit people begin to be Scrupolous (sic) of the Continental Bills, and are looking out for marks, but by reason we

While there are no direct estimates of the volume of counterfeit money produced and circulated, there is ample evidence from both sides of the Atlantic that the amounts involved were considerable; no country in the eighteenth and early nineteenth centuries, Gordon Wood wrote, 'had more of it' than America.[7] Benjamin Franklin was in no doubt as to the purpose, scale, and impact of British counterfeiting or that New York was the centre of the conspiracy. '[Paper currency] being the instrument with which we combated our enemies, they resolved to deprive us of its use by depreciating it; and the most effectual means they could contrive was to counterfeit it. The artists they employed performed so well, that immense quantities of these counterfeits, which issued from the British government in New York, were circulated among the inhabitants of all the States, before the fraud was detected. This operated considerably in depreciating the whole mass, first, by the vast additional quantity, and next by the uncertainty in distinguishing the true from the false; and the depreciation was a loss to all and the ruin of many. It is true our enemies gained a vast deal of our property by the operation; but it did not go into the hands of our particular creditors; so their demands still subsisted, and we were still abused for not paying our debts!'[8]

Knowledge of direct British involvement in the practice was brought to the attention of George Washington in 1779. Writing to the Continental Congress he reported that, 'I have received a letter from a confidential correspondent in New York … the most important part of [which] relates to the indefatigable endeavours of the enemy to increase the depreciation of our currency, by increasing its quantity of counterfeits.'[9] The

have no Standard of the former emissions, we are not able to Detect them if there are any, and I have some reason to Suspect there are Some & that they came from New York.'

[7] G. Wood, "American Dream Money," *The New York Review* (10 November 2011).

[8] 'The Retort Courteous' (1786), *The Writings of Benjamin Franklin*, Vol. 10 (Ed.) A. Smyth, (New York, NY: MacMillan Co., 1907) p. 111. Newman produces a list of colonial newspapers carrying advertisements to the effect that counterfeit Congress notes could be obtained for the price of the paper they were printed on. E. Newman, "Counterfeit Continental Currency Goes to War," *The Numismatist* (January/February 1957). One North Carolina commentator claimed that counterfeit money was so widespread that the 'only means of distinguishing the difference was said to lie in the superior execution of the spurious bills,' cited in B. Ratchford, American State Debts (Durham, N.C.: Duke University Press, 1941), p. 36.

[9] *The Writings of George Washington*, Vol. vi (Ed.) J. Sparks, (Boston, MA: Russell, Odiorne, and Metcalf, 1834), p.413. Washington expressed concern over counterfeit currency even earlier. In a letter to John Hancock (18–19 April 1777), he enclosed 'a Copy of

correspondent has not been identified but other sources confirm the validity of his report. What is known is that the Glencairn, a British ship *en route* from Glasgow to British-occupied New York, was captured by an American frigate, and the following details were sent to the Continental Congress. 'On board the Glencairn, a person says he had in charge a box, which was to be delivered to some person in New York, but upon our coming up with them and the ship striking, threw it overboard; upon which we went immediately after it, and with difficulty got it before it sunk, when upon examination we found it contained materials for counterfeiting our currency, consisting of types, paper with silk and isinglass in it &c. We have however determined to secure the person, as we believe him to be the sole intender of the villainy: The box we have on board and shall bring it with us to Boston.'[10]

Newman concludes that since New York was the Glencairn's destination 'the counterfeiting of Continental paper money was intended rather than the counterfeiting of any separate state issue. This is also corroborated by the paper containing mica and silk. The inclusion of type indicated a desire to improve the quality of counterfeits since most counterfeits of earlier Continental issues were made from engraved copper plates and were more readily distinguishable from the genuine notes than typeset counterfeits. As to whether the captured passenger was "the sole intender of the villainy" is an opinion which, no doubt, was modified by the American authorities on further investigation.'[11] Scott maintains the centrality of New York was longstanding, and while legislation was enacted making counterfeiting a capital crime, the authorities do not seem to have been successful in suppressing the practice. 'The eventual enactment of the death penalty for the crime is not surprising but rather the fact that only one conviction under that law is recorded in the minutes of the Supreme Court of New York. It is, however, quite likely that there were other convictions in the courts … where several of the cases were tried, although the records of those trials are no longer extant. Nevertheless, it

an Advertisement published in Gains paper (NY) of the 14th which shews that no Artifices are left untried by the Enemy to injure us. Before the appearance of this unparalleled peice (sic), I had heard, that a person was gone from York to Rhode Island with a Quantity of Counterfeit Money.' *Founders Online,* (National Archives, https://founders.archives.gov/documents/Washington/03-09-02-0184).

[10] E. Newman, "The Successful British Counterfeiting of American Paper Money During the American Revolution," *British Numismatic Journal,* 7 (1959) 174–8, p. 181.

[11] Ibid. Also the source for the capture of the Glencairn.

remains true that the Americans were far less successful in apprehending and prosecuting the culprits than were the British agents in disseminating the counterfeits.'[12]

There are no quantitative estimates of the impact the British policy of counterfeiting had on the American economy. Newman argued that the 'degree of effectiveness of these activities cannot be measured other than by recognizing that American paper money depreciated most when British counterfeiting activity was at its height. Following a $40 for $1 exchange ordered by the Continental Congress in 1779, the entire $200,000,000 issued by the United States of America became worthless in 1781 and has never been redeemed in whole or in part. Admittedly the quantities of authorized paper money depreciated by virtue of its own abundance, but the speed with which prices rose and paper money became unacceptable was materially stimulated by British counterfeiting activity.'[13] The British must have been satisfied with the results, as the policy was duplicated against the French. It appears to have similarly impressed Americans, as during the Civil War, Northern entrepreneurs emulated the British example by printing enormous quantities of bogus Confederate notes (Table 15.1).[14]

The above table shows the amount of 'bills of credit' issued by the Continental Congress between 1775 and 1789. Both the number and specie value of the emission fluctuated within a given year, notwithstanding the monotonic depreciation shown in the table. By the end of the period the Continental was worth about 2 cents. Baack has shown that the declining trend was reversed during the course of 1778 owing to three developments: the defeat of British forces at the battle of Saratoga (October 1777), the signing of the Franco-American alliance (February 1778), and the receipt of Lord North's peace offer two months later.[15]

[12] K. Scott, "Counterfeiting in New York during the Revolution" *New York Historical Society Quarterly*, **42** (1958) 221–260, pp. 257–258.

[13] Newman, 'British Counterfeiting,' p.174.

[14] On France see, E. Levasseur, "The Assignats: A Study, in the Finances of the French Revolution," *Journal of Political Economy*, **2** (1894) 179–202. On the Confederacy see D. Weidenmeir, "Bogus Money Matters: Sam Upham and his Confederate Counterfeiting Business," *Business and Economic History*, **28** (1999), pp. 313–324.

[15] B. Baack, "America's First Monetary Policy: Inflation and Seigniorage during the Revolutionary War," *Financial History Review*, **15** (2008) 107–121, p. 113, fig. 3.

Table 15.1 Annual supply of continental dollars, 1775–1779

Year	*Nominal amount*	*Specie value*	*Depreciation*
1775	$6,000,000	$6,000,000	1.00
1776	19,000,000	15,350,000	1.23
1777	13,000,000	4,040,000	3.23
1778	63,500,00	10,380,000	6.12
1779	180,000,000	5,270,000	34.16
Total	241,500,000	41,020,000	5.89

Source: C. Bullock, *The Finances of the United States from 1775–1789 with Special Reference to the Budget, Bulletin of the University of Wisconsin*, **1** (1895) 117–273, p. 135. Grubb revises the 1979 estimate downwards to $98.6 million, thus reducing supply to $200.05 million. F. Grubb, "The Distribution of Congressional Spending During the American Revolution, 1775–1780: The Problem of Geographic Balance" NBER Working Paper 14,267 (August 2008), p. 26, Table 3

Note: The total indicated is overstated since many notes were either withdrawn or exchanged. Bullock estimates the amount in circulation probably amounted to no more that $200 million. The total amount, which included state currency issues, and loan office certificates increased the total amount outstanding by one half, that is, $300 million

Baack argues, in keeping with McCandless' analysis,[16] that 'during the war, the single most important indicator of future government expenditures is the process of the war itself. Because of this, it is the war news and its effects on people's expectations that move currency prices and move them much more violently than actual expenditures or actual money issues do,' raising expectations of an end to the War, which given 'the Continental Congress dependent upon currency for revenue, ... (implied) lower future issues of the Continental Dollar.'[17] In the event, conciliation was rejected, the War resumed, as did further emissions causing the Continental to resume its previous declining trajectory.

Individual states likewise issued fiat money, with amounts varying from state. The amount of state paper money issues totalled just over $200 million between 1775 and 1783. Virginia alone accounted for more than four-fifths of the total; North and South Carlina were the second largest issuers. Outside of the south, Massachusetts and Pennsylvania accounted

[16] G. McCandless, "Money, Expectations, and the US Civil War," *American Economic Review*, **86** (1996) 661–67, which empirically tests Mitchell's earlier argument that expectations of future government behaviour were important in determining the current price of currency. War news was one of the important predictors of that future government behaviour. W. Mitchell, *A History of the Greenbacks* (Chicago, Il: University of Chicago Press, 1903).

[17] Baack, 'America's First Monetary Policy,' p. 115.

Table 15.2 Annual state issues of paper money, 1775–1783 (thousands of dollars)

State	*1775*	*1776*	*1777*	*1778*	*1779*	*1780*	*1781*	*1783*	*Total*
NH	133	145	11	120		145			643
VT							84		84
MA	1000	667		667		1534			3868
CT	500	367	17			633			1517
RI	200	567	182		133	67			1148
NY	112	637					411		1161
PA	420	227	532			1516	1330	300	4325
DE	80		66						146
NJ		467		681		600	800	85	2632
MD	535	535				320	533		1924
NC*	125	1250		2125	1250	3100		250	8100
SC*	1120	942	615	1062	5000				8739
VA	1167	1667	2700	2300	3300	40,000	116,700		167,834
Total	*5392*	*7471*	*4123*	*6955*	*9683*	*47,915*	*119,858*	*635*	*202,031*
Cum.	5392	12,863	16,986	23,941	33,624	81,539	201,397	202,031	

Source: B. Ratchford, *American State Debts* (Durham, N.C.: Duke University Press, 1941), p. 34, Table 3

for the largest issuances. The figures cannot be accepted at face value. Those for Virginia, above all, the figures for 1780 and 1781 have been described as 'fantastic' and, in any event, relate to the amounts authorised by the state legislature and not the amounts actually printed. The data for North and South Carolina are equally suspect, where again the estimates refer to authorisations rather than emissions. For all three southern states, the reported figures are caveated as follows: 'there are few reliable records of the amounts actually issued,' and in several instances the amounts which might be issued 'were dependent upon on certain contingencies, and in one case the governor and council of North Carolina were empowered to issue as many bills as they thought necessary.'[18] What gives these figures credibility is that they correspond almost exactly with Thomas Jefferson's estimate of $200 million as the total amount of state issues. It is, of course, possible that Ratchford's adjustments were meant to bring his estimates in line with those of Jefferson (Table 15.2).

The vast quantities of paper money issued naturally resulted in depreciation, which typically varied with the amounts issued and further

[18] B. Ratchford, *American State Debts* (Durham, N.C.: Duke University Press, 1941), p. 34, Table 3.

compounded by the way in which individual states redeemed or, in some instances, repudiated the outstanding amounts. Virginia provides an extreme example of repudiation, offering citizens a loan certificate for 1 dollar for every 1000 dollars surrendered. 'A millionaire in paper money, in other words, would get $1000.' Virginia's approach may be compared with Maryland, where redemptions were made at the rate of forty to one or Connecticut which honoured its obligations at a one-to-one rate of exchange.[19] The following table[20] and chart illustrate the rate of depreciation of the Continental dollar and the paper currencies issued by three southern states; the figures indicate how many state currencies would be required to purchase what a $100 in silver would buy (Chart 15.1):

	Maryland	Virginia	N. Carolina
1977	400	400	300
1778	600	600	550
1779	4150	4000	3000
1780	10,000	7500	20,000
1781	18,000	100,000	72,500

In principle, we would expect the rate of inflation to correspond with the rate of monetary creation. The relationship between money supply growth rates and inflation in the Colonial Era is contentious, notwithstanding attempts to limit price increases via wage and price controls.[21] Hugh Rockoff tested the Quantity Theory of Money hypothesis that asserts that variations in prices are related more or less uniquely to variations in the money supply.[22] Based upon the same data as contained in the above two tables, Rockoff concluded 'that a simple version of the quantity theory of money goes a long way toward explaining the resulting inflation.'

Alas, his results do not support his conclusion, which may reflect shortcomings in the data used to test the theory, or that other influences of

[19] A. Nevins, *American States Before and After the Revolution*, p. 486. Nevins provides a detailed state by state account of paper money issues and redemption procedures.

[20] J. McCusker, *How Much Is That in Real Money? A Historical Price Index for Use as a Deflator of Money Values in the Economy of the United States* (American Antiquarian Society, 2001), Table C2.

[21] J. Grossman, "Wage and price controls during the American Revolution," *Monthly Labor Review*, 96 (1973) 3–10.

[22] H. Rockoff, "War and Inflation in the United States from the Revolution to the Persian Gulf War," in *Economic History of Warfare and State Formation*, (Eds.) J. Eloranta, E, Golson, A. Markevich, N. Wolf, (Springer: Singapore, 2019,) Fig. 1, 'Money and Inflation during the Revolutionary War.'

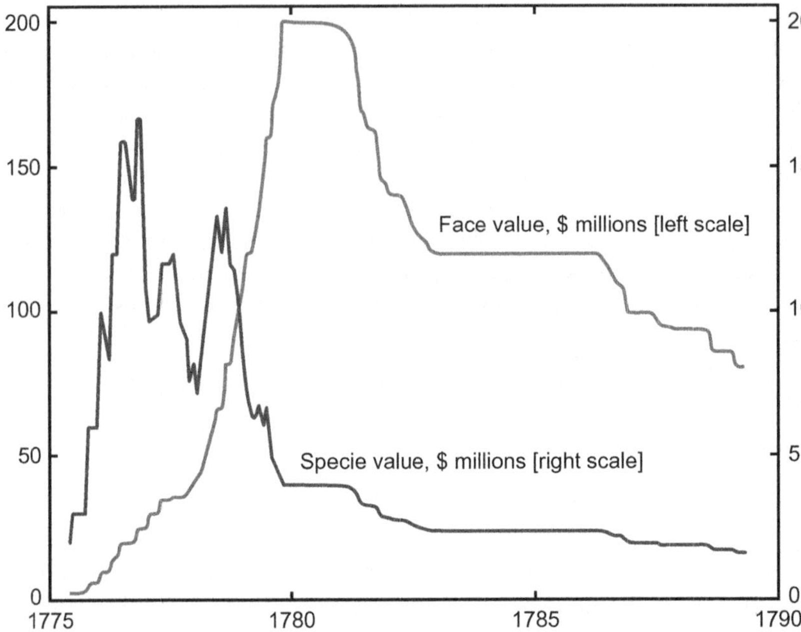

Chart 15.1 Nominal and Specie Value of Continental Dollars. (Source: G. Hall and T. Sargent, "Fiscal Discriminations in Three Wars," *Journal of Monetary Economics*, **61** (2014) 148–166)

equal or greater significance were neglected. First, the issuance data are subject to the limitations noted above, and while the amount of currency a state legislature authorised may affect inflationary expectations, it is the amount actually issued that drives prices. Second, the data for several states are combined into a single measure, which could only be justified if the states constituted a common currency area. The data shown for Massachusetts include that state's own rate of currency issuance together with the amounts created by New Hampshire and Rhode Island. Given the disparity in state size, it is possible that monetary developments in Massachusetts affected prices in neighbouring states. The same, however, cannot be said for Connecticut and New York or Pennsylvania and Delaware, where again state issuances are combined. And, finally, the correlation between Rockoff's two measures, at 0.327, is not statistically significant. The result may, accordingly, reflect either data limitations that once corrected will reveal the validity of the underlying theory or, alternatively, it may support James Madison's view that the value of paper money 'depends on the credit of the State issuing it, and on the time of its redemption; and is no otherwise affected by the quantity than as the quantity may be supposed to endanger or postpone the redemption.'[23]

During the early 1780s, the United States had neither a securities market, a commercial banking system (though three banks organised), nor a central bank resembling the Bank of England. The national currency had collapsed, and in 1790, the United States, having collected only $162,200 in tariffs, faced default on its debts. By 1800, however, the country had a modern financial system. During the 1790s, Congress chartered a national bank, the Federal government assumed payment of war debts and funded them at par, tax revenues grew to $10.8 million and paid most government expenditures, and a securities market trading in government bonds and a few corporate equities developed in each large American town.[24]

[23] Cited in A. Bolles, *The Financial History of the United States; From 1774–1789* (New York, NY: D. Appleton and Company, 1879), p. 147.

[24] Kulikoff, 'First National Depression,' p. 151. Albert Gallatin, Hamilton's successor as Secretary of the Treasury, had by 1808 reduced the federal debt-to-GDP ratio by an estimated 50 per cent or so, including the additional debt from the Louisiana Purchase. P. Hildebrand, "Albert Gallatin, one of the financial founding fathers—what can we learn from him today?" Speech at the Swiss-American Chamber of Commerce, Geneva, 10 September 2008. Hildebrand attributes to Gallatin two major achievements: 'First, there is Gallatin's singular success in his pursuit of debt reduction. Gallatin took advantage of prosperous and relatively peaceful times to reduce the public debt of the emerging United States. The second key legacy of Albert Gallatin's efforts is the way in which he reinforced the financial institutions set up by Alexander Hamilton and made skilful use of them.' Gallatin was Treasury Secretary from 1801 to 1814. At the start of his term of office, the public debt of the United States amounted $83.0 million; by 1812 it had been reduced by nearly 50 per cent to $45.2 million. When he left office in 1814, outstanding debt had risen to $81.5 million, reflecting increased borrowing from the public to finance the War of 1812. Historical data public debt are available at www.treasurydirect.gov/govt/reports/pd/histdebt/histdebt_histo1.htm).

CHAPTER 16

Trade and Trade Policy

The War drastically altered the pattern of the new Republic's trade. Under the colonial regime, direct American trade was restricted to Britain's other regional colonies and to the metropole itself, the latter including trade destined for other parts of Europe. Following the start of hostilities, all trade with Great Britain and its colonies was banned. Exports accordingly would be expected to have declined, even more so taking account of British port blockades. Published data do not exist for the war years, which has forced scholars to develop 'conjectural' estimates of the impact the conflict had on American exports. The following table presents one set of such estimates, which suggest the negative impact was massive, with average annual shipments of America's principal commodity exports (tobacco, rice, grains, indigo, fish, and meat) all declining by 80–100 per cent from their pre-war levels; the same appears to have been true for invisible exports, which slumped by 87 per cent.[1]

It would appear, however, that once hostilities ended American exports more than recovered their pre-war levels. Freed from the constraints imposed on the colonies by the British government Americans developed 'new' markets or, perhaps more accurately, countries with which they could now trade with legally but with which formerly such traded was carried on illicitly, via smuggling, for example. The pre-war comparisons regarded trade with all third party non-British entities as trade with

[1] Kulikoff, 'America's First National Depression,' p. 137, Table 7.1.

G. Pollio, *The Rise and Fall of Britain's North American Empire*,
https://doi.org/10.1007/978-3-031-07484-4_16

England, so that it is impossible to determine precisely the extent of such trade. This would be especially true with respect to Northern European countries, principally France and Holland, which post-war accounted for 16 per cent of the new Republic's exports. Trade with southern Europe, by contrast, actually increased by more than a third, although its share remained unchanged at 14 per cent. Europe thus accounted for three-fifths of total American markets and thus constituted its principal geographic market.

Independence, of course, gave the former English colonies the right to set its own trade policy, and among the first acts approved by the American Congress was the Tariff Act of 1789 that imposed both *ad valorem* and specific duties on imports.[2] There are three principal objectives restrictive policies can serve, which Douglas Irwin describes as the 'three Rs of trade policy, namely, revenue, restriction and reciprocity.'[3] While not necessarily inconsistent, they can at times be mutually exclusive, owing to the specific political objectives the policy is meant to promote. This is best understood within the context of policy differences that arose between the two leading political parties, the Federalists and Republicans (Table 16.1).

> Seeing imports as the critical tax base on which he planned to finance government expenditures and fund the public debt, Hamilton advocated modest, non-discriminatory import duties to ensure a steady stream of revenue into the Treasury coffers. He also wanted a stable commercial relationship with Britain to avoid any conflict that might disrupt imports and diminish customs revenue. By contrast, Jefferson and Madison saw trade policy as an instrument for achieving reciprocity, a weapon to be wielded against what they perceived to be Britain's grossly unfair discrimination against U.S. commerce. They sought to impose countervailing restrictions in an effort to force Britain to improve its treatment of U.S. goods and shipping in its home and colonial markets.[4]

[2] D. Irwin, "The Aftermath of Hamilton's 'Report on Manufactures,'" *Journal of Economic History*, **64** (2004), 800–821, presents a comparative analysis of the rates in the 1789 and subsequent Acts, p. 812, Table 2.

[3] D. Irwin, "Trade Policy in American Economic History," *Annual Review of Economics*, **12** (2020) 23–44, p. 24.

[4] D. Irwin, "Revenue or Reciprocity? Founding Feuds over Early U.S. Trade Policy," in *Founding Choices: American Economic Policy in the 1790s*. D. Irwin and R. Sylla (Eds.) (Chicago, IL: University of Chicago Press, 2010), pp. 89–90. A key implication of Irwin's position is that Hamilton was prepared to tolerate Britain's discriminatory policies against America.

Table 16.1 Geographic and commodity distribution of American trade, pre- and post-revolutionary war

Annual average exports: Thirteen Colonies 1768–1772 and the United States, 1790–1792 (thousands of pounds sterling: 1768–1772 prices)

	1768–1172		*1790–1792*	
Destination	*Value*	*Per cent*	*Value*	*Per cent*
Britain and Ireland	1616	58	1234	31
Northern Europe	–		643	16
Southern Europe	406	14	557	14
British West Indies	759[a]	27	402	10
Foreign West Indies			956	24
Africa	21	1	42	1
Canada	–		60	2
Other	–		59	1
Total	2802	100	3953	100

Principal commodity exports

Commodity	*1768–1772*	*1790–1792*
Tobacco	766	964
Beef, pork, bread, etc.	410	712
Grains	509	670
Dried fish	154	187
Indigo	113	101
Per cent of total exports	69.7	77.7

Source: J. Shepherd and G. Walton, "Economic Change after the American Revolution: Pre- and Post-War Comparisons of Maritime Shipping and Trade, *Explorations in Economic History*, **13** (1976) 397–422

[a]Includes British and foreign West Indies

Notwithstanding that Alexander Hamilton favoured bounties 'as the most efficacious means of encouraging manufactures,'[5] the United States only infrequently relied on them to encourage exports, but for fiscal

[5] *Report on Manufactures.* In this respect Hamilton differed from Adam Smith who objected to bounties because they forced industry 'not only into a channel that is less advantageous, but into one that is actually disadvantageous.' 'it is not the interest of merchants and manufacturers, the great inventors of all these expedients, that the home market should be overstocked with their goods, an event which a bounty upon production might sometimes occasion' (WN: II:13–14).

reasons, never on a large scale; import restrictions, by contrast, were confined more or less exclusively to tariffs, which unlike bounties, that increased expenditure, had the additional advantage of producing revenues which, as Secretary of the Treasury, was Hamilton's main concern.

The Tariff Act of 1789 could be, according to Irwin's schema, best regarded as a revenue measure, although others have argued for a broader view. They aver instead that it was meant equally to raise revenues ***and*** protect domestic industry, a conclusion supported by its preamble—(an Act) 'necessary for the support of government, for the discharge of the debts of the United States, and the encouragement and protection of manufactures'—and the scope of its coverage, with many of the enumerated goods selected specifically because they competed with domestic production. However, the secondary importance of protectionist objectives is underscored by the priority accorded to the Act's revenue raising aspects, while the rates adopted were too low to serve as effective protective measures.[6]

But perhaps the strongest argument favouring the singular importance of the revenue aspects of trade policy was that Alexander Hamilton, then Secretary of the Treasury, was selected to present the Federalist view on the relationship between trade and industrial development. Hamilton's views were set out in his now famous *Report of Manufactures* (1790) and are often singled out as having established the intellectual and political rationale for the application of high tariffs against foreign goods, policies that generally were rejected at the time even if they subsequently served as the foundation for future legislation.[7] Such views are inconsistent. Hamilton's main aim as Secretary of the Treasury was to provide the government with revenues required to service its debt and cover its current expenditure. High tariffs would have frustrated attainment of those

[6] J. Dobson, *Two Centuries of Tariffs*. US International Trade Commission (Washington, D.C.: Government Printing Office), p. 8. See also J. Nelson, "Alexander Hamilton and American Manufacturing: A Reexamination," *Journal of American History*, **65** (1979) 971–995, 'The slight increases in the tariff that [Hamilton] recommended were predicated upon the declining cost of imports and hence were of little protective value,' p. 977.

[7] 'Despite ... Hamilton's enthusiastic advocacy of protective tariffs, the Nation as a whole exhibited little interest in using high tariffs to stimulate manufacturing at home. The eloquent arguments Hamilton marshalled were generally neglected during his lifetime, but they would be revived and used effectively by later advocates of tariff protection,' Dobson, 'Two Centuries of Tariffs', p. 8.

objectives by discouraging consumption of imports, encouraging smuggling, or both. Instead, he favoured moderate rates that would minimise such risks.

Thomas Jefferson believed that manufacturing industry threatened the values of an agrarian way of life,[8] a perspective rejected by Hamilton, who considered that a country in which both sectors flourish was superior to one in which only one or the other existed.[9] 'Particular encouragements of particular manufactures may be of a Nature to sacrifice the interests of landholders to those of manufacturers; But it is nevertheless a maxim well established by experience, and generally acknowledged, where there has been sufficient experience, that the aggregate prosperity of manufactures, and the aggregate prosperity of Agriculture are intimately connected. In the Course of the discussion which has had place, various weighty considerations have been adduced operating in support of that maxim. Perhaps the superior steadiness of the demand of a domestic market for the surplus produce of the soil, is alone a convincing argument of its truth.'

Hamilton further identified several advantages connected with the development of manufacturing industry including, inter alia, an extension of the division of labour, greater mechanisation, creation of additional employment opportunities, and attracting skilled immigrants. He next discusses two broad considerations that explain why countries adopt protectionism policies, observing that each arises for opposite reasons and thus differentially affects the pace of industrial development. The first, the so-called infant industry justification, asserts that emerging industries need to be insulated against foreign competition until such time as they can

[8] '[The] cultivators of the earth are the most valuable citizens. They are the most vigorous, the most independent, the most virtuous, and they are tied to their country, and wedded to its liberty and interests, by the most lasting bonds .... I consider the class of artificers as the panders of vice, and the instruments by which the liberties of a country are generally overturned.' Jefferson to John Jay, (1785) cited in M. Frisch, "Hamilton's Report on Manufactures and Political Philosophy," *Publius*, **78** (1978) 129–139, p. 130.

[9] 'It is not uncommon,' Hamilton wrote, 'to meet with an opinion that though the promoting of manufactures, may be the interest of a part of the union, it is contrary to that of another part. The northern and southern regions are sometimes represented as having adverse interests in this respect. Those are called manufacturing, these agricultural states, and a species of opposition is imagined to subsist between the manufacturing and agricultural interests. The idea of an opposition between those two interests is the common error of the early periods of every country, but experience gradually dissipates it.'

achieve the necessary degree of maturity enabling them to compete successfully against long established industries elsewhere. In Hamilton's view infant industry trade policies are designed to encourage, not protect, local manufacturing industry, and thus are independent of protectionist measures adopted elsewhere.

> When a domestic manufacture has attained to perfection, and has engaged in the prosecution of it a competent number of Persons, it invariably becomes cheaper. Being free from the heavy charges, which attend the importation of foreign commodities, it can be afforded, and accordingly seldom or never fails to be sold Cheaper, in process of time, than was the foreign Article for which it is a substitute. The internal competition, which takes place, soon does away every thing like Monopoly, and by degrees reduces the price of the Article to the *minimum* of a reasonable profit on the Capital employed. This accords with the reason of the thing and with experience.

Hamilton had little further to say about infant industries focusing instead on what he considered to be the more common and pernicious alternative, namely, that trade restraints constitute a legitimate response to protectionist measures adopted by other countries that inhibit domestic industrial development. 'It is well known ... that certain nations grant bounties on the exportation of particular commodities, to enable their own workmen to undersell and supplant all competitors, in the countries to which those commodities are sent. Hence the undertakers of a new manufacture have to contend not only with the natural disadvantages of a new undertaking, but with the gratuities and remunerations which other governments bestow. To be enabled to contend with success, it is evident, that the interference and aid of their own government are indispensable.' Free trade was the preferred option, but the reality of protectionism elsewhere that made it an impossibility was widespread among the Republic's Founding Fathers.

Recent research provides a more nuanced understanding of the ways restrictive policies affected industrial production. More to the point, it has been shown that the measures adopted during the Federal period had a positive impact on infant industries, but adversely affected trade-dependent sectors,[10] a not entirely unexpected result. Finally, as to whether the 'more

[10] 'The trade disruptions appear to have had large but temporary effects on production by domestic infant industries and trade-dependent industries. Yet because infant production was

moderate' import duties favoured by Hamilton and the Federalists, or the more restrictive policies adopted by the Republicans, had the greater impact on American industrial production, the available evidence indicates that the growth rate of industrial production, at *c.* 5 per cent annum, was virtually identical over the two political sub-periods, in fact little different than the growth rate achieved over the entire 125 year studied by Davis.[11] This suggests that notwithstanding the vagaries of American trade policies, they appear to have had little or no lasting impact on the pace of industrialisation.

It is likely that little change in the direction of trade policy would have occurred following the transition from a Federalist to a Republican agenda, had not a series of European developments intervened that threatened America's international commercial interests. The most important of these include France's attempt in the late 1790s to disrupt the Republic's trade with Great Britain; Great Britain's policies in the following decade that restricted American trade with Europe; and, finally, America' s embargo against, and the subsequent more stringent no-trade policy towards, Britain that culminated in the War of 1812. External pressures not only increased the need for "new" market sources of revenue but also highlighted the dangers inherent in America's dependence on imports as the principal source for manufactures (Chart 16.1).

Fiscal pressures, however, remained paramount. The immediate need was to fund the surge in Federal indebtedness resulting from the 1812 war, the total cost of which has been estimated at $90 million[12] (equivalent to $1.6 billion in 2020 prices), the bulk of which was financed by debt—the national debt rose almost threefold between 1811 and 1815 to *c.* $127 million[13]—the balance through a combination of seigniorage

permanently higher and trade-dependent production was permanently lower after the resumption of normal trade, other factors such as the shifts in the composition of demand, technological change, and a different structure of manufactured imports under the Tariff of 1816 may have been responsible for this reallocation,' D. Irwin and J. Davis, "Trade Disruptions and America's Early Industrialization," NBER Working Paper no. 9944 (August 2003).

[11] Davis, 'Annual Index,' p. 1189, Table 3.

[12] S. Daggett "Costs of Major U.S. Wars," *Congressional Research Service*, (2010), Table 1, p. 1 (accessed at: https://sgp.fas.org/crs/natsec/RS22926.pdf).

[13] B. Ratchford, "History of the Federal Debt in the United States," *American Economic Review*, 37 (1947) 131–141, p. 131.

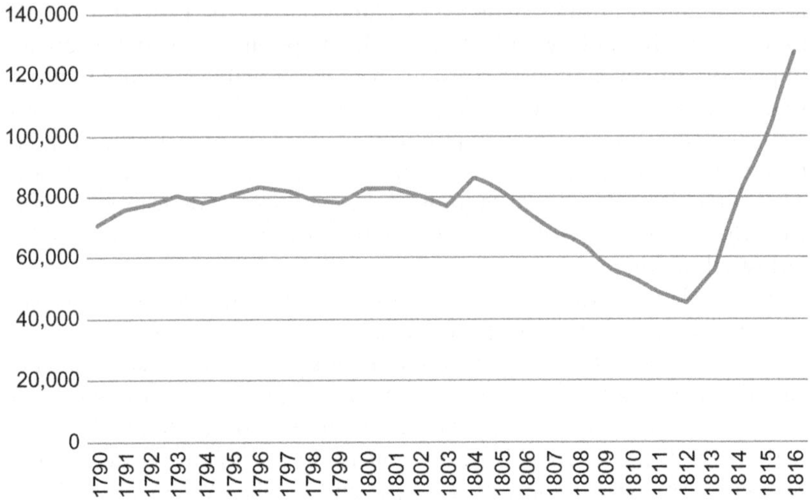

Chart 16.1 Federal debt outstanding, 1790–1816 (thousand dollars). (Source: US Treasury Department)

(inflation), taxes, land grants and letters of marque.[14] A second concern was fears that the end of the war would result in a resumption of imports that threatened the viability of war-nurtured industries in the Northeast, notwithstanding that import volumes were central to the growth of Federal revenues.[15] To address these dual risks, Congress passed the Tariff Act of 1816 that rewrote the entire tariff schedule, increasing average rates by two-fifths compared worth those applying prior to the war.[16] Taussig concluded 'that the restrictive legislation of 1808–15 was ... equivalent to extreme protection. The consequent rise of a considerable class of manufacturers, whose success depended largely on the continuance of protection, formed the basis of a strong movement for more decided limitation of foreign competition.'[17] This objective was

[14] H. Rockoff, "War and Inflation in the United States from the Revolution to the First Iraq War," NBER Working Paper 21,221 (May 2015), p. 48.

[15] Concerns over the risks posed by a resumption were not fanciful. As the price of imports fell 28 per cent from 1814 to 1816, industrial production declined 7 per cent in 1816 as vulnerable firms went bankrupt and shut down. Irwin, 'Clashing over Commerce' p. 126.

[16] Dobson, 'Two Centuries of Tariffs,' pp. 8–9.

[17] Taussig, 'Tariff History, p. 23.

facilitated by the post-War disappearance of the Federalist party from national politics, leaving Congress without an organised political party in favour of low tariffs and open commerce.[18]

[18] Irwin, 'Clashing over Commerce,' p. 127. Hamilton's resistance to broad demand for protection for manufacturing industry appears to have been a factor in desertions from the Federalist party. 'Those measures a government commonly enacted in a private enterprise economy to stimulate manufacturing, favourable tariffs, direct loans and grants, and internal improvements, Hamilton could not attempt. As his political economy compelled him to act against the manufacturers' interests, many responded by deserting his party and opposing his program.' Nelson, 'Alexander Hamilton and American Manufacturing,' p. 994.

Conclusion

Britain's mainland colonies differed fundamentally from those in the Caribbean, the former represented permanent settlements, the latter commercial assets. British citizens in increasing numbers together with other Europeans were attracted by the opportunities presented by the mainland colonies. Many paid their own passage; those without means entered into agreements with merchants that in effect repaid voyage costs via a fixed-term labour supply contract; others arrived as slaves from West Africa purchased either for 'cash' (in the form of cowrie shells) or goods, above all textiles, firearms, and gunpowder. It is the latter category of immigrants that has attracted the lion's share of scholarly attention. Some studies focus on the narrower question of the microeconomic aspects of slave labour, others on the broader issues arising out of the trade. For some, slavery was the decisive factor driving Britain's Industrial Revolution, for others it was responsible more broadly for the rise of American capitalism. These topics now dominate early colonial history, but there are other, important aspects of the colonial economy that deserve equal attention if we are to arrive at a balanced assessment of the region's growth and development.

The first century and half of colonial America's existence attracted little attention from the British government; indeed, the period up to the French and Indian Wars has been characterised as one of 'salutary neglect.' This is not to say the British government was indifferent to what transpired in its

G. Pollio, *The Rise and Fall of Britain's North American Empire*, https://doi.org/10.1007/978-3-031-07484-4

American colonies, only that it recognised that a policy of letting the colonies get on with their own business was more conducive to British interests than a policy of active intervention in their affairs. Later governments took a less benign view of Britain's territories in the New World, indeed, viewing them more as a liability than an asset. In pressing its demands that the mainland colonies should contribute more towards the costs of running the empire, especially as much of the revenue raised would be used to defend and administer the colonies. The colonists, by contrast, argued the proposed fiscal measures were incompatible with British law. As no Americans sat in Parliament, it could not accept that the government had the right to tax mainland colonies without their consent. In effect, colonial Americans challenged the premise that underpinned each revenue measure, namely, the supremacy of Parliament in all matters affecting the colonies.

Each subsequent revenue measure was resisted and ultimately rescinded by Parliament, largely because the increasingly strident responses of the Americans posed a threat to British prosperity. The British government thus faced two options: it could either recognise that no revenue measure would ever be acceptable without the consent of the colonists or it could use force to compel compliance, which under the circumstances invited the risk of rebellion. Pushed to the limit, Parliament enacted the Coercive Acts ruling out the possibility of finding a mutually acceptable compromise and in consequence tipped the scales in favour of Revolution.

The War that ensued was extremely costly and paid for mainly via monetary creation owing to the absence of alternative financial resources. True, Americans were able to raise funds in foreign markets, especially from France, Holland, and, to a lesser extent, Spain, but the amounts, although not insignificant, nevertheless covered only a modest share of the new Republic's financial requirements. Sequestration of Loyalist property emerged as a third financial alternative, although the political and psychological benefits of confiscation appear to have outweighed the material gains, which in any event varied considerably among individual states.

The War caused a significant economic contraction, deeper than the Depression of the 1930s, and drastically altered the distribution of national wealth, which prior to the Revolution was perhaps the most equitable in the world. It also undermined the Articles of Confederation, the agreement among the thirteen States that amounted to the Republic's first constitution. The War underscored the Articles' deficiencies leading in turn to the Constitutional Convention in 1787 that established a federal government operating under the terms of the newly adopted Constitution.

Index

A

Adams, John
  and representation, 172
American Civil War, impact of abolition, 66

B

Boston
  Non-Importation Agreement, 157
  tea and smuggling, 119–124
Burke, Edmund, 7

C

Confiscation, 190–194
  implementation, 190–194
  and redistribution, 189
  revenue, 190–194
Cotton
  impact of; abolition of slavery, 66; British production constraints, 54
  importance to economic growth, 71

E

Economic impact
  of Revolutionary War, 203
  of slave trade, 49

F

Fiat money
  definition, 214
  and depreciation, 220–223
  supply of, 220–223
  See also Revolutionary War
French and Indian War, The significance of, 100

H

Hamilton, Alexander
  and debt sequestration, 198
  post-war financial reforms, 225, 226, 228
  proposed tariffs, 4
  and tariffs impact on development, 88, 226–230

G. Pollio, *The Rise and Fall of Britain's North American Empire*,
https://doi.org/10.1007/978-3-031-07484-4

I
Industrial development
constrained by British, 75
critical factors enabling, 85–88
iron, 77
shipping, 83

J
Jefferson, Thomas
and land ownership, 184

L
Labour sources in Colonial America
indentured servitude, 16
slaves, 19
Land ownership and suffrage, 189
Land values
and demographic pressures, 91
and imperial land policy, 91
and speculative investment, 91

M
Mercantilist constraints, 75–77
See also Industrial development
Molasses Act, 1733
and opposition to, 101

N
New History of Capitalism, critique of, 55
Nonimportation, 158–159
colonial reactions, 162
economic impact, 160
and interest groups, 158–159
See also Revenue and Trade Policies

P
Parliamentary representation
attitudes to, 2
opposition to, 5, 103–105
Post-Revolution trade and trade policy, 225–233
Tariff Act of 1789, 228

R
Repudiation, 195–202
and debt sequestration, 196
definition, 195
and impact of inflation, 196
and resolution, 202
sums involved, 196
Revenue and Trade Policies, 12, 112
adoption by Jeffersonian Republicans, 4
attitudes towards, 8
impact of rising prosperity, 10
impact on Rebellion, 12, 171
Revolution and aftermath, 175
attempts at conciliation, 170
and British sympathisers, 182
costs of, 178–182
Revolutionary War
and counterfeiting of currency, 215–218
and foreign loans, 203–205
and impact of French support, 208
monetary creation and financing of, 215–218

S
Salutary neglect, definition of, 75
Seven Years War, The
costs of, 105
impact of cost of, 107–111

Slavery
and American economic growth, 73
cotton production and exports, 57
efficiency of, 56
impact on industrial revolution, 64
profitability, 58–63
relationship to textile industry, 55
Slave trade, 52
finance of, 31
historic traffic in, 19
and mortality rate, 30
of native Americans, 20
profitability, 47
rights to trade, 27
in West Africa, 21
Smith, Adam
attitude to representation, 6, 169
and benefit of trade, 9
and disbenefit of slave trade, 49
and loss of the colonies, 169
Spanish America and rights to supply slaves, 28
Stamp Act 1765, 148
definition of, 132
impact of, 129; land conveyances, 136; payment in sterling, 148; printers, 133–136
and justification for opposition, 1
lack of authority for, 128
objectives of, 127, 133
and remittance, 131, 132
resistance to, 111
Stationing of troops and resentment, 100
Sugar Act, 1766
and resentment of, 102
Sugar production and impact on demand for slaves, 21

T
Tax measures, 1
costs and benefits of, 2
See also Revenue and trade policies
Tenanting of land, extent of, 92–95
Townshend duties, 123, 149–156
colonial reactions to, 149–156
and complexity of legislation, 153
and parliamentary supremacy, 149
revenues raised by, 151
See also Tax measures
Trade and Navigation Acts, 3, 115–125
colonial reactions, 163
support for independence, 115–125
See also Revenue and trade policies
Treaty of Amity
and debt repayment
See also Repudiation
Treaty of Paris, The
and inclusion of debt repayment, 199

Z
Zong, the
notorious court case, 37

The manufacturer's authorised representative in the EU is Springer Nature Customer Service Centre GmbH, Europaplatz 3, 69115 Heidelberg, Germany. If you have any concerns regarding our products, please contact ProductSafety@springernature.com

Printed and bound by CPI Group (UK) Ltd, Croydon, CR0 4YY

30/09/2026

02225490-0005